AF594576

CHASING THE SHADOW

CHASING THE SHADOW

MICKEY MARCUS'S 200 DAYS OF DESTINY

STEVEN L. OSSAD

UNIVERSITY OF MISSOURI PRESS
COLUMBIA

University of Missouri Press, Columbia, Missouri 65211
Printed and bound in the United States of America
 First printing, 2024.

Library of Congress Cataloging-in-Publication Data

Names: Ossad, Steven L., author.
Title: Chasing the shadow : Mickey Marcus's 200 days of destiny / Steven L. Ossad.
Other titles: Mickey Marcus's 200 days of destiny
Description: Columbia : University of Missouri Press, 2024. |
Series: American military experience | Includes bibliographical references and index.
Identifiers: LCCN 2024026885 (print) | LCCN 2024026886 (ebook) | ISBN 9780826223180 (hardback) | ISBN 9780826275073 (ebook)
Subjects: LCSH: Marcus, David, 1901-1948. | United States. Army--Officers--Biography. | Israel. Tseva haganah le-Yiśra'el--Officers--Biography. | Jews--United States--Biography. | United States. War Department. Civil Affairs Division--History. | United States--History--1933-1945. | Jerusalem--History--Siege, 1948.
Classification: LCC E745.M35 O88 2025 (print) | LCC E745.M35 (ebook) | DDC 973.918092 [B]--dc23/eng/20240809
LC record available at https://lccn.loc.gov/2024026885
LC ebook record available at https://lccn.loc.gov/2024026886

∞™ This paper meets the requirements of the American National Standard for Permanence of Paper for Printed Library Materials, Z39.48, 1984.

Typeface: Artifex CF and Garamond

THE AMERICAN MILITARY EXPERIENCE SERIES
JOHN C. MCMANUS, SERIES EDITOR

The books in this series portray and analyze the experience of Americans in military service during war and peacetime from the onset of the twentieth century to the present. The series emphasizes the profound impact wars have had on nearly every aspect of recent American history and considers the significant effects of modern conflict on combatants and noncombatants alike. Titles in the series include accounts of battles, campaigns, and wars; unit histories; biographical and autobiographical narratives; investigations of technology and warfare; studies of the social and economic consequences of war; and in general, the best recent scholarship on Americans in the modern armed forces. The books in the series are written and designed for a diverse audience that encompasses nonspecialists as well as expert readers.

Selected titles from this series:

No Sacrifice Too Great: The 1st Infantry Division in World War II
Gregory Fontenot

Patton's War: An American General's Combat Leadership, Volume 2: August–December 1944
Kevin M. Hymel

Patton's War: An American General's Combat Leadership, Volume 1: November 1942–July 1944
Kevin M. Hymel

Patton: Battling with History
J. Furman Daniel

Lessons Unlearned: The U.S. Army's Role in Creating the Forever Wars in Afghanistan and Iraq
Pat Proctor

Loss and Redemption at St. Vith: The 7th Armored Division in the Battle of the Bulge
Gregory Fontenot

Military Realism: The Logic and Limits of Force and Innovation in the US Army
Peter Campbell

Omar Nelson Bradley: America's GI General, 1893–1981
Steven L. Ossad

The First Infantry Division and the US Army Transformed: Road to Victory in Desert Storm, 1970–1991
Gregory Fontenot

Dick Cole's War: Doolittle Raider, Hump Pilot, Air Commando
Dennis R. Okerstrom

For my parents

During the flight to Palestine, I asked Mickey what made him agree to come. He rolled up his sleeve, pointed to his arm, and replied, "Because the blood of Abraham flows in my veins."

I believe his shooting was divine intervention. And he felt it on the flight. This is one of those uncanny things when a person suddenly feels that his luck is up. Sometimes when I remember this, I feel shivers.

Later I asked, where should we bury you if you die? And he replied, "At West Point, that's where everyone goes."

—*Shlomo Shamir*

CONTENTS

ILLUSTRATIONS

FOREWORD

David Daniel "Mickey" Marcus has a unique place in the history of the twentieth century, and this first comprehensive and critical biography very much shows why that is true. He had an amazing career in the US Army during World War II and an equally remarkable role as a shaper of Israel's army.

Born in Manhattan near the turn of the twentieth century, Mickey Marcus was a first-generation American who carved out a path at West Point, as a lawyer, in NYC politics, during World War II and after, where his amazing talents as a planner and a trainer marked him for distinction. No one had better organizational skills or was better at planning, designing, and implementing realistic training for soldiers going into combat.

After working in Germany during the occupation, Mickey organized the army's new War Crimes Branch, preparing for the trials that would ultimately be held in Europe and the Pacific after the Nuremberg Trials. His work in the postwar occupation of Germany and his achievements in establishing the legal framework and mechanisms of prosecuting war crimes mark high points in an amazing career.

After returning to private practice in 1947, and during the run-up to the partition of Palestine, he was recruited to help build a modern army for Israel. After touring the British-occupied country and preparing reports and training manuals, Mickey made a quick trip back to the United States before returning to Palestine before the Declaration of Israel's Independence on May 14, 1948. During the weeks of foreign invasion that followed, he exercised the talents that led him to a position of responsibility and trust among Israel's high command. On June 10, 1948, tragically just before a UN ceasefire, Mickey was accidentally killed, a great shock to all who knew him.

My own interest in Mickey Marcus goes back many years—from the time I first saw the film *Cast a Giant Shadow*, which is loosely based on his exploits. After I learned that Mickey was an attorney and had been a uniformed lawyer in the US Army, his life became even more interesting to me, as I too had a career as a soldier and army attorney. Although I have also worked in the area of war crimes, I am no Mickey Marcus, but his accomplishments as a man, a soldier, and an attorney were a model for me and others to emulate.

More than seventy-five years have passed since Mickey left his mark, and he has been forgotten by most Americans and Israelis, but he deserves to be remembered. This first serious and balanced biography will go a long way to make that happen.

—Colonel Fred L. Borch III, US Army (ret'd)

INTRODUCTION

> I was privileged to meet Colonel Marcus many times during his short period of service with Israel. He was my closest adviser on many occasions and in many informal discussions. I admired his judgment, vision, and inspiring argument. With these personal attributes and his realistic approach to military problems he made an outstanding contribution to the development of Israel's war machine.
>
> —Israel Defense Forces chief of staff
> Yaacov Dori, June 1949

The Crucial Outsider at Exactly the Decisive Moment, 1948

In war and revolution, a single person marked by *fortuna* and possessing the character required by the moment can influence the birth of nations. Quickly understanding the battlefield and political forces arrayed and grasping the dynamics of decision-making on both sides of the hill, such a person radiates energy and personal dynamism. Accepted even by hard partisan adversaries in the councils of power, their influence may be subtle but gains force in retrospect. That is not an argument for a great person view of history, but a plain observed fact drawing from many spheres of human activity.

Mickey Marcus was exactly that kind of person. A wartime associate in the American high command, no stranger to the great and famous, told Mickey's best friend that he was "the most unforgettable man I've ever met."[1] That oft-quoted recollection echoes in the few accounts of those who knew him face-to-face and recorded their impressions, especially during his final two hundred days. Even after three-quarters of a century and with a scant written record, the image radiates. Mickey was the type of character whose life, due to their charisma, their near mythic aura, and their total adherence to the task at hand, invites embellishment, inspiring tall tales ten feet high—even movies. But why?

If David Daniel "Mickey" Marcus, code name Michael Stone, had not agreed to drop everything in 1948 to fight for Israel's survival and independence, that nation would have been born weaker and with Jerusalem besieged. More than one hundred thousand isolated Jews would have been at the mercy of Transjordan's Arab Legion, local and foreign extremist Muslim militias, and violent and religiously inflamed neighbors. When Mickey entered this fight, a twenty-five-year period of British colonial rule over local Jewish and Arab inhabitants, after centuries of Ottoman occupation and suppression, was ending. A brand-new UN without any history of peacekeeping was trying to partition the land between those inhabitants, who were fighting their own civil war. Intelligence professionals universally predicted the quick defeat of any Jewish provisional government. Memories of the Jews' ordeal only a few years before, the British policy against immigration of Holocaust survivors to Palestine, and the pronouncements of every Arab leader about the fate of the Jews already living in Palestine—the Yishuv, as they were called—leave little doubt about the stakes.

David Marcus knew from direct personal knowledge of secret intelligence about the Holocaust, and most profoundly from a visit to Dachau just days after its liberation, that—in the words of Thucydides—the fate of the weak and defeated is to suffer what they must at the hands of those who can do as they will.[2] Had Mickey Marcus, code name Michael Stone, never had his brief brush with destiny, the position of modern Israel would have been more perilous than it was after the first round of fighting in mid-June 1948. Modern Jewish sovereignty over the promised land—as well as Zionism itself—might have suffered mortal blows soon after its victory declaration, for a third and final time.

The core question of this biography, then, is how did this late convert to Zionism, a middle-aged Jewish American lawyer and politician with a distinguished but noncombat World War II record, come to hold a position of respect, authority, and command in the nascent Israeli army? And how was he able in such a brief time to help unify, inspire, and rally that very young army's feuding internal factions in time to field a professionally organized fighting force exactly at the crucial turn of Israel's history? More concretely, how did, first, the principles he embodied, real and constructed; second, the doctrine and manuals he authored; and third, the passion for training he promoted continue to influence the Israel Defense Forces (IDF) and support the mutual national security interests at the core of American support for Israel?

Military, civil, and religious institutions in Israel and the United States have maintained the image of Aluf Michael Stone as the man who broke the siege of Jerusalem, the most visible of all those who came to fight for Israel from outside: David Daniel "Mickey" Marcus, West Point boxing champion, fearless Fed, New York City prison commissioner, local war hero, and Soldier for All Humanity, the epitaph on his West Point gravestone.

Almost from the moment of his death, Mickey has been called an American Marquis de Lafayette, Tadeusz Kościuszko, and Friedrich Wilhelm von Steuben, the drill master of Valley Forge, rolled into one, each moniker in some ways apt, especially the last. Mickey was the most trusted foreign military adviser of the nation's founding father David Ben-Gurion—Israel's George Washington, the longtime Palestine-based Zionist leader in charge of the largest underground Palestinian Jewish militia, the Haganah (Hebrew for "the Defense"). He was the most famous member of the Machal, some thirty-five hundred volunteers who came from outside to fight for Israel, forming a very loose group.[3]

That Mickey Marcus was even associated with the actual Machal organization officially formed by the provisional government after Israeli independence, or that he could be called a volunteer at all, remains arguable, since he was a professional military consultant under contract to the Jewish Agency. As the man who recruited him makes clear, he was identified as part of the search through sympathizers of the Haganah, and in the end recruited and paid like an American general from the time he arrived in Israel until his death there.[4]

Mickey was the first Jewish soldier called *aluf* (variously translated from Hebrew as "general," "count," "duke," "lord," or "captain of a thousand") by the official order of Israel's first commander-in-chief. David Ben-Gurion picked the man and the moment, but he drew a veil over the identity of his hand-picked *aluf.* Almost no one beyond the top command and field officers and a few journalists knew the identity of the American warrior, and once word leaked out of high-ranking outsiders in the top ranks of the Haganah, the ring of secrecy around Marcus drew even tighter.[5]

The Keepers of the Shadow, the Makers of Movies, Friends and Protectors of Legacy

With that partly clandestine and tragic end, it's not surprising that the life of David "Mickey" Marcus has become the stuff of legends and myths, even fantasy, conspiracy, wild exaggeration, and untethered embellishment. The early strands of the heroic image came together in Edward Berkman's 1962 biography of Marcus, *Cast a Giant Shadow*, and Melville Shavelson's 1966 film of the same name, loosely based on Berkman's book. The image of Marcus created by Jewish American actor Kirk Douglas in the film version dominates most evocations of the man, for good or ill. These days, reactions to the book or movie rest mostly on current headlines rather than the historical context of the struggle in which Marcus died, or the events that cast him as a real-life player in an event marked by many evocations of destiny.[6]

Hollywood's big-screen portrayal only fortified the outright fictions of the book and even manages to add completely fabricated backstories, mixing powerful imaginings of dramatic events with a gross misreading of other historical details and characters. Mickey's widow Emma provided much family material to Berkman and went along completely with the Hollywood version of Mickey's story. Even when pressed by the objections of actual participants in the events the film portrayed, especially Moshe Sharett, one of Israel's founders and its second prime minister, she refused to interfere in either the book or movie about her husband. She undoubtedly realized that the star-studded Hollywood movie would help preserve Mickey's legacy, and in a completely favorable light. In this, she was correct. As in the case of the movie *Patton* (1970), which has shaped Americans' collective memory of not only the mercurial General George Patton but also his contemporary subordinate turned boss, Omar Bradley, the film version of *Cast a Giant Shadow* has cemented a heroic image of the complex character embedded in the accepted version of Mickey's life—and death.[7]

The film partly reveals how the lasting image of Mickey Marcus was shaped by the state of the movie business of the time, as well as notions of heroism. Several years after the publication of Berkman's biography, screenwriter Shavelson optioned the book after Metro-Goldwyn-Mayer declined it. Despite his pitches, industry executives, particularly Jews, turned him down. He believed the reluctance was due to "the fear that permeates this industry" and concerns about appropriation of film assets in Egypt, adding that "the pogrom mentality has not yet vanished from Hollywood." Even after World War II the industry wasn't ready to feature a Jewish battlefield hero. Shavelson finally convinced John Wayne, promising him a significant supporting role as a composite of Patton and General Maxwell D. Taylor, which in turn swayed Harold Mirisch and his Universal Artists associates. They had, like MGM, previously rejected the film idea. When Frank Sinatra, Angie Dickinson, and other bankable names signed on, it was a done deal.[8]

The film's locations included sites in New York and Israel that lent official support to the effort. When Emma visited Israel and was asked about Mickey's fictional love interest in the film, played by sultry Senta Berger, she responded, "Well, I don't know if anything like that happened, but it could have. I have only one request, don't make him dull." As context, Emma's recollections in her letters show a keen interest in her husband's flirting, which was frequent.[9]

The film garnered mixed reviews. The *New York Times* said Marcus "emerges as a contrived hero" in "a confusing, often superficial biography." The *Los Angeles Times* said, similarly, that the movie took the "all but incredible" Mickey Marcus to a level "simply too hard to believe," concluding that "in attempting to tell us too much, [it] has not told us enough." They got it right. The film foreshadowed polarized politics at the San Sebastian International Film Festival in Spain, where "boos were mixed with cheers at the end of the showing."[10]

If the movie shaped the image of Marcus, the most important person in Mickey's life except for Emma was Charles G. "Steve" Stevenson Jr., who remained at the front rank of the keepers of the shadow. Steve is a crucial character in Mickey's story, and he is there at every important moment of his life: the two were teammates and close friends at their alma maters Brooklyn Boys High School and West Point, roommates, best men to each other at their weddings, and today lie side by side in the West Point cemetery. Steve's important wartime position as executive officer of the Pond—the unofficial name of the US Army's secret intelligence unit G-2 (General Staff, Intelligence) and rival to the Office of Strategic Services (OSS)—and his continuing efforts to memorialize his friend also raise fascinating questions, especially about Mickey's last days: how he was able to travel back and forth between the United States and British-ruled Palestine after the partition vote, and what, exactly, he was doing in Washington and New York City in April 1948 and early May, just before the final British withdrawal.

Equally fascinating questions arise about Mickey's boss at the Pentagon, Major General John Hilldring, and his secret role during this period. In the debates on the partition of Palestine in late 1947 and in the aftermath of the UN vote, Hilldring was publicly described as the State Department's unofficial channel to the Jewish Agency and liaison with American Jewry. In late March, the department was considering how the Jews in Palestine would react to American pressure and concluded that they would more easily accept bad news from someone sympathetic rather than from State professionals who most Jews saw as biased, if not actual anti-Semites. Hilldring was briefly named an assistant secretary of state just before independence, and there was speculation that he helped the Jewish side in the debate around Truman's recognition of Israel.[11]

From the time Marcus transferred to the Pentagon in 1943, Hilldring nurtured his right-hand man, and he played a greater than hitherto examined role in Mickey's last days, being his main contact in the US government before and immediately after Israel's independence. When Marcus was actively trying to recruit military consultants, he cited Hilldring's support to prospective prospects.[12] One of the last letters Mickey wrote, dated May 16, 1948—two days after Israel declared its independence, and describing the battlefield situation—was to Hilldring, sent to him via Haganah courier. In it he assured his old boss that Israel would hold fast, push back its enemies, and defend its territory—until help arrived from outside. Marcus anticipated, or prayed, that American arms and economic aid would be forthcoming, but that didn't happen.[13] Hilldring never took up his State Department appointment, and he faded from the Palestine issue. In the end, America gave Israel a terrific diplomatic gift, but for a long time, hampered by embargoes and presidential politics, it did not send military or economic aid. Mickey's full hopes were not fulfilled.

With Israel once more in a war for survival, and America now its vital partner, amid changing political fortunes, it's not only a good idea to revisit this fascinating character, but also vital to understanding today's headlines.

CHASING THE SHADOW

PROLOGUE

The Return Bout

> Mick's uproarious laughter became his hallmark. It was never stilled. It broke down all barriers of rank and protocol. Because of his warmth and human fellowship, he won the affection of his associates as few men have ever done before in the Army.
>
> —Charles G. "Steve" Stevenson, Class of 1924

Indoor Meet, Old Gymnasium,
US Military Academy, New York, March 25, 1922

Towering above the gymnasium, five rows of seats lined the running track balcony. Sitting in the center and flanked by the academy elite and high-ranking visitors, Superintendent Brigadier General Douglas MacArthur '03 surveyed his handiwork. An avid sponsor of all intramural sports since his arrival in 1919, MacArthur was the driving force in expanding the army's official intercollegiate program. Never missed a bout.

Consistent with the expected demand, the venue for the premier event of the indoor meet of 1922 shifted from the small boxing hall where the prelims were held. A specially constructed steel-supported boxing ring was bolted to the large second-floor basketball court. The crowd knew they were watching two of the best college boxers in the country—and, as it happened, two of the best in West Point and intercollegiate boxing history. Squaring off in a much-anticipated return match, undefeated sometime welterweight David Daniel "Mickey" Marcus '24 faced John W. "Jazz" Harmony '23, who had suffered his only defeat at Mickey's hands in a legendary bout the year before.[1] The 1922 *Howitzer* yearbook described the long-awaited rematch: "The best in the last four years; best in the spirit of friendly rivalry between the classes; best in closeness and uncertainty of the outcome, and best in quality of the work of the contestants. . . . The highlight was the welterweight bout, as each fighter was an expert glove pusher, and each was backed to a man by his class."[2]

Fig. 1. Mickey as intercollegiate welterweight boxing champion, 1923. Military History Institute

Support was not limited to boisterous outbursts of class spirit. Gambling, officially forbidden at the academy but quietly tolerated, reached historic intensity, even though cash was banned on campus. The currency of choice was future rations of apple pie and ice cream, with the stakes ranging from a week's issue to "all in"—a six-month wager. Desperate cadets might bet their milk rations, although they traded at a steep discount to sweets. Everyone had a stake in the outcome, but Mickey's classmates dominated the betting. Four hundred strong, and until then the largest in West Point's history, the "Thundering

Herd" took their name from the noise they made clambering over the lumber brought in to build housing to accommodate them.

Standing in Harmony's corner, John Valentine "Frenchy" Grombach '23, a future intercollegiate heavyweight champion, journalist, media executive, and world-class spy chief, whispered encouragement to his fighter. Frenchy, later the founder of the Pond, the US Army's G-2 secret intelligence unit during World War II, was a son of France's consul in New Orleans, a natural brawler, braggart, and bully who had famously worked as a bouncer in a Bourbon Street brothel before his appointment to the academy. He knew the styles of both boxers and had watched them slug it out in a dozen practice bouts. The physical differences were stark, as Frenchy recalled.

"Marcus was dark-skinned, with very black hair and piercing dark eyes. He was very heavily built—tremendous shoulders, chest, arms, and stocky legs as well. Harmony had very white skin, gray eyes, brown hair, and a typical Irish face. The strong overhead boxing lights—this was before the invention of cold lighting—accentuated the differences in coloring between the two men."[3]

Jazz moved gracefully, like a ballet dancer, with a weaving and rolling rhythm. A veteran NCO quartermaster of the Great War, appointed to the academy directly from the ranks, he had polished his boxing skills in the service and was technically proficient, as well as lighter and nimbler on his feet than his shorter opponent. Never had he failed to respond to the "outburst of cheering with which the Corps greeted his appearance by giving his customary clever exhibition of hit and duck."[4]

Mickey was an aggressive freestyle puncher, lacking refinement but, powered by his extraordinary upper body, capable of inflicting and absorbing terrific punishment. A gymnast and weightlifter, he was markedly slower than his opponent but far from sluggish, able to move quickly when he sensed the kill. Mickey's fighting signature was a "pile-driving left that he usually started from the floor," and he was so renowned that a "murmur ran through the crowd whether it connected or not." The Thundering Herd was confident that their classmate's crushing left would batter the agile and talented sharpshooter into submission. The only question was whether Mickey could make the weight. That issue was resolved as both men came trotting up from the locker room into the ring. The three-thousand-strong crowd roared.[5]

Referee Billy Cavanaugh, short, squat, and known for decades professionally as "Billy Glover," drew the fighters to him and issued instructions for the three-round bout. Hired just before MacArthur's arrival, Cavanaugh had been recruited as the founding coach of the army's team, molding a catalogue of champions for almost three decades. Standing with two of his best fighters, he ticked off the old Marquis of Queensberry rules: a knockdown ended a round, followed by a one-minute rest; a knockdown scored as a knockout if the boxer could not get back into the ring after one minute.[6]

At the bell, both fighters came out swinging. Mickey went on the offense and "threw punches mostly roundhouse from all angles and continually." Jazz, still smarting from his previous humiliation by a lowly plebe who still stood undefeated, pursued the risky strategy of going toe-to-toe with the slugger, exchanging blows and hitting back with precision and force when he could. "It was as if a glove factory exploded," one team member said. In defiance of academy rules against rowdy spectator conduct, the cadets were screaming so loudly that those absent unfortunates walking punishment tours a quarter mile away at the South Barracks heard the yelling.

In the first round, Mickey had the better of Jazz, who took punishment for getting too close to the street fighter. In the excitement, few fans noticed that Mickey took a conventional right-hand stance with his left arm extended, rather than a southpaw stance, and used his deadly left sparingly and without the usual power. Frenchy, tending to his man, noticed the move, but seeing that Jazz suffered nonetheless, advised him to stop trading punches and box at a greater range, only closing when an opening developed.

It worked. In the second round Harmony kept his distance, evaded Micky's probing hooks and crosses, and went into a clinch whenever he was trapped against the ropes. Mickey fought the same fight as the first round but did only minor damage to his opponent and still seemed hesitant. No one doubted that Jazz had the edge, and the tension rose as the final, and decisive, round began.

Initially Mickey went on the defensive, moving cautiously, aimlessly; then suddenly he attacked with his left. Although he ducked, Jazz took the punch to the top of his head, a blow so powerful it propelled him halfway across the ring. A quarter century later, retired major general Harmony recalled the moment: "I can still feel that poleaxing left. I attribute my bull neck to it."

The Thundering Herd went crazy. They chanted like a blood-drunk Colosseum audience waiting for the final devastating blow that would end the fight—and deliver the sweets. It never came. That was the only time Mickey employed his devastating left. Jazz recovered his bearings, and Mickey resumed leading with his right, which Jazz easily evaded or blocked before going into a clinch. The judges conferred and ordered a rare fourth round. It played out much like the third. Mickey never used his left. Jazz scored at long range but with obvious effect. The decision for Harmony rendered the Thundering Herd silent as the prospect of victory sweetened by apple pie ala mode quickly turned to bitterness in the mouth.

After Cavanaugh raised Harmony's arm, the loser crossed the ring and, breaking into his well-known grin, extended both gloves in a show of congratulations. Harmony returned the gesture, but when Mickey flinched on contact with his left glove, the surgeon noticed, and trailed along as Cavanaugh accompanied his fighters to the Old Gym locker room. The surgeon examined Mickey's left arm, immediately identifying a serious and obviously very painful wrist dislocation. Mickey admitted that he had fallen during that afternoon's horse-riding practice and that the injury occurred then.[7]

The implication was clear. Cadet Marcus had entered the ring knowing he was injured, thereby taking a great personal risk. When he explained, without the seriousness warranted, that the pain was tolerable until he connected with Jazz's head in the third round, the doctor was not amused. After some harsh words from Cavanaugh,

Mickey again dissolved into smiles and headed for South Barracks, accompanied by his closest friends since Brooklyn Boys High School, Steve Stevenson and George Smith, roommates and so-called wives in what the Thundering Herd called the "Suite of Three Faiths." Word quickly got around about what had happened, and esteem for Mickey only grew, especially as his athletic career reached new heights in gymnastics in his upper-class years. Undoubtedly, some cadets made up their boxing losses on the bout with Harmony by betting on other Mickey contests.

What does the incident reveal about the character of the man, and as a predictor of future events and decisions? And what does it say about the inner life, the moral and intellectual core, of Mickey Marcus, and how and why he died on a hillside outside Jerusalem, at the pinnacle of his life and the moment that Jewish sovereignty was restored, as it was lost, in war? Those questions are partly answered in his story, even as that war continues.

When the Thundering Herd began to reconnect early in World War II, exchanging self-censored information about what they were doing, Lowell "Wampus" Limpus, ex. '24, kept classmates posted. Voted honorary member of the class and then military editor of the *New York Daily News* during the war, Wampus referred to his pal Mickey's role in the Civil Affairs Branch as "right beside the throne and under the gun," writing in the alumni notes of his growing influence, "He still packs a lot of punch."[8]

This prologue is largely based on West Point *Howitzer* yearbooks (1921–24) and "Class of 1924 Notes" in *Assembly*, the West Point alumni magazine, as well as the eyewitness account of John V. Grombach, also a West Point boxing champion who was commanding officer of the US Army's Secret Intelligence Service in World War II. His executive officer was Charles "Steve" Stevenson. Besides materials from Ted Berkman's book *Cast a Giant Shadow* and the Berkman Papers, other sources include Stevenson, "Marcus Obituary"; Limpus, "This Was Mickey Marcus," *Saturday Evening Post*, December 4, 1948; and Red Reeder (Mickey's friend, wounded war hero, and later coach and chronicler of West Point athletics), *Heroes and Leaders of West Point* (New York: Thomas Nelson, 1970), 101–9.

CHAPTER 1

The Early Years

> From the day we got to camp, the Jewish boys were under constant attack. We faced ridicule, like being called Jew bastards and physical confrontations, with little Mick faring the worst because he fought back.
>
> —Noah Chase, boyhood friend, 1957

Lower East Side Tenement, Hester Street, Manhattan, Early Twentieth Century

As far back as anyone could remember, nobody called him David, or anything close. His first nickname, Little Mike, courtesy of idolized older brother Big Mike, in time gave way to Mikey, and finally Mickey. Sometimes he signed his letters to his wife from the field "Mici." His gravestone reads "Micky." A very few from boyhood or the Point, chiefly Steve Stevenson, called him Mick. At the end of his life he passed into history and imagery with a made-up code name, Michael "Mickey" Stone, but even in that official fiction, the Mickey people knew endures.[1]

David Daniel Marcus had the classic American rise to legend. He was born on the anniversary of George Washington's birthday, February 22, 1901, in a back-facing fifth-floor apartment at 103 Hester Street on Manhattan's Lower East Side, the youngest son of five surviving children of Mordecai (Max) and Leah (nee Goldstein) Marcus. Penniless and uneducated immigrants from Iasu, Romania, the Marcuses arrived legally in New York Harbor on the SS *Amsterdam* in 1900. They were fleeing rising fears of renewed anti-Jewish pogroms and seeking a better chance in life for their children. Both hailed from large families, many of whose members eventually came to America.[2]

Max operated a vegetable pushcart on Orchard Street and did well enough to buy a stall in the Washington Street market. In 1906 he moved his family to Williams Avenue in the East New York section of Brooklyn. Prospects looked good until Max succumbed to illness, probably tuberculosis, and died in 1910, casting the family into poverty and forcing them into a tenement between the BMT subway and the Long Island Rail Road, the proverbial wrong side of two tracks. The three older sons rallied, led by the oldest Michael, Big Mike, nineteen, who undertook the main family responsibilities and became close to his youngest brother, who trailed after him constantly. Although the background of poverty is a theme in the Marcus story, that is not the lingering recollection of some close to him back then. Julius Freeman, from whom Mickey was "virtually inseparable" during childhood, described him as "expansive and extroverted," someone who easily mingled at parties, had an "easy laugh—booming and infectious," and "frequently teased his mother and sisters."[3]

The Marcus family were early congregants of Union Temple in Brooklyn, one of the oldest and most prominent Reform synagogues in the United States.[4] At Union, Mickey received a Hebrew school education and attended daily prayers with his brothers for a year after Max's death. Mickey was a bar mitzvah and mastered the basics of Torah study, Jewish traditions, and beliefs, especially the premier legal text, the Talmud, and its commentators. If he knew the Hebrew alphabet and any of the language—and there is much evidence to the contrary—he used it only for basic prayers. And even if he knew any of those prayers by heart, he certainly didn't speak or understand the spoken language as it was in the mid-twentieth century, nor was he able to read it except in a prayer book. Most important, there is no evidence that he had strong feelings about Zionism, Middle Eastern politics, or the fate of Jews in Europe generally as he grew to adulthood.

During his career he had broad-based Jewish community associations, but his earliest awareness of a broader historical Zionist narrative was the ubiquitous blue Jewish National Fund charity box in his house, contributions to which were earmarked for land development, especially planting trees on Jewish-owned land in British-ruled Palestine.[5]

On the ethnically defined streets of Brooklyn, an awareness of what it meant to be Jewish at the start of the twentieth century came early and hard. The promise of America, opportunity held out to all, had not been realized in the crowded neighborhoods still fed by immigration. Straining under the frictions sparked by so many different peoples packed into a small space, the streets became a battlefield where the inevitable ethnic turf wars, stoked by greed and racial hatred, were waged. Bullying, theft, and worse were common, even daily, occurrences. And soon after his father died, Mickey began to experience the hostility in his community.

At a visit to the Jewish Educational Alliance building, Mickey was scanning the bulletin board, which was always covered with notices of meetings and classes. A small ad grabbed his attention: a New York welfare group was offering a free two-week stay at Camp Shepperd Knapp in Litchfield, Connecticut, for undernourished children. Mickey knew what that meant and, noting his own thin arms and legs and recalling comments from his brothers and mother about his weight, wondered if he fit the description. He collected the forms and took them home for Big Mike, now his guardian, to sign. After a thorough health evaluation, Mickey was one of ten children selected from the Brownsville section of Brooklyn. One of the others, Noah Chase, would recount the experience to Mickey's widow Emma more than fifty years later.

In total, there were about a hundred Jewish children among the six hundred selected to attend the camp that year. While the charity was nondiscriminatory, it seemed to Mickey and Noah that the requirement for undernourishment was much less stringent for the Christian boys. But that wasn't the worst injustice. As Noah remembered, "From the day we got to camp, the Jewish boys were under constant attack. We faced ridicule, like being called sheeney bastards, and physical confrontations with little Mick faring the worst because he fought back." The counselors, all of whom were gentiles, observed only that the Marcus child was the common factor in many disputes. Their idea of discipline? Noah bitterly recalled, "Poor Mickey & me had more castor oil in those two weeks than some kids take all their lives."

Mickey's longed-for escape from a life of poverty, with the chance to savor—if only for a moment—delicacies he would crave for the rest of his life, turned into a nightmare. Yet it had a profound impact on him. Sitting on his bunk and applying a bandage to his bloody nose and lip, he defiantly swore to Noah, "I'm going to build up my muscles . . . make them so hard that I'll be able to defend myself against anybody." Not long after, he began accompanying Big Mike to the local gym, where, true to his oath, he dedicated himself to physical exercise and developing his strength.[6]

A favorite terrain for the infliction of terror on the helpless by local bullies was the subway, the easiest victims being elderly religious Jews, whose distinctive clothing and facial hair made them easily recognizable targets. The tactic was to surround the victim and start yanking on his beard—in a terrifying foreshadowing of a favorite Nazi humiliation and torture—until the robbery and the humiliation was complete. Determined to fight back, Big Mike, with his brothers alongside him, formed and led a group of Jewish toughs looking for payback, organizing a series of ambushes on bullies targeting Jews, eventually clearing away the threat. It wasn't long before young Mickey, short, strong, and scrappy, joined his brothers in defense of their people.

Big Mike had dabbled in boxing before his father's death, and afterward, despite the cost, managed to maintain steady attendance at a local gym. He recognized Mickey's potential early and gave him his first boxing lessons, encouraging his little brother's interest in developing his upper torso and building up his stamina. By the time Mickey was sixteen, his body was "hard as nails." The two brothers developed a lifelong love of boxing and gymnastics, which had a visible impact on both their physiques, the subject of much family joking and quiet pride.[7]

Fig. 2. Steve Stevenson, left, and Mickey, second from right, at Boys High, 1918. Special Collections, West Point

Solid academic performance, paired with strong athletic ability and a genial, easygoing personality, proved to be Mickey's ticket to assimilation and community success. First at Public School 109 and then at Boys High School (now Boys and Girls High School) in Brooklyn, Mickey was a consistent, if not outstanding, student and an avid participant in team sports. Then one of the top schools in New York City, Boys High boasted a celebrated Romanesque Revival building, with gables, dormers, and a corner campanile topped by a pyramid roof. In the confines of Boys High and on its playing field, it students could temporarily escape the reality of poverty and the hardship and prejudice on the streets outside. The school was also a kind of melting pot, a place where young people who would not normally socialize, or even cross paths, learned to see past their differences and form a sense of community.

Mickey developed lasting friendships at Boys High, most especially with Steve Stevenson, his closest friend, high school teammate, college and bachelor roommate, and lifelong confidant. Both boys were members of the high school Arista academic honor society and played together in team sports. By the time the United States entered World

War I in April 1917, Mickey had decided to try to gain admission to West Point and forge a career as a soldier. For his part, Steve had known early in life that he wanted to follow his father and enter West Point, something that must have influenced his best friend as well. Marcus family lore had it that when Big Mike took young Mickey to movie matinees and the trailer featured West Point's Corps of Cadets, Mickey would express his desire to be among them.[8]

Prospects for appointment to West Point were difficult enough, even for legacy candidates. Adding to that was the anti-Semitism deeply ingrained in the Regular Army at the time, a factor that the Marcus family, with no apparent political influence, let alone leverage, had no means to offset. Stevenson got the West Point and movie trailer story from Big Mike, but offered no explanation for how Mickey—or he himself, for that matter—had gotten appointed to the academy. "All I know," he wrote,

> is that Mick was appointed from what was then the 8th Congressional District of Brooklyn by Congressman Cleary in the Bay Ridge section of Brooklyn where I resided. Mick must have had some help to get an appointment from the Congressman of that district which is on the other side of Brooklyn from where he lived. I could not get an appointment from Congressman Cleary because he was a Democrat, and my folks were Republican. I got my appointment from Congressman Siegel of the 20th Congressional District on the East Side of New York City. The irony of it is that it would have been more logical for Mick to get his appointment from Congressman Siegel of the East Side where he was born, and it would have been more logical for me to get my appointment from Congressman Cleary in Bay Ridge where I had lived since I was one year old. Mike really knows something about this but prefers to remain silent. I never asked Mickey about it. It is just one of those questions which will have to remain unanswered.[9]

In his senior year Mickey was voted Best Athlete, as well as captain of both the baseball and football teams. The 1918 Boys High yearbook, the *Recorder*, trumpeted his ambition and intended destination in capital letters: West Point. The prospect of a free education was undoubtedly another factor in his plans, as was the natural patriotism generated by the Great War. Nevertheless, Mickey's decision caused consternation in his mother and other family members, to whom the idea of military service summoned up men in uniform, indifferent to or active participants in pogroms and other harsh actions against Jews.[10]

Various accounts suggest that it was Mickey's athletic or academic prowess that led to his appointment, but Steve clearly implies that there was more—even something sensitive politically, or illegal—involved. Shlomo Shamir alluded to this in his recollection of conversations with Mickey in which the Brooklyn native suggested that he had a tough time getting into West Point.[11]

After graduating from Boys High in January 1919, followed by a year at City College of New York, mostly studying mathematics, Mickey got a lucky break. An excellent performance on the competitive entrance exam and the coincidence of his application with a very brief window of West Point expansion in the spring of 1920 enhanced his chances, and he won the coveted appointment for entrance to the US Military Academy. Because of a nationwide polio outbreak on top of the lingering Spanish influenza pandemic, new cadets were ordered to report two weeks later than usual. On July 1, 1920, Big Mike accompanied Mickey on the New Jersey ferry to Weehawken. As the boarding of the train to Highland Falls, New York, was being announced, big and little brother embraced. Big Mike handed Mickey a ten-dollar bill, saying "Be a good boy, Mick—and don't get into any fights." At the Point, Mickey happily joined his best friends from Boys High, George Smith and Steve Stevenson, and left civilian life behind to join the long gray line.[12]

West Point, July 1, 1920: The Most Democratic Institution in the United States

The long gray line of us stretches
Through the years of a century told,
And the last one feels to the marrow
The grip of your far-off hold.

—"The Corps," US Military Academy hymn

Situated on a commanding plateau on the west bank of the Hudson River, West Point was a key objective of both sides during the Revolutionary War. Washington rated it the most important strategic position in America, selecting Lieutenant Colonel Thaddeus Kosciuszko, a Polish military engineer and hero of Saratoga, to design the defenses in 1778. The next year Washington made his headquarters there, and engineers constructed fortifications, extending an iron chain across the Hudson to command all river traffic. West Point was never taken by the British, despite the treason of its commander, General Benedict Arnold, and remains the oldest continuously occupied military post in the United States.[13]

Even during the American Revolution, Washington and others realized that their recent reliance on foreign experts in technical fields, like engineering and artillery, was a weakness and a battlefield liability, and he urged the creation of an academy devoted to the "practical and theoretical training of cadets for military service." President Thomas Jefferson signed legislation establishing the US Military Academy in 1802 at West Point. Soon afterward, the institution was lucky to have a leader that, to borrow a nautical metaphor, set it on a course it still follows. Colonel Sylvanus Thayer, superintendent from 1817 to 1833, upgraded academic standards, made military discipline and training a leadership function, and firmly established the principle that honorable conduct is the most vital measure of an officer's worth.[14]

Consistent with the needs of a young nation, the West Point curriculum was based on civil engineering and the sciences. Throughout the country's first century, academy graduates did the surveying on land and sea, built railways, bridges, harbors, and roads. Graduates gained experience and recognition for their skill and professionalism during the Mexican and Indian Wars, and they dominated the officer corps of both sides during the Civil War, especially those officers who had been commissioned into the Corps of Engineers, then the most prestigious of the branches and the signal of early promise. Gradually, the development of other professional and staff schools in the various branches of the service led to pressure for a broadening of the curriculum, aligning it more closely to traditional American colleges. There are few universities where its history and the role of its graduates in shaping it better exemplify the soul of the institution.[15]

Office of the Superintendent,
West Point, New York, Fall 1920

To rebuild the corps, the US Military Academy administration in 1920 had just admitted the largest number of plebes ever to its class of 1924: 425 cadets, a 65 percent jump from the year before. The next year the army would reverse course under budgetary and political pressure, and admissions would drop 50 percent, back to prewar levels, where they would stay for a decade. There was, then, a one-year window of opportunity through which Mickey barely squeaked, thus ensuring the poor young man from Brooklyn a free education and a lifelong connection to the military. Without West Point, there would be no military icon Mickey Marcus. It was a necessary but not completely sufficient condition.

Facing a threefold jump in demand for instructors, the math department reached out to former students. At the request of Colonel Charles P. Echols, class of '94, Major Omar "Brad" Bradley '15 returned in the fall of 1920 as an instructor to West Point, where he taught Mickey, Steve Stevenson, Lowell "Wampus" Limpus, Buck

Lanham, and many other members of the class.[16] Just five years out of the academy, Bradley had to catch up quickly, like many of the other graduates brought back by the army to teach. At first he was barely able to stay ahead of the class of '24 plebes.

The state of the school at the time was, in a word, chaos. During the recently concluded world war, the Corps of Cadets had been gutted by five accelerated graduations, transfers of instructors, and other disruptions caused by the US Army's participation in the world conflict. Tactical officers (TACs), also recent alumni—the enforcers of academy discipline, as well as instructors in the military arts and assistant coaches for sports teams, among other duties—had been dispersed. When Bradley arrived from an ROTC assignment in South Dakota, the academy was halfway through the controversial superintendency (1919–22) of Brigadier General Douglas "Mac" MacArthur '03, an often-decorated battlefield hero of the Great War who had been personally selected by Army Chief of Staff Peyton Marsh to modernize and expand the academy, bringing the school into the twentieth century two decades after it started.[17] At the same time as Mac returned to the academy to lead it, Major Jacob "Jake" Devers '09, who would later command the Sixth Army Group in Europe in World War II, was assigned as leader of the field artillery instructors. Major Courtney Hodges, ex '08, and like Mac a highly decorated veteran of World War I, also returned as an infantry instructor and a tactical officer (TAC). Brad got on well with fellow infantryman Courtney Hodges, forging a friendship and later a working relationship that lasted their whole lives with Hodges eventually serving under Bradley in World War II. Like classmate Dwight D. "Ike" Eisenhower '15, he had no use for Jake Devers, who he considered pompous and arrogant.

MacArthur made it his mission to revolutionize the West Point curriculum, which lagged by every academic and pedagogic measure compared to peer civilian institutions in the United States at that time. Given the institution's historic institutional resistance to change, he knew that his proposals would provoke severe reactions, especially from the faculty. Many of them had taught MacArthur but had never personally experienced combat or a modern academic environment. These men viewed him as a threat to both the established order of the institution and the power of West Point's Academic Board.

In this standoff, MacArthur's personality didn't help. Although he was idolized by the cadets as a genuine war hero and the very embodiment of the corps—Mickey expressed his admiration of MacArthur often—the superintendent was aloof and reclusive, rarely seen on campus except at sports events, which he relished.

Many alumni had mixed feelings about the new administration and viewed some of the more unpleasant aspects of life at the academy with a mixture of nostalgia and survivor's pride. They sided with the conservatives on culture issues but recognized the Point's academic and military shortcomings. Bradley and Devers both cheered the new emphasis on physical fitness and the expansion of the intramural sports program, as well as the revitalization of the curriculum, which emphasized math to the detriment of the humanities. More puritanical by nature than most of his colleagues, Bradley balked at some measures to ease discipline, like ending the smoking ban (he didn't smoke, himself). He initially viewed greater freedom with passes to New York City skeptically, fearing an increase in discipline issues that never materialized, and thought that Macarthur's loosening of restrictions struck at the very foundation that made the institution something special. Devers, much more of a scholar warrior, supported the educational reforms and cheered public attempts to ease the harsh environment for plebes and lower classmen.

Nothing, however, aroused more controversy on campus and the alumni network than MacArthur's attempts to shut down the summer camp on West Point's parade field, the Plain, and abolish hazing, which had gained public attention after the widely reported suicide of a plebe in the press. Macarthur viewed the summer camp as useless from a military training perspective and a boondoggle for the faculty and staff, but the hazing issue he took more personally. As a cadet and son of a well-known Civil War hero, he'd had a particularly brutal experience during the initial rite of passage known as Beast Barracks in his first weeks as a plebe, tormented by hardcore TACs who drew their inspiration for abuse from John "Blackjack" Pershing '86.[18]

The president of his class and first captain of the corps, Pershing had returned to the academy a decade and a half later as a merciless disciplinarian, hated by those he encountered as "cold as ice." His tenure as a TAC was notorious. After he bragged to a young lady that he had "cowed the entire Corps," the cadets retaliated by giving him the silent treatment, refusing to converse with him except for official business, a rare sanction against a superior officer. When he entered the dining hall on duty, they sat at attention, refusing to eat. Yet even though Pershing himself was gone by the time Macarthur arrived, there were still admirers and practitioners of his hazing style at West Point.[19]

It would only take a few years for the disapproval of Macarthur's revolutionary ideas among old graduates and the Academic Board to find a sponsor. When General Pershing became chief of staff of the army in 1922, Macarthur's fate was sealed, and he was ousted from the academy that spring. Those in Pershing's orbit, most importantly George C. Marshall, would later fall in 1930, when MacArthur became chief of staff.

The new super named by Pershing, Major General Fred W. Sladen '90, was, according to Bradley, a disciplinarian and "really one of the fine officers we had in those days," with a wry sense of humor. One Sunday, shortly after he arrived during Mickey's second year, Sladen invited Will Rogers to entertain the cadets. Rogers won over the corps right away at his host's expense, cracking, "Well, I see General Sladen is trying to do for you in four years what it took him five years to do." That was true for a surprising number of generals; Bradley found that out of the major generals in the army at that time, sixteen out of twenty-one had spent five years at the Point, as had Patton.[20] It certainly wasn't lost on anyone, especially the cadets, that MacArthur, by contrast, had graduated at the top of his class, and many, including Devers, lamented the change in intellectual orientation.[21]

The new superintendent rewound the clock, with the hearty approval of the higher ranks and alumni. Hazing, Beast Barracks, and the summer camp on the Plain all returned to their previous levels of intensity. Congress, in no mood for expensive new schemes, shelved all of MacArthur's ambitious expansion plans. A return to previous routine became the order of the day. Nevertheless, a modernized curriculum and intramural sports programs endured as MacArthur's legacy.

Mickey and Steve Stevenson arrived at the academy a full academic year after Macarthur arrived, just as his policies were taking hold and shaking up the place. Just months after the big fight with Harmony, Macarthur was gone.

"The Thundering Herd": US Military Academy at West Point, Highland Falls, NY, July 1, 1920

From the beginning at Beast Barracks, Mickey became a prime hazing target. It wasn't only his high-pitched voice. By then he had transformed his body into a tailor's nightmare and was issued a blouse with a collar several sizes too big, to fit his barrel-like chest and bulging shoulders. Upperclassmen took special pleasure inflicting on him a particularly humiliating form of abuse, forcing him to tuck his chin back into the collar and calling him "Tom Jenkins's plebe," a reference to the legendary wrestling coach Tom Jenkins, who had a nasty habit of publicly ridiculing heavyset cadets. Mickey's laugh, a universal object of recollection, intensified the fervor of those with a natural proclivity for sanctioned insults.[22]

In some things, everyone was equal in misery. One particularly hard-nosed tactical officer stood out during their first days. Major Simon Bolivar Buckner Jr., later commander of Tenth Army on Okinawa and highest-ranking general killed in World War II by enemy fire, while overseeing physical training one very hot summer day, ordered the plebes to run "up a terrifically steep hill on which man after man just fainted from the heat and the labor." Just as plebe morale hit bottom, with many considering resignation, the TACs returned to their normal duties, and upperclassmen took over the hazing with the fury of those who had recently suffered and enjoyed the pain of others.[23]

Thundering Herd classmate Czar Dyer stood next to Mickey in their first formation as plebes in Company F on the very day they entered the academy. The two bonded as squad mates on the hikes that summer, especially on the killer hike with Major Buckner. Marcus and Dyer became special targets of Edward Shelley Gibson '22, a hard-bitten decorated World War I veteran from West Virginia, who demanded they report to him for weeks to stand plastered against his wall during every available minute each day. "Gibson had the unique distinction of being the only mortal that Mickey ever thoroughly detested," Dyer would later write.[24]

Two distinctive characteristics of Mickey were often mentioned: his uproarious laugh and his habit of using the parting salutation "Cheerio." According to Stevenson, the former "broke down all barriers of rank and protocol and won the affection of his associates as few men have ever done in the Army."[25] Emma wasn't sure when the young Mickey started saying "Cheerio." She once asked one of Mickey's work colleagues and friends, NYC detective Frank Grottano, about it. Mickey picked up his trademark greeting a decade after attending West Point, Grottano told her: "A British delegation toured the NYC prisons to make a comparison with their institutions. One of them instead of saying goodbye said, cheerio. It tickled Mickey's fancy as he mimicked the visitor and began to use the word himself until his cheery cheerio became his own—a spontaneous and natural greeting."[26]

But whenever that good spirit arose, at the beginning of his first year Cadet Marcus was a prime target for "crawling," another academy term for hazing, as Stevenson reported in a letter to his sister dated September 3, 1920: "We get treated like animals now. We never appear outside of our rooms unless it's necessary. They crawl us for everything, but at the table we suffer the most. We must sit so straight we can hardly eat. . . . Marcus came to the Mess Hall one day with a little piece of lint on his head and they bawled him out for coming to mess covered with rags. Mickey wasn't bothered a bit. He just laughs at every upper classman who tries to crawl him."[27]

Mickey and his suite mates got used to the steady stream of upperclassmen who came by to rattle him and try to push him to the breaking point. Not all of them were malevolent, though, and one who took a special interest in his fellow Brooklynite was Second Classman Harry Albert '22, who was cadet sergeant in Company F and kept an eye on him. It was beneath the dignity of some to crawl a plebe, but Albert watched over him with "dignified condescension" to make sure he grew up properly. That never seemed to happen, though, and Mici (how he signed his letters to Albert) was "always either grinning or laughing out loud with that peculiar high-pitched cackling laughter." At that point Albert's interest became frustration with Mici's general sloppiness. "I did not know that under his Plebe-skins were the shoulder muscles of the boxer-gymnast; and I mistook his bulging shoulder and back muscles under his loose-fitting Plebe-skins, for indifference to posture."[28]

In front of the mess hall, as the company was lining up after dinner to march back to barracks, Albert heard Mici's laugh. By this time totally fed up with his attitude, and as a matter of pride and duty to straighten out the incorrigible plebe, Albert confronted his charge, saying, as he would later recount, "Mr. Dum john, wipe that smile off,"

> which he tried to do, but didn't quite succeed. Albert ran his fingernails along his braid, and uncovered soup stains.
>
> "You're a disgrace, Mister, and I'm ashamed of you." Mickey began to smile. "Wipe that grin off," which he made a valiant effort to do, but couldn't quite make it; so, I went after him again and ordered.
>
> "Take your hand and wipe it off, do you hear? Now throw it down and step on it!"
>
> I will say this much for him, that he obeyed my order about going through the motions of wiping off the grin, throwing it down and stepping on it, only to hear him burst out laughing with that inimitable high-pitched cackle that we who knew him could never fail to recognize as his trademark. At this point my

> patience and dignity were exhausted. Here was my Plebe making a monkey out of me, a Sargeant, in front of the other Plebes, so I go up and I says to him,
>
> "Mr. Dum john, if you don't stop this grinning, I'll have the whole corps of cadets after you. I'm ashamed of you!"
>
> And to that remark from me, Mr. Marcus gave the classic rejoinder, so typical of the fearlessness and cheerfulness of his nature:
>
> "Sir, no matter what you do to me, I cannot stop smiling."[29]

When Mickey became an upperclassman, he did not let his harsh experience poison his attitude toward the concept of hazing. According to Stevenson, Mickey "played it down the middle when he became an upperclassman. He certainly did not make life miserable for Plebes or crawl them hard. On the other extreme he did not go out of his way to ease their burdens. He helped those that needed help and corrected those that needed correction, when these cases came to his attention, but I do not recall that he went overboard in either direction." In his last year, Mickey still racked up more than three dozen demerits.[30]

Emma Chaisson Marcus

In his sophomore year Mickey started to move away from boxing just as Army began to make its mark in intercollegiate sports. He joined the gymnastics team, and by his senior year was Army's best horizontal bar gymnast. His feats on the boards were hailed by the *Howitzer* yearbook as "unequaled in years," winning for him more recognition and an invitation to the Olympic tryouts. In the summer of his sophomore year, he also met Emma Chaisson, the cousin of a friend, at a party. He was checking out the older girls but was immediately taken by Emma's beauty and musical gifts, and she by the romance of a handsome cadet in uniform. For more than a quarter century, and in many and varied circumstances, Mickey's achievements as a West Point athlete—as well as his Roaring Twenties antics on the dance floor with girlfriend Emma—and his extraordinary physique would be recalled, in tranquility and on battlefields.[31]

David Marcus and Emma Chaisson (1905–1982) shared a mutual belief that their relationship was encompassed by the Yiddish word *beshert*, derived from the Middle High German *beschern*, "preordained or allotted." Simply put, two people described as *beshert* are meant for each other, what some today might call soulmates. There is ample proof that the concept goes beyond any one culture, ethnicity, or people. From the moment the shy sixteen-year-old girl glimpsed the athletic cadet in uniform at a party, they were *beshert*, and everyone knew it, later including members of the underground government of Israel.

After her husband's death, Emma Marcus exerted the kind of control of his image that put her firmly in an American military tradition of steely-willed, competent widows—Libby Custer, LaSalle Pickett, and Kitty Buhler Bradley, to name just a few—women whose lives were defined by the nurturing, protection, and sometimes active marketing of their husbands' public image and legacy. For three and a half decades Emma successfully maneuvered lawyers, writers, filmmakers, veterans' groups, and the wily politicians of two nations into entrenching and polishing the image of her beloved husband.

West Point eventually became the focal point for Mickey's American military legacy, as well as a common Israel diplomatic stop. Claiming Marcus as their own, the American Veterans of Israel, official successor to the various Machal organizations, with the support of the West Point rabbis, Israeli government officials, Jewish veterans, and others, in the 1960s began holding an annual Marcus memorial service. On Sunday, June 10, 1985, at a special ceremony at the West Point Cemetery, the government of Israel placed an official commemorative plaque on Marcus's tombstone. Since then, numerous officials from Israel have visited the grave, including ambassadors, officers, prime ministers, and presidents.[32]

In the end, though, nothing softened the fact that Emma had, for much of her adult life, been left behind to grieve alone. She never remarried and remained an elementary school teacher. Plagued by illness and blindness in later years, and living near poverty, she still held a special position in the eyes of her Brooklyn community, those in Israel who knew her husband, and Mickey's friends and West Point classmates and their wives, especially Steve Stevenson's bride, Mair. The couples are buried side by side.

On June 1, 1924, after an address by Chief of Staff John J. Pershing, David Marcus graduated 145th of 406 in his class. His yearbook *Howitzer* page, written by Lowell "Wampus" Limpus '24, is remarkably prescient, praising the warmth of his personality, his cheerful disposition, his achievements as a boxing and gymnastic competitor, and his support—often at the expense of his class standing—for cadets experiencing difficulty. He was always there for friends, in class, on the playing field, or in any way he could. The voice of Limpus, who struggled in Omar Bradley's math class, always needing extra help and getting it from Mickey, echoes in this yearbook profile, which captures the essence of Marcus's expansive concept of service and sacrifice.[33]

Fig. 3. Mickey's official US Military Academy portrait. West Point Museum

Duty, Honor, Country. The ethos of West Point created Mickey Marcus, American hero. At the center of Marcus's life, and manifest in all aspects of it, was the near-organic sense of personal obligation expressed in the academy's motto, with its evocation of transcendent responsibilities. For Mickey, the obligations and sacrifice implied by the motto draw legitimacy and authority from trusted institutions like his alma mater, from the American promise of equal justice under law and freedom from religious persecution, and from a keen recognition that free people take responsibility for their actions. In this book's opening vignette, the context is a minor sports drama, but the reason that Marcus chose the path he took in life is clearest in just such settings, right up through his last two hundred days.

Honor and integrity are manifest first, and—in the most defining sense, by words and promises at the highest level—matching ideals. Mickey risked his military career the day of the boxing bout because he had said that he would fight, and the accident in the West Point stables that afternoon changed nothing. He would have fought with a broken arm. The hard lessons of assimilation for Jewish immigrants in the tenements of early twentieth-century Brooklyn emerge, drilled into Mickey by his revered older brother Big Mike, and made real by the open anti-Semitism they experienced on the streets: never let down your family, school, team, yourself, no matter the sacrifice or pain. Or anyone else's. Never join the oppressors. Learn how to best stand and fight, long odds or short, broken or whole, even with defeat staring you in the face. Personal will to prevail is more than an abstraction in any struggle. When World War II descended on Mickey Marcus's world, and again when the struggle of the Jewish people to reestablish sovereignty over their claimed land reached the critical moment, many strands of identity, personal history, and politics came together in Mickey Marcus.

Unrelenting pride and vanity, as well as self-deprecation, permeates his story, and the rivalry with Jazz Harmony displayed them all. As Mickey said about the decision to go to British Mandate Palestine, after he unsuccessfully tried to recruit several others, "I may not be the best man for the job but I'm the only one willing to go."[34] That was the same thing he said to Steve Stevenson after the fight. Who else would, or could, battle Harmony for the honor of the Thundering Herd? And Mickey certainly appreciated the grand gesture, honed by years of service as a high-level War Department General Staff officer in wartime Washington, routinely interacting with the secretaries of state and war, the army chief of staff, and top Allied officers. And his ease in social situations was also enhanced by his West Point reputation and his instinct for comity and comradeship. Somehow he always managed to arrange the delivery of the best single malt scotch available at numerous wartime conferences, even at the embarkation port just before D-Day.

Finally, even before West Point, there is the flirtation with—almost a longing for—danger, a restlessness of unbridled spirit, that Marcus displayed in other situations, and that his wife Emma would later openly liken to a "rendezvous with death," the now famous phrase of a long-forgotten poem. It is this that drew to him the war correspondents who were around Marcus during his final days, especially the greatest combat photographer of the century, Robert Capa. In Marcus, Capa saw some kind of American echo of himself, and he warned Mickey that he was getting close to the edge, just as he had in the ring that day back at West Point. By ignoring the very real possibility that he could end his military career by boxing while injured, and later by visiting dangerous war fronts in a vicious civil war marked by atrocity, Mickey mocked fate to write his own destiny. In the end, though he had left the life of a soldier long before, he reached the gateway to a professional officer's success, the brigadier's star—yet even that isn't so simple. When he did walk away from something, however, it was always on his own, personally reckoned terms.

Fort Jay, Governors Island, Manhattan Harbor, Company H, Sixteenth Infantry, Fall 1924

Mickey and Steve, after a brief leave, and now newly commissioned Regular Army second lieutenants of infantry, reported to Fort Jay,

Governors Island, Manhattan Harbor as platoon leaders in Company H, Third Battalion, Sixteenth Infantry. The assignment was a lucky break, landing the two of them close to home, Emma, and Mair, now Steve's steady girlfriend. Roommates once again, Mickey and Steve picked up a fourth-hand Dodge so beat up that the only way into it was by climbing over its jammed and twisted doors. The picture of the elegant Emma struggling to enter the contraption was the subject of singular ribbing. As bachelors stationed on a small island dominated by Regular Army mores and traditional social conventions, the new arrivals quickly became targets of the base matchmakers. The car made escape easier, but the badgering stopped when the post ladies learned that the two new lieutenants had steady girlfriends whom they were likely to marry.[35]

Service in the interwar army had its professional challenges. Recently transferred to Manhattan, the Sixteenth Infantry had a distinguished record in World War I, fighting as part of the First Infantry Division, the "Big Red One." The division's motto was (and remains) "No mission too difficult, no sacrifice too great—Duty First." The Sixteenth was part of the first US unit committed to battle, so many of its peacetime enlisted men, NCOs, and company grade officers were combat veterans. It was later dubbed "New York's Own" by Mayor Fiorello La Guardia, and "The Sidewalks of New York" became its regimental song. As a group the Sixteenth was insular; it bore a proud reputation that would last through World War II, and did not welcome outsiders, including local West Point–trained men.[36]

Limpus, a combat veteran who knew the context better than most, described Mickey's first encounter with the hard-edged men under his command as one that established the young officer's reputation for an unconventional, if effective, style of leadership. The story would become standard in West Point lore, although John Valentine "Frenchy" Grombach, who was also on the base at the time, questioned its details.[37] Finding himself in command of tough regulars, according to Limpus, Mickey gathered his men, who were not prepared for this squat, top-heavy, newly minted shavetail lieutenant, shouting at them in a high-pitched voice that became even more piercing with anger. When he shouted the order, “Squads right, march!” he was greeted with raucous laughter and vulgar shouts. It was an act of gross insubordination and a direct challenge to his authority, one demanding an immediate and decisive response.

Mickey ordered the men to march behind the stables, formed them into a circle, took position in the center, and addressed the platoon, focusing his intense gaze on the obvious ringleaders, one at a time.

“I can see I’m going to have trouble with you,” he said. “We’ll settle it now.” Then, stripping off his shirt, he sauntered up to the largest man in the group, the one who had laughed loudest and longest, and got right in his face.

“Let’s forget about rank. I don’t like to be laughed at, and I can lick any man who tries it. Do you believe that?”

The large and tough-looking private, eyeing the much shorter young officer, gave an honest answer: “No sir, not if you mean that about forgetting about rank.”

Mickey didn’t hesitate. “OK, let’s get going.”

Immediately the soldier lunged at Mickey, who avoided the thrust, then decked the larger man, knocking him out cold with his pulverizing left. Mickey slowly put back on his blouse, adjusted his Sam Browne belt, and faced the now silent and respectful soldiers, the timber of his voice no longer a laughing matter,

“From now on you men had better remember one thing. This is my kind of company punishment. I’m not going to bother with kitchen police and things like that. Now take that man back to the barracks and cut out the nonsense. I don’t like trouble.”[38]

The tactic worked. Laughter and derision evaporated that day, and Mickey’s platoon became the best disciplined unit in the regiment. During his two years in the Regulars, he participated in the normal peacetime routine of the 1920s: individual weapons, squad, and platoon training in all weather. That was integrated with periods in the field, operating in larger units with the Organized Reserve Corps (ORC), local ROTC school formations, and summers at the Civilian Military Training Camp at Camp Dix, New Jersey. During this period, in order to make money, Mickey began to box professionally in Brooklyn and Long Island under the ring name of Danny Mars. That lasted until his commanding officer saw him in the ring.[39]

By the spring of 1926, after two years of night classes at Brooklyn Law along with his daytime duties, and much soul-searching, Mickey resigned from the Regulars, applying for a commission in the ORC as a second lieutenant in the field artillery. With the Regular Army shrinking, and opportunities for promotion disappearing, dozens of his classmates made the same choice, including Steve Stevenson and Frenchy Grombach. Many would return to service during World War II, including dozens who held command and staff positions, and more than a dozen generals.[40]

There was more involved in the decision. His last duty assignment was slated to be Panama, and that didn't fit his plans with Emma. Even so, that might have been tolerable except for a major professional problem. The story was recounted by his classmate Czar Dyer, then a second lieutenant serving at Camp Dix, who ran into Mickey while commanding the Signal Corps detachment there. Dyer described driving "a thoroughly blue Mickey" to the railroad station at Trenton on his very last night in the army. Contrary to classmate Lowell Limpus's account, Dyer claims that Mick said he was leaving principally because his battalion commander, Lieutenant Colonel Nicholas W. Campanole, was a tyrant who had driven him ragged with his crazy and conflicting orders.[41] Dyer, who in 1929 also left service as a second lieutenant for his own reasons, confirmed that characterization. After resigning, Mickey continued studying law, got a job, and after a five-year courtship married Emma, who was working as a fifth-grade teacher. By then she was a skilled pianist, which enriched Mickey's passion for opera, and for a long time she filled their home with music.[42]

Fig. 4. Mickey with his bride, Emma, on their wedding day, July 3, 1927. Military History Institute

Deputy Prison Commissioner, Welfare Island, NYC, January 24, 1934

In 1928, Marcus challenged Democrat Murray Ahearn for the New York State Assembly seat of Brooklyn's Kings County Second District on the Republican ticket. Mickey lost the election but gained admirers and important contacts during the race. Soon after, he became eligible for a job as a junior lawyer in the US Treasury Department, and then as an assistant US attorney under district attorney George Z. Medalie, an ambitious Jewish politician who ran the Justice Department's Southern District of New York office. The working relationship between Medalie and Marcus developed into a friendship, including exchanges of letters during World War II, that would last for the rest of their lives.[43]

One of Mickey's closest associates at the DA's office was Thomas E. Dewey, chief of the bootlegging division, and on his way to fame also as a racket-busting Manhattan DA, governor of New York, and Republican presidential candidate during Mickey's final days in 1948. "Everybody loved Mickey Marcus because he genuinely with all his heart, liked everybody," said Dewey. "The feeling we all had for him can more properly be described as an abiding affection. Any conversation with him was animating and stimulating." The two spent most of their time tracking down violations of Prohibition, with no small amount of irony, as most of Mickey's office mates enjoyed social drinking, none more than Mickey himself.[44]

When former World War I army pilot and Republican congressman Fiorello La Guardia won election as mayor of New York on a reform, antimachine ticket in 1933, Mickey became a front-row participant in the exciting reformist Republican City Fusion Party administration. His name had first been passed to La Guardia by Limpus, who was then covering city government for the *New York Daily News*. He was visiting the US attorney's office one afternoon in 1932 when he witnessed a confrontation between Mickey and some fixers involved in a prohibition case, during which Mickey threw the men out of his office. Limpus described the encounter the next day to his lunch partner, then congressman Fiorello La Guardia.

Months later, on the night of the mayoral election, the victor invited the newsman to his place and over drinks asked him about the honest DA he had mentioned months before. Reference checks with both Medalie and Dewey affirmed Limpus's recommendation of the candidate for the position the new mayor had in mind. Later in a face-to-face interview, "The Hat," as a cartoonist nicknamed La Guardia because of his fondness for ten-gallon headwear, put it to Mickey, looking deep into his eyes:

"I'm searching for a Deputy Commissioner for New York City's prison system to run things. I particularly want an honest man."

Returning the stare, Mickey replied, "You're looking at one."

Mickey had supported La Guardia's election but had no plans to enter politics and was at the same time thinking of leaving government service to go into private law practice with Arthur H. Schwartz, another prosecutor and rising Republican star. Later, Schwartz would play a role in supporting the legacy of Mickey Marcus in the early years after his death. When La Guardia made his surprise approach, it upended Mickey's plans, something that would mark his life more than once. Emma was not happy but gave way. The Hat, who had much in common as well as stark personality differences with Marcus, was a persuasive man.

Mickey assumed the job as acting prison commissioner on December 27, 1933, effective until the arrival of nationally known penologist Austin H. MacCormick, who was wrapping up matters at his federal prison job. On January 1, 1934, Mickey officially became first deputy, the person running day-to-day operations. As it happened, MacCormick fell ill with a chronic condition shortly after his arrival and dramatic debut, so Mickey would be de facto commissioner until he officially assumed the title of commissioner more than six years later. It's not clear how sudden MacCormack's illness was, or whether The Hat had known about it when hand-picking Mickey for the job of number two. [45] Steve and Mair Stevenson were in Times Square on New Year's Eve when they saw Mickey's name flashed across the skyscraper lights and immediately sent a congratulatory telegram to the new deputy commissioner.[46]

Mickey had already begun work on a spectacular program of reform, displaying the planning genius that would characterize both his political and military careers. Taking direct aim at the top of the long-entrenched corrupt Tammany Hall–backed prison administration, Marcus envisioned a highly visible and dramatic demonstration of Mayor La Guardia's determination to change things fast. In a highly targeted operation, the new administration would take down the corrupt leadership of the most visible and notorious of the dozen and a half institutions that made up the NYC prison system. One of them, Welfare Island (now Roosevelt Island), had a rotten reputation stretching back a half century, having been described as the "worst prison in the city" by Marcus's predecessor, a respected professional who had tried unsuccessfully, if sincerely, to garner support for reforms in the previous humiliated administration.[47]

Not only did the prisons in NYC reek of systemic corruption, but the rot reached all the way to the top administrators. By the time MacCormick arrived at his post, announcing a major personnel shake-up in his department and promising to purge all grafters, Marcus was already gathering evidence that would "go right down the line" to rid the department of its bad actors. Two separate gangster mobs had corrupted the authorities at Welfare Island, including the deputy warden, some jailers, and the medical staff, who, acting as precursors of a scene from the film *Casino*, were permitting certain criminal prisoners to use the hospital facilities for their own personal comfort and profit. To make room for the top crooks, sick and injured inmates were thrown out of their hospital beds and scattered around the ordinary cell dormitories. After only three weeks on the job, Marcus was ready to move, and he personally led the raid on Welfare Island. He hoped his action would expose the full extent of the corruption and threat to the security of the citizens in the prison, and then clean it up, exactly as the new mayor had promised.[48]

In the early morning of January 24, 1934, an armed seventy-man posse of wardens and plainclothes and uniformed police officers, with journalists in tow, all of them personally organized by Marcus, descended clandestinely on the small island in the East River. There was no breach of security. Part serious business and part performative publicity stunt, the action featured the swashbuckling young reformer and former boxing champion physically confronting thugs and corrupt officials alike. Mickey was the first man through the prison doors. He bolted up the stairs to find Joie Rao, one of the mob leaders, sitting in a barber's chair in a hospital ward, being shaved by a capo. Mickey grabbed the gangster's shirt collar, pulled him up, and hustled him off to an ordinary cell.

Operating in secrecy and with military precision, MacCormick and Marcus were on the spot, dividing their tasks, the commissioner manning the forward HQ and the deputy leading the raiding party. The immediate goal was to detain corrupt deputy warden Daniel Sheehan and return all prisoners to normal detention, beginning with the kingpins of the two gangster mobs that had practically taken over the hospital facility. Evidence already collected by Marcus suggested that the raid would uncover various types of contraband, including drugs and weapons. When they discovered the stache, the photographers were ready—just as Mickey had planned.[49]

The carefully choreographed twenty-four-hour-long raid, along with ongoing exposés of local Democrat-protected prison corruption and drug dealing, fueled headlines for weeks. It was a good start to the promised cleanup, as the prison had been a target of reformists of every description since the end of the nineteenth century, when it was known as Blackwell Island.[50] During the investigation that followed the raid, further shakeups at the prison engulfed the doctors, other keepers, and eventually the warden himself.[51]

Later the story became the source for the Warner Bros. stock movie *Blackwell's Island* (1939), with the popular young Jewish American actor John Garfield perfectly cast as the Mickey-inspired zealous, punch-throwing journalist reformer. Mickey was paid as a technical adviser on the project and treated to an all-expenses-paid stay in Hollywood hosted by the Warner studio. In an interview with a local city correspondent, he described his vacation, his first in four years: "I lived at the Hollywood Athletic Club for $2.50 a day, including a swim in the outdoor pool each morning. Mr. Jack Warner did things on a magnificent scale. He sent me out and back on the Super Chief, even had radios on it! I listened to Tristan on the way back. Some opera!" Emma didn't go, and she was angry with Mickey, who unilaterally decided, without even discussing it, that it wasn't worth her taking time off work. These unilateral decisions involving her were not unique.[52]

During this period Mickey spent a lot of after-hour time in the office compiling statistics relating to criminal behavior, which he proudly showed to his former law professor Franklin F. Russell. Russell suggested that Mickey ask New York University whether they would accept his research for credit towards a doctorate in penology. Mickey followed his advice but felt duty-bound to show it to his boss, Mayor La Guardia, because, as the professor noted, "Mickey was a straight shooter and didn't pull any punches and the statistics and his conclusions would hurt some people." His controversial research focused on certain categories of crimes and the ethnicity of offenders, finding correlations he considered significant, though joking that "he himself was half Irish and half Jewish and therefore could hardly be accused of being prejudiced against the Jewish or the Irish, which he told me with the great gusto that only he could use in telling a story." It was a joke he told often, varying his half self-identity depending on his audience. When Mickey showed the thesis to The Hat, he was duly impressed, declaring, "Mickey, we're having an election in a few weeks. It would be a wonderful thing to have this thesis published by a member of my administration. All it would do is lose me the Italian, Irish, Jewish and Negro votes."[53]

La Guardia's growing confidence in Marcus was nevertheless reflected in Mickey's appointment in the summer of 1936 as a temporary magistrate, the youngest in the city's history, to help relieve an excessive case backlog in the crowded Manhattan courts. His office celebrated the appointment, his friends giving him a judge's robe and gavel. Mickey was a great boss, and Rose Sanker, his secretary, was one of his biggest fans. "During baseball season," she wrote to Emma, "DM was always presented with season complimentary tickets but seldom used them. He was always thoughtful about giving different personnel a chance to be excused for an afternoon and spend an enjoyable time at the game. Who wouldn't love a man like that?"[54]

Back at the job after his month-long stint at the court, Marcus collaborated closely with special prosecutor Tom Dewey in an operation that eventually led to the shutdown of Charles "Lucky" Luciano's prostitution ring. Dewey's office issued a statement shortly afterward to personally "express my admiration and appreciation for the cooperation of David Marcus, Deputy Commissioner of Corrections. The handling of more than one hundred thirty prisoners, including one hundred twenty material witnesses, in the various jails in this city has been a major problem calling for almost daily conferences and extraordinary cooperation on his part. This, he has given, in unstinted measure, and without his help, this case would not have been brought to a successful conclusion."[55]

Mickey was now one of the most visible members of the La Guardia bipartisan Fusion government and enjoyed the public confidence of the mayor. He also was beginning to develop a national reputation as a prison reformist. After he'd been running the department for six years, on April 22, 1940, La Guardia finally appointed him to the top spot as commissioner of corrections.[56]

Fig. 5. Mayor Fiorello La Guardia swears in Mickey as prison commissioner as Emma looks on, April 1940. Special Collections, West Point

CHAPTER 2

World War II

Just got back from 21,000 miles of flight from Washington to Miami–Puerto Rico–British Guyana–Natal–Accra–Khartoum–Cairo–Jerusalem–Iran–Cairo–Tunis–Palermo–Naples–Bari–Brindisi–Palermo–Algiers–Marrakesh–Dakar–Natal–Guyana–Puerto Rico–Washington.

—Letter from Mici to Emma, December 18, 1943

Mr. Fixit, Twenty-Seventh Infantry Division, New York National Guard, August 1940

Following the news reports from Europe, especially after Germany started to make aggressive moves, Mickey became convinced that war with Hitler was inevitable and desirable before all civilization was destroyed, and that he wanted to be in uniform when it happened. Emma also attributed his early zeal to gratitude to America for providing him with a free education at Boys High and West Point and a sense of obligation to repay his country with what he knew would be wartime service. Like many of his fellow West Point–trained citizens at the onset of the war who had not remained professionals, and echoing the beginning of the Civil War, Mickey used his political, business, and school connections to get an appointment in his local state militia, in this case his NY National Guard division. He had maintained his Organized Reserve Corps (ORC) commission as a field artillery officer since 1926, and his friend and confidant Colonel Arthur V. McDermott, judge advocate general of the New York National Guard, recommended him to Major General William N. Haskell, commanding Twenty-Seventh Infantry Division. Mickey also knew the general's son, Colonel John F. Haskell '25, a slightly younger West Pointer who, like Mickey, resigned during the late 1920s and then left a high-powered Wall Street job to rejoin the Twenty-Seventh Infantry Division (ID) and serve as executive officer to his father.

Just four months before his appointment as prison commissioner in August 1939 Mickey was commissioned captain in the Judge Advocate General's Corps, New York National Guard. Established in 1775, the US Army's Judge Advocate General (JAG) Corps runs the largest and one of the oldest law firms in the United States and sets the rules and regulations for all such military organizations, including the National Guard. The duties of a US Army infantry division JAG in World War II spanned the full range of legal issues, but the most important was providing legal advice to the division commander and staff. This included military, administrative, and contract law questions as well as representation in legal proceedings, police, courts-martial, administrative hearings, and contract disputes. The JAG supervised legal research and drafting, training and mentoring staff, and legal assistance to soldiers and families, and served as the division's ethics officer. Depending on circumstances, the JAG might also be called upon to render advice on intelligence, counterintelligence, and security matters, as well as the rules of warfare. The division JAG made sure that all department operations were fully compliant with applicable law, no matter the jurisdiction or complexities.[1]

The transfer earlier from the field artillery ORC to JAG, NY National Guard, facilitated Mickey's quick transition to more active military involvement, and he was there when the Twenty-Seventh was sworn into federal service on October 15, 1940, a year after the invasion of Poland by Germany and the Soviet Union. That same day the division left by train for the large infantry training center at Fort McClellan, Alabama. Emma was at the train station amidst a tumultuous scene and their goodbye kiss made the newspaper. Mickey's reasons for leaving his job were not entirely appreciated by La Guardia and friends, not to mention Emma, who once again was unhappy about one of his unilateral decisions made without discussion with her.[2]

La Guardia, upset and concerned that his loyal cabinet member might not return to his job once discharged from the army, tried to persuade Mickey to accept his salary as prison commissioner while in uniform. Mickey flatly refused the offer of double-dipping, calling it "dishonest," feeling that it would compromise his conduct and obscure his basic loyalty. He did, however, know how to maintain relationships, and when the salary incident went public with a negative slant on the Big Hat, Mickey defended him and La Guardia, as big-hearted as his commissioner, penned a note saluting Mickey's sense of duty and honor.[3]

During his time at Fort McClellan, Mickey developed a close working relationship with Major General Haskell, who said of their service together, "It seemed to me that when any particularly bothersome matter came to my desk, the first man I would send for would be Colonel Marcus for his recommendation." Mickey also deepened his friendship with Haskell's son John. In the war, the younger Haskell would be severely wounded in combat while serving in Europe with a secret radio intelligence unit called Force T, losing a leg but recovering and going on to enjoy a renewed and distinguished financial career.[4]

One of Mickey's ancillary assignments was division headquarters commandant, in which he was responsible for the smooth operation of the nerve center of the division. Every detail within the HQ perimeter except discipline and training falls under the commandant's authority. Ensuring local security, managing dining facilities, overseeing vehicles, and maintaining sanitation standards are high on the list of routine but vital duties. Organizing and shepherding inspections by high-ranking VIPs was common before the attack on Pearl Harbor when interest in the peacetime expansion was high, and before the pressures of wartime curtailed the visits. Mickey welcomed members of Congress, prominent businessmen, high-ranking officers, government officials, especially New Yorkers, and well-known journalists who visited Fort McClellan often.[5]

Upon Federal mobilization, MG Haskell's mission was to build a well-trained combat-ready division and bring it up to wartime strength. To do so, he would have to improve Fort McClellan as a place in which to live and train. When Haskell first arrived, the men of the regiments were quartered on the fringe of the main post in squad tents pitched on wooden platforms. The officer's housing wasn't much better. His staff addressed the reality that the fort was unprepared for the projected influx of new troops and lacked sufficient housing, training grounds and facilities, uniforms, weapons, and other equipment to achieve their basic goals. The first step was to erect a temporary wooden mess hall at the end of each company street, with a latrine at the opposite end. Within a month of the arrival at the fort of the Twenty-Seventh Division, the army's previous plans for expansion started to bear fruit, with the soldiers moving into more permanent structures on the main post.

Fig. 6. Mickey at Fort McClellan as JAG and HQ commandant, Twenty-Seventh Infantry Division, late 1940. Military History Institute

Fort McClellan remained one of the largest and most important infantry training facilities during the war, and after nine months of training, on June 27, 1941, the division became a part of VIII Corps, Second Army.

The staff and soldiers of the mobilized National Guard divisions were inexperienced in large-unit operations and unfamiliar with the complexities of modern maneuver warfare and its demands. Many of the long-serving officers owed their positions to political influence and cronyism rather than actual competence or experience. The rapidity of the army's mobilization had aggravated those limitations, but the weeding-out process led to constant officer changes and reorganization. The turnover and shifting of troops from one division to another necessitated almost continual training in the field through large-scale maneuvers conducted at the army level in the southern United States. General Dwight D. Eisenhower, who gained top-level attention during service then as a general staff colonel, praised the results of the maneuvers, especially the development of teamwork, while uncovering officers unfit for command.[6]

On November 2, 1941, the sixty-three-year-old General Haskell, long a fixture of the NY Guard hierarchy, was finally relieved of command and, along with JAG Lieutenant Colonel Marcus, assigned to temporary duty at the War Department. An extensive inspection tour of installations in preparation for Haskell's next assignment followed. Before leaving, Haskell penned a memo to his friend General Ben Lear, who had commanded the US Second Army maneuvers to which the Twenty-Seventh Division was attached, about officers who would be fit for higher-level responsibilities: "Lt. Col. Marcus is a reliable and efficient officer. He is endowed with the highest standards of respect and commitment which are reflected in his daily behavior. He holds a number of positions and as such he conducted successful negotiations while drafting many contracts. In general, he is a commander and an officer with abilities in many and varied fields. I strongly recommend that he be promoted to the rank of colonel."[7]

While Mickey was on tour with Haskell, his successor as commander of the Twenty-Seventh, Brigadier General Ralph McT. Pennell, took over. He had led the division's Fifty-Second Field Artillery Brigade and was promoted to major general in February 1942. The next month Pennell took formal command of the division at its new headquarters at Fort Ord, alongside Monterey Bay, where it had been ordered following the attack on Pearl Harbor. He immediately requested that Lieutenant Colonel Marcus return to the division, which he did while the Twenty-Seventh awaited orders to ship out. During this period, the main staff focus was on reaching authorized field strength after discharges, transfers, and promotions, before the division boarded ships bound for Hawaii on February 27, 1942.[8]

The division remained on Oahu, where it was reduced to three infantry regiments and fourteen thousand men in authorized strength, dismantling the four-brigade structure. Mickey got his first experience in civil affairs as executive officer to General McPennell and responsible for military government and all Hawaiian Island provost marshal (criminal) affairs, including liaison with all the relevant civilian agencies. The islands had been under military rule since the Pearl Harbor attack, and Mickey was exposed to every aspect of rule under martial law.[9]

The actual role of the division office of the provost marshal is multifaceted and can vary with the division's location. The office is responsible for policy, planning, oversight, and budgeting for military police and law enforcement, including criminal investigations, forensics, corrections, facility and high-value personnel security. In counterintelligence operations, the provost marshal coordinated efforts with the War Department and local police. Typical investigations spanned a range of petty misconduct, desertion, and more serious offenses, including violent crimes. Because Hawaii was under martial law, Mickey's duties there also focused on espionage, sabotage, and other major security breaches.[10]

Mickey's oversight extended to the management of military prisons and temporary stockades, where he ensured the welfare and proper confinement of detainees awaiting trial or punishment. In this role, he sharpened and deepened his experience, adding the skills of professional military officer to his civilian experience. Beyond the confines of military discipline, the office of the provost marshal general played a pivotal role in the logistic aspects of the division's movements, including military traffic. Mickey's service in Hawaii was his first introduction to civil affairs in a friendly but occupied military location (the territory was under martial law), balancing military objectives with the interests of civilians, mediating disputes, and maintaining harmonious relations with civil authorities.[11]

Commander, Twenty-Seventh ID
Ranger School, Oahu, Hawaii, Early 1943

In the early months of the war, as defeat piled on defeat and General George C. Marshall and Lieutenant General Lesley J. McNair, the organizational genius, combed through generals to find fighting division commanders, rapid turnover in division and corps command continued. Major General Ralph C. Smith, who would eventually lead the Twenty-Seventh ID into combat at Makin Island and controversy at Saipan, took over from McPennell on November 20, 1942, bringing with him his own chief of staff, Colonel Albert K. Stebbins '24, a member of the Thundering Herd who relieved Colonel John Haskell. He left for the War Department to help establish an independent Civil Affairs Division.

Because of its early deployment to the Pacific Theater of Operations, the Twenty-Seventh ID could not rotate through the amphibious and special combat training given to units stationed in the United States and scheduled for amphibious combat later in the war. Ralph C. Smith, who took command of the division in November 1942, was an outsider in the chauvinistic New York National Guard unit, and as such was determined to establish his mark and make sure his men received equivalent training to that received by stateside soldiers. He had no illusions about the task, although he underestimated the extent of Regular Army resentment against the guard, or later the problems of joint command with the US Navy.[12]

Fig. 7. Major General Ralph C. Smith, commanding Twenty-Seventh Infantry Division. US Army

Ralph Corbett Smith was born in South Omaha, Nebraska, in 1893. He was an early aviation enthusiast—so early that he was taught to fly by Orville Wright. Commissioned a second lieutenant in 1916, he went on General John Pershing's punitive expedition against Pancho Villa in Mexico and then served in France, where he was wounded in the Meuse-Argonne offensive and twice decorated for bravery. During the interwar period he developed a reputation as an educator before taking command of the Twenty-Seventh Infantry Division in late 1942. His division fought in the Gilbert Islands in 1943, and a year later at Saipan in the Mariannas. During that battle, he was relieved of command by his corps commander, Marine lieutenant general Holland M. Smith, in a bitter interservice controversy but was later cleared by an army inquiry. After the war Ralph Smith was military attaché at the US Embassy in Paris and at CARE, the postwar humanitarian aid group, where he was chief of mission for France. At his passing, he was the oldest surviving general officer of the US Army.[13]

On the advice of his staff officers and longtimers in the division, several of whom had been in the Thundering Herd or been cadets with Mickey, Smith picked his JAG to organize a Twenty-Seventh ID Ranger school. Mickey developed the curriculum and selected instructors for the basic amphibious training course for eight thousand men in the three fighting regiments and direct support units. Retired colonel Fred Borch, the leading scholar of the US Army JAG Corps, zeroed in on the professional divide that Mickey crossed, musing, "One wonders what infantry officers thought of an Army lawyer organizing and running Ranger training of some 8,000 men during those months." Mickey's inspiration for tough training as he set about developing and instructing his Ranger training course was William Orlando Darby and his Ranger battalions, which had been officially activated in June 1942. Darby trained his men for close combat in all kinds of terrain and worked them to a peak of physical fitness and readiness. He had chosen the Ranger moniker to honor Rogers's Rangers, a company of light infantry that fought in the French and Indian War and gained renown for very deep penetration raids.[14]

One constant in Mickey's experience, reinforced during his extensive tour of training facilities with General Haskell just before the war, was the poor physical condition of most soldiers, even those far along in basic training. The Ranger course Marcus designed included intense physical conditioning and intensive training in small-unit tactics appropriate to different terrain for an offensive force, as well as for commando-type and active defense warfare, such as raids, ambushes, communications attacks, and killing up close. As he had early in his army career, to inspire his troops Mickey joined them in the most strenuous training, holding his own with men more than half his age. He engaged in the activity full bore, and in so doing toughened up his own body, returning to a rigorous training schedule and diet control.

This very brief assignment, which was limited to the Twenty-Seventh ID, gave rise to the wild claim that Mickey ran Ranger school training for the whole army, or even that he founded the Rangers, adding to the many tall tales and exaggerations stretched past breaking that surrounded the man. Using his training experience as justification,

Marcus tried to talk the army into giving him a field command with a Ranger unit, but not unlike the most famous Ranger of all, Bill Darby '27, he was unsuccessful in his early attempts to get into combat.[15]

Civil Affairs Division, Pentagon, Washington, DC, April 1943

Just as he was wrapping up Ranger school and readying the division for combat deployment in the Central Pacific, Mickey's career took another unexpected twist. After recommendations from Haskell back in Washington, he was transferred in March 1943 to the newly created Civil Affairs Division (CAD)—designated as G-5, "General Staff, Civil Affairs and Military Government," in the general staff corps organization chart—under Major General John H. Hilldring. When Marcus left Hawaii to return to Washington, DC, General Smith wrote in a letter of commendation, "Your most outstanding achievement is the superior work you have done in organizing and directing the 27th Division Ranger School. Your own splendid leadership and personal example of physical prowess made this school a great success. You have shown that you know the business of soldiering and tactical leading of troops."[16]

Mickey's new boss, John Hilldring, was a University of Connecticut graduate and World War I veteran of the Third Infantry Division, holder of a DSC, whose performance and demeanor as an instructor at the Infantry School at Fort Benning, Georgia in 1932 impressed Lieutenant Colonel George C. Marshall, then head of the school's academic department. A respected and discreet military administrator, Hilldring was then serving in the War Department as G-1, chief of personnel, a politically sensitive job for which he was ideally suited.

His new mission was to "advise the Secretary of War [Henry L.] Stimson regarding policies in areas occupied by United States military forces, maintain close cooperation with United States and Allied combat forces, and with appropriate civilian agencies at Washington, and represent the War Department in relations with inter-Allied boards concerning problems of military occupation."[17] Later, he explained to his staff that their function was to conduct the planning, policymaking, supervision, and coordination of all matters concerning military government, and regulating all army agencies concerned with military government. A few months later, the Combined Chiefs of Staff created a combined civil affairs committee in Washington, DC. While field responsibility for operations would pass to the theater commanders during and after combat, including for these matters, when the military situation was right, CAD would ensure that operational planning before the fighting also considered what would happen after.[18]

Fig. 8. Major General John H. Hilldring, head of civil affairs and military government. Military History Institute

The new department had its own difficult administrative path to general staff recognition. After the creation of the Army Service Forces (ASF) in March 1942, the War Department began preparing for the military governance of areas taken from the Axis powers. The provost marshal general's office developed training proposals that led to the establishment of the School of Military Government at the University of Virginia in May 1942. This office also formed a planning unit in

Washington. Actual US military government operations began six months later, during Operation Torch in November 1942, in North Africa but under British command. One of the key policy questions was the status of French Morocco and Algeria and whether their mandate included both administering liberated people and ruling conquered territory.

In late 1942 President Roosevelt established the Office of Foreign Relief and Rehabilitation Operations (OFRRO) within the State Department, led by former governor Herbert H. Lehman. This office planned relief for areas freed from Axis control and worked closely with the ASF. Lehman was frustrated by organizational problems stemming from overlap between the provost marshal general's office, the secretary of war's office, and the State Department. At that point, Roosevelt and Marshall decided to establish a separate Civil Affairs Division at the General Staff of the Army level to oversee civil affairs planning and training, including setup of G-5 staff sections at army units down the order of battle to division level. Eventually, as the Allies found it increasingly difficult to agree on common objectives beyond defeating Germany, soldiers assumed roles in civilian administration that crossed over into policy.

In practice, the anti-Nazi alliance vision of a postwar order emerged with only vague directions from higher-ups. Problems framed by diplomatic language did not include specific measures to achieve lofty aims as wartime allies once again became competitors, opponents, and enemies, but that would come later. After the War Department formed CAD in the War Department Special Staff, the provost marshal general continued to have responsibility for training military government officials, but CAD became the main planner for all civil and military government policies. Other divisions in the Service Forces headquarters also contributed to that planning, overseeing various responsibilities in supply, personnel, labor, and currency. All these units operated under the general policies set by CAD, and Marcus was frequently the point of contact.[19]

Mickey's first job at the new organization was head of the Government Section, based on his political experience and reputation, and then as executive officer to General Hilldring, and finally, for the remainder of the war, as the head of CAD's powerful Planning Division. Hilldring, who had chronic heart problems, relied on Mickey from the beginning, an almost identical replay of Mickey's experience as deputy to prison commissioner MacCormick back in New York City. For two years Hilldring made speeches and outlined policy on a leisurely schedule, while Mickey ran the department day to day.

CAD historian Edgar L. Erickson testified to the scope of Mickey's influence: "He was in on all the major directives on military government issued by the United States through the Joint and Combined Chiefs of Staff. Marcus did so much of his work 'off the cuff' he left very little in the way of records that specifically tied him to various planning actions. That was one of the headaches encountered in trying to run down his responsibility for CAD actions."[20] Once again, in Lowell "Wampus" Limpus's phrase, Mickey assumed the role of the "power behind the throne," with a minimum paper trail, a role at which he clearly excelled. His boss reported directly to Chief of Staff George C. Marshall, frequently through Mickey as liaison, sometimes in face-to-face meetings.

Hilldring's health problems, although persistent, did not prevent his contributions over the next decade and a half as a soldier, diplomat, and businessman. He would also head up the investigation into and prosecution of those who had committed war crimes in the American-occupied sector of Germany and administer refugee affairs there. He and Marcus maintained direct personal contact right up until the latter's death. Finally, as is now clear, Hilldring played a confidential, if not entirely covert, role in Mickey's recruitment efforts for the Haganah and in the maneuvering leading up to Israel's independence.[21]

Just as La Guardia felt more secure with the intense, gesticulating, and brilliant deputy watching his jails, the top army echelon, including those around Marshall, found reassurance in Mickey's presence as Hilldring's right-hand man. Quick to appreciate his tireless energy and competence, Hilldring finally succeeded in gaining Mickey's promotion to full colonel in July 1943, noting, "If the Civil Affairs Division did a satisfactory job after a late start, it was largely because of the far-seeing and imaginative planning of Colonel Marcus." In less than four years, Mickey had risen from captain to full colonel, a rare feat for a noncombat officer.[22]

During this period CAD concentrated on the post invasion occupation of Sicily, its first major planning operation. There was no confusion about the status of the objective: it was enemy territory. The British Fifteenth Army Group was responsible for military government policies and execution overall, with US Seventh Army responsible for its sector after Sicily was cleared of German troops and the Italians there surrendered. Although Mickey was later cited for his role in drafting the Italian surrender document, and played a classified role in Italy, there is no evidence that he was in Sicily, or the Italian mainland, after the invasion at Salerno in September 1943, but it can't be ruled out. While representing CAD in Washington and at the major wartime conferences, Colonel Marcus participated directly in sensitive negotiations with high-ranking US government officials, including President Roosevelt, Secretary of War Stimson, and their advisers, as well as officials in Allied governments and agencies in which US civil affairs doctrine was formulated and managed.[23]

The Cairo and Tehran Conferences, November–December 1943

From late November to December 1, 1943, President Franklin D. Roosevelt met with Chinese president Chiang Kai-shek and British prime minister Winston Churchill in Cairo. The conference was a stopover for Roosevelt and Churchill on the way to meet Soviet leader Joseph Stalin in Tehran. In Cairo, Roosevelt outlined his vision for postwar Asia, in which the Republic of China would be one of the "Four Policemen" responsible for keeping the peace.

To secure his vision, Roosevelt sought a commitment from Chiang that China would not try to expand across the continent or control nations in Southeast Asia that were already in the process of decolonialization. In return, Roosevelt offered to guarantee that the territories stolen from China by Japan, including Manchuria, Taiwan, and the

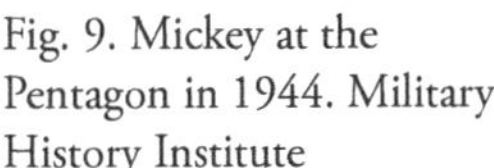
Fig. 9. Mickey at the Pentagon in 1944. Military History Institute

Pescadores, would be returned to Chinese sovereignty. Roosevelt also wanted Chiang's support for a trusteeship to ease the transformation of the European colonial territories after the war. Marcus provided advice to his delegation about the legal underpinnings of these arrangements, but they failed to gain the support of the British or French, and events rendered all these efforts moot. Although Roosevelt, Churchill, and Chiang had common interests, they also had vastly different objectives. For one thing, Chiang wanted to reopen the Burma Road, which had been a major supply line from India to China, an effort that the British were reluctant to support for their own reasons.

Nevertheless, Roosevelt shrewdly guessed that promises to aid China in reopening its supply lines were more important to the Chinese than the actual execution: a demonstration of the Republic of China's importance to the US government would hopefully boost sagging Chinese morale. The resulting Cairo Declaration, jointly released by the United States, the Republic of China, and Great Britain on December 1, 1943, pledged to eject Japanese forces from all the territories they had conquered, including China, Korea, and the Pacific Islands. Before the conference concluded, Mickey consulted those assembled on war crimes and surrender policy.[24]

On the heels of the Cairo talks, the Tehran Conference—held in Iran from November 28 to December 1, 1943—commenced with Roosevelt and Churchill meeting with Soviet premier Joseph Stalin. In Tehran, the "Big Three" strategized their military actions against Germany and, secondarily, Japan and took time to deliberate on post–World War II arrangements. One of the most significant achievements of the conference was mutual commitment to Operation Overlord, the amphibious invasion of northern France then slated for May 1944. In a show of solidarity and strategy, the Soviets pledged to launch a large and near simultaneous offensive on the eastern front. Mickey was there representing Hilldring and thus was privy to the secrets. The Soviet offensive, it was hoped, would divert German attention and forces away from the impending Allied invasion in France. Furthermore, in a crucial agreement, Stalin promised to join the Allies in their war against Japan once Germany had been defeated. In exchange, Roosevelt assured Stalin postwar control over specific territories, including the Kuril Islands and the southern half of Sakhalin, as well and access to vital ports in northern China.

The fate of postwar Eastern Europe, particularly the borders of and other arrangements for Poland and Germany, was another central topic of discussion. Stalin proposed a shift in Poland's eastern borders that would align with an established line. To compensate Poland for this territorial adjustment, it was agreed that the German-Polish border would move westward to the Oder and Neisse Rivers. This decision would, however, only be formally ratified at the Potsdam Conference in 1945. In a significant diplomatic move, Roosevelt managed to secure a promise from Stalin that the Baltic states of Lithuania, Latvia, and Estonia would be reincorporated into the Soviet Union only after a public referendum, albeit one held under Soviet conditions. Marcus contributed to discussions about election structures.

The three leaders also touched upon the division of postwar Germany into separate zones occupied by the Allied powers. It was at Tehran, too, that Roosevelt shared his vision for the formation of the United Nations, emphasizing a leadership structure in which the United States, Britain, China, and the Soviet Union would play dominant roles in maintaining global peace and security. By the end of the conference, Roosevelt felt he had achieved many of his objectives. He had secured the Soviet Union's commitment to join the war against Japan and garnered support for the centerpiece of his postwar vision, a global government organization backed by the major powers. He believed that through direct negotiations and promises, he had built a foundation of trust with Stalin—even if history would later prove that trust misplaced. Stalin also made significant gains at the meeting, especially concerning Eastern Europe, setting the stage for the geopolitical dynamics of the postwar era.[25]

SHAEF, Norwich House, St. James Park, London, late May 1944

In early May 1944, after one year in the Civil Affairs Division, Mickey knew that the Allies' cross-channel invasion of France was just weeks away.[26] The expanding importance of CAD in Allied invasion, conquest, and occupation planning—and the key role played by its dynamic and inexhaustible planning genius—was reaching a defining moment. Just three months after the small CAD cadre at Eisenhower's Supreme Headquarters Allied Expeditionary Forces (SHAEF) became a full G-5 section, the First US Army Group (FUSAG) and US First Army (FUSA), both under command of Lieutenant General Omar Bradley, followed SHAEF by raising the status and authority of their CAD sections, at least on paper.[27]

These purely administrative changes were accompanied by a rising level of activity in the field. All over southern England, the entire CAD establishment—the European Civil Affairs Regiments (ECAR), companies, and detachments that had been enlisted, trained, and deployed to England during the past year—was assigned to various corps, divisions, and subordinate units for the invasion. By D-Day, fifty detachments of 1,300 men with equipment and weapons— sidearms—were attached to First Army. A similar number of detachments were later attached to Third Army.[28] By the end of the war, the CAD infrastructure in Omar Bradley's Twelfth Army Group, comprising 1.23 million men organized into four field armies, fifteen corps, and sixty-five infantry, armored, and airborne divisions, would total twelve thousand CAD personnel in hundreds of separate ECAR units.[29]

After all the staff work, planning, manual drafting, meetings, telephone conferences, memos, and tens of thousands of staff man-hours, the whole structure was about to go operational, with the invasion just weeks away. CAD was facing questions from all fronts, but especially from Eisenhower's headquarters, SHAEF, which was charged with coordinating the efforts of the British Twenty-First Army Group and the US First Army. There were also issues to be resolved with relevant political agencies, touching issues of command authority, security, and other immediate occupation requirements. With so many powerful actors and diverse interests on the stage, the potential for inter-Allied conflict was intense. It was Mickey's goodwill with the British, who credited him with a "co-operative and liberal outlook," that helped secure agreement on many combined (and maddening) planning problems. British respect for the American negotiator eventually led them to award him the stunning blue ribbon and cameo of a military Commander of the Order of the British Empire.[30]

Operation Overlord planning was reaching a climax, and all action shifted to London. Though still in Washington, Mickey knew he needed to act quickly. All eyes were on "the far shore," and he wanted to get there as soon as possible to observe for himself the results of his past year's work. All he needed to do was persuade his boss to allow him to go to London as the War Department liaison officer to G-5 at SHAEF. The initial conversation in what turned out to be Mickey's ticket to London took place during a late-morning coffee break while

Hilldring and Marcus stood cramped in the far corner of a jammed fourth-floor snack bar at the brand-new Pentagon building built by Brigadier General Leslie Groves, who would later run the atomic bomb program.[31]

There is no doubt that a restlessness of spirit, at best barely controlled, coupled with a hunger for adventure—as well as a touch of vanity—played a role in Mickey's desire to see firsthand what was happening. There was also a strong professional case for the presence of a top-ranking liaison officer on the scene. Marcus had been a witness to the results of his planning for the conquest and rule of Italy, but the disappointing theater-wide CAD experience gained in the Mediterranean—mostly a British-handled affair—had afforded him only a glimpse of the manifold problems likely to follow the liberation of France and western Europe.[32] CAD had been involved in the Overlord plan, and now the field armies were about to invade. That meant that unless those CAD plans worked from the outset, things would have to change quickly, ideally with the input of someone with authority who could identify the problems early and expedite their resolution. Issues of combined Allied planning did not make the task easier, making the presence of an American liaison officer with stature and sufficient gravitas on the scene helpful when dealing with British leaders—some of whom could be, to put it gently, headstrong.

Mickey had already tangled with America's most important ally during the Italian campaign, as well as in the initial stages of Operation Neptune planning—the naval component of the invasion, which would transport the troops across the Channel and land them on the beaches. There were sharp debates over French policy and the degree to which the United States should recognize any one politician or faction, especially de Gaulle and his party.[33] During a protracted bureaucratic debate in Washington with British representatives about whether a satellite planning group of the Combined Civil Affairs Committee should be set up in London, Mickey at first opposed the idea. Concerned that it would delay planning and coordination, he later acquiesced, explaining his frustration and change of heart: "The

British have refused to take affirmative action in the Combined Civil Affairs Committee (CCAC) meetings which has resulted in complete frustration with nothing having been accomplished for months. London is the only remedy and if not accepted the CCAC would cease to exist." After Marcus gave the go-ahead to the London branch, the British resumed full cooperation.[34]

Mickey wanted to be in France when the first CAD detachments arrived, just after the landings of the combat troops in Normandy. We take this dimension of warfare— specific requirements for civilian relief, refugees, infrastructure support, health, security, lost property claims, governance, and so on—largely for granted now. In early June 1944, however, American civil affairs policy and procedures for both liberated and enemy territory were as untested as the large citizen-soldier army raised and poised to attack *Festung Europa*.

The scale of Overlord was enormous even for a specialized unit like Civil Affairs. On D-Day and during the opening days of the operation, dozens of specially trained teams of mostly reserve officers and enlisted men were gathered, assigned disembarkation locations and schedules, and soon found themselves governing villages, towns, provinces, and cities, including liberated capitals. Mickey aptly pointed out the wisdom of conducting an on-the-spot evaluation as soon as the first large target area, Carentan, was liberated. However unlikely it seemed, rapid fine-tuning or even radical alteration might prove necessary.

There was certainly a bureaucratic justification for dispatching a liaison officer with full War Department authority to tie up loose ends in the days before the cross-Channel attack. It would also be good advertising for SHAEF to have a top War Department officer on hand, touring a few good-sized occupied towns. The CAD sections of First Army and Twelfth Army Group were transitioning to combat operations, so close observation of those units in England and during the first days of the invasion would provide useful information for future operations in other theaters, especially the Pacific, all within Mickey's responsibility as chief of planning.[35] And there was also the matter of the unpredictable de Gaulle and potential actions of his Free French movement which might complicate the combined Allied civil affairs efforts. These factors made on-the-spot information gathering critical. Hilldring agreed it was in CAD's interest to see how the policies were initially received in France.[36]

Colonel William Chanler, Hilldring's deputy, agreed that Marcus could be spared for a few weeks, including an initial tour of the invasion beaches in Normandy. Then Marcus could get back to his desk to continue planning for the final year of the global war, including surrender strategy for Germany and Japan, postwar occupation, war crimes trials, and the establishment of a United Nations organization. It made good sense to send Marcus, who knew most of the principals. No fanfare—just a few weeks out of the office, "showing the flag" at SHAEF, and logging some deserved downtime for Mickey, who was working at a furious pace and would appreciate a few weeks of wartime London nightlife.

Colonel Marcus set out for temporary duty at G-5, SHAEF, via priority air transport, on May 8, 1944, drafting his own orders with authority to "provide liaison, and act as observer in the implementation of military government policies for France."[37] The CA officers at Bushy Park outside downtown London had reason to applaud Mickey as choice for liaison officer. For one thing, as colleagues who had attended the great wartime conferences with him recalled, he had access to single malt scotch of the highest quality by the case and was always available for socializing at any hour when off duty.[38]

Detachment C2B1, Newton Abbot, England, late May—early June 1944

After arriving in England, Mickey dived into a mountain of paperwork, as well as constant meetings, minor crises, and hastily arranged phone conferences. He coordinated his activities with Brigadier General Julius C. Holmes, deputy G-5, SHAEF, and the senior American CAD officer in the European Theater of Operations (ETO). It was busy in the echelons just below. After a period as a planning section, First US Army Group (soon renamed Twelfth Army Group), G-5 section, overseeing some seventy-five men, was busy assigning advance teams of about a dozen men to each corps and division of the invasion forces to administer CA policies at the lower levels of command.[39]

Meanwhile, Mickey was making plans for his own tour of the first liberated towns. He was "bigoted" (that is, privy to the key details of Operation Overlord) and knew the invasion date for Overlord as well as the order of battle, especially which commanders would be engaged early. He found his instrument. Major General Maxwell D. Taylor, 101st Airborne Division commander, two years his senior at the academy, as well as a very good friend of Hilldring, would be his ticket to France.

Like others at West Point during the early 1920s, Max Taylor was a big Mickey fan during the early days of intercollegiate boxing and remembered his epic bouts, as well as his antics on the dance floor. It would be an easy matter for Mickey to engineer the proper transfers through him. Taylor's 101st Airborne was part of Major General J. Lawton "Lightning Joe" Collins's US VII Corps, the first of the three American invasion corps scheduled to occupy a large French city, the port of Cherbourg. Spearheaded by two American paratroop divisions making a night drop early in the morning of D-Day, the fifty thousand men of VII Corps would strike near dawn, led by assault companies of the 4th Infantry Division on Utah Beach. Mickey attached himself to 101st Airborne HQ and would land by boat on D+2 with some of the first CA soldiers coming in behind the combat troops.[40]

Major John J. Maginnis, a fifty-year-old coal dealer and reserve officer with solid Republican credentials from Worcester, Massachusetts, was one of those men assigned to the 101st Airborne.[41] A veteran of the Great War and a onetime student at the Sorbonne, Maginnis was based in Shrivenham in Berkshire, some eighty miles west of London, by the end of January 1944. Situated on the grounds of a former private school for girls, the crowded base had been set up during the summer of 1942 and was the first stop of the European field experience for thousands of G-5 personnel, including the now-famous Monuments Men.[42] Shrivenham offered none of the amenities expected by officers;

everyone below the rank of lieutenant colonel was obliged to share quarters with at least a dozen other men.[43]

Morale was a big problem. General Dwight D. Eisenhower, head of SHAEF, responding to the problem by visiting the base a day before Mickey arrived in London, calling the soldiers "as modern as radar and just as important to the command" and repeating his oft-stated dictum that the job of soldiers was to defeat the enemy. Rejecting any political agenda for G-5, he firmly reminded the officers of their highest priority: "You are not politicians, or anything else, but soldiers."[44] G-5, like everything in war, was subordinate to military necessity, and while humanitarian results were a good thing, the object of all, especially for the soldier, was victory as fast as possible.[45]

In mid-April 1944 Major Maginnis took command of Detachment C2B1, fourteen officers and men, and moved to Newton Abbot, VII Corps headquarters, on the southwestern coast of England in Devonshire, sixty miles west of Southampton. Compared to Shrivenham, the place was a paradise, just down the road from Torquay, the "Riviera of England." Not least of the town's attractions were the constantly crowded and pulsating bars at the Central and Imperial Hotels. There was lots of drinking: everyone knew what was coming.[46]

.On May 20, 1944, Maginnis was summoned to the forward headquarters of VII Corps at Plymouth at 1000 hours and ushered into a conference room dug into the granite of the old caves at harborside. As he waited, enlisted men stripped the conference room of maps, charts, photos, and documents, since Maginnis was not "bigoted." The naturally cooled room held the senior American civil affairs brass then gathered in the ETO: Colonel Dell B. Hardin, G-5, VII Corps; Brigadier General Julius C. Holmes, deputy G-5, SHAEF, top American G-5 in Europe; Colonel Cornelius Ryan, G-5, Twelfth Army Group; and Colonel David Marcus, G-5, Chief of Planning, War Department.[47]

General Holmes told Maginnis his unit would be assigned to HQ 101st Airborne Division and the first G-5 detachment operating in France. His mission was to run a good-sized town (name classified until D minus one) in a strategic location. Colonel Marcus would join the detachment at the end of May as an observer. Normally such an important officer would be attached to a higher headquarters, but Mickey had insisted on being with the first field unit to go in on the invasion over the beach. The potential for conflict was obvious, as General Holmes pointedly reminded the visiting staff colonel that Major Maginnis was in command. Mickey, grateful to be a part of the whole thing, smiled and said he understood, but clearly his paper trail of transfers from Washington to SHAEF to VII Corps to 101st Airborne had been noticed as the work of an energetic and assertive officer, exactly the type of person to pop up when least expected.[48]

Mickey joined Maginnis at Newton Abbot on May 28, 1944, a beautiful spring Sunday. Pulling up in a general staff car, he leaped from the vehicle with a smile and outstretched hand. Cutting a very different figure from their first encounter, he wore an ill-fitting field uniform without insignia or patches, "all of it brand new and none of it seeming to conform to the contours of his body. He was short in stature, his dark hair was short and thinning, his face had the suggestion of a smile on it, even in repose, and his most noticeable feature was his broad, powerful upper body."[49]

In their first face-to-face talk, described by Maginnis as "casual," Mickey made it clear that he was not there to interfere and was prepared to help in any way he could. In an extraordinary act of personal leadership, both unexpected and unorthodox (not to mention a court-martial offense), Mickey bigoted Maginnis on the spot, pointing out on the map where they were going and telling him the invasion date, as well as his own mission: to observe and report to the Pentagon on the operations of G-5 units at all levels, particularly those occupying the first liberated towns, as well as to assess the political atmosphere in US-liberated areas, especially the extent to which the population accepted de Gaulle and his followers. French internal politics had continued to require much G-5 attention since Operation Torch, a year and a half before.[50]

That last part was problematic. Despite his obvious intelligence and his deep involvement in the minutiae of French politics, Mickey had no facility with the French language and would not be able to talk with the locals. He often complained, "I wish to hell I could talk to these people; I'd like to get to know them better." Using a phrase Maginnis called a "Marcusism," Mickey went deeper: "Through an interpreter you can find out the way to the railroad station alright, but not the way to a man's heart." He envied his fellow officers' language ability, saying that "it puts you on the inside."[51] Mickey's friend Red Reeder, the disabled war hero and legendary West Point coach and author, remembered Marcus's frustration with French as his academic weakness.[52]

From the very beginning of their brief but intense association, the outgoing and socially adept New Yorker, crime-busting attorney, and drinking pal of La Guardia, and prison reformer Marcus and John J. Maginnis, the reserved New England businessman, Rotarian, and loyal Republican stalwart, got along amazingly well. They shared many interests and experiences, personal, political, and military: attendance at the Civilian Military Training Camp preparedness camps, participation—not always successful—in local city electoral politics, stints of reserve training, solid marriages, and strong ties to school, community, church, and synagogue. The binding tension of imminent danger, their mutual dedication to the mission, and the intensity of direct participation in epoch-shaping events drew them together in grave purpose. Walking in the ancient English town of Totnes, complete with narrow streets, castle, guildhall, and gate, Mickey struggled to recall an extraordinary sunset in Oahu; Maginnis recalled that he "relied on a word he used rarely but tellingly when reaching for a superlative to describe a person, thing, or situation; 'magic.' "[53]

There were light moments as well. As evidence of Mickey's resourcefulness, distinctive personality, and ability to wield the tools of Washington power, even on the verge of the momentous invasion, with transport at an absolute top need basis only, he had somehow, true to form, managed to bring a case of single malt scotch with him from London. During an evening visit to the temporary home of the Sandifords, a bombed-out London couple whom Maginnis had befriended, Mickey presented his hosts with a bottle. It was polished off by the time the officers left that evening. Mickey felt bad about being someone who takes back gifts and the next morning dropped off another bottle. The pattern repeated for a few more days, until one evening the officers didn't appear, nor the next night, and the Sandifords got to keep their gift unshared.[54]

Southampton, England, June 4, 1944

Late in the warm, bright afternoon of June 4, after a brief detour to see Stonehenge, Mickey arrived at Southampton for embarkation, but foul weather was to delay the invasion. The detachment were given tent assignments, blankets, and anti-gas impregnated clothing, then waited. All were armed. Mickey, who had qualified as marksman at West Point, slung a carbine over his shoulder.

The next day Mickey was taking a shower when he suddenly started talking in a loud voice to his stall companion, Major Maginnis: "Too bad about the 9th Infantry Division."

"What's the matter with it?"

"Kind of falling apart from what I hear."

"Really? What happened to it?"

"Regimental commanders—especially the 47th—are giving them trouble!"

A head with an outraged expression popped up over the stall divider, and Mickey, feigning surprise, greeted the angry eavesdropper.

"Why Georgie Smythe, what are you doing here?"

Colonel George Smythe, West Point '24 of the Thundering Herd and famed football player, was commander of the Forty-Seventh Infantry Regiment and on the threshold of a distinguished combat record as well as important postwar G-5 jobs. He shouted back, "Mickey Marcus, what are you doing here—only soldiers are allowed in here."

It was not the only such spontaneous encounter Maginnis would witness over the next several weeks.[55] That night, after the reunited classmates had eaten dinner together, two couriers from First Army G-2 arrived and delivered a sealed packet about Carentan, containing lists of city officials, a history of the town, economic data, and maps. A small rural town, Carentan sat astride the road linking the major towns of Normandy from Caen in the east to the port of Cherbourg on the northern coast of the Cotentin peninsula. The railroad also passed through Carentan, an important commerce and communications hub with its own inland port for ships small enough to navigate its shallow canal. Rich dairy country surrounded the town, the output of which was processed by the US-owned Carnation Milk Company. Mickey believed from his first look at the Overlord maps that Carentan would be one of the most important objectives in the invasion because it lay on the very narrow seam between the Omaha (V Corps) and Utah (VII Corps) assault beaches, making it a natural weak spot.[56]

Sweating out the delay, Mickey found a novel use for some of the US-issued franc notes in the G-2 packet slated for civilian compensation claims. He started writing personal greetings to friends and relatives across the face of the currency, shifting from fifty-franc notes to the two-franc denomination only when he realized with embarrassment that he had to pay for the personal souvenirs. His summation: "Planning good; execution sloppy."[57] Meanwhile, the constant humming of engines overhead lasted throughout the next day, confirming that the invasion was on. Two days later, on the morning of June 8, the advance party boarded ship along with elements of the Fourth Infantry Division. Their large amphibious vessel held amphibious ships like DUKWs and LCTs ("landing craft, tanks") for the trip across the channel to Utah Beach.

Utah Beach, VII Corps, Audouville-la-Hubert, June 8, 1944

As they left port, leaning over the railing on the landing craft in which they were riding, Maginnis turned to his companion and said, "Mickey, this is the second time in my life that I am sailing out of Southampton for France and war." Turning very serious, Mickey replied, "John, the reason we have a great country is because of people like you who are willing to make sacrifices."[58]

After a rough and uncomfortable crossing, their LCT made for shore in the rain amid sporadic artillery fire and enemy strafing. Dumped in the surf far off the beach, their jeep was swamped, and Mickey waded ashore in water up to his chest, lugging his briefcase and gas mask to the VII Corps rally point. That was the closest to a bath Mickey would get in a week. Up on the beach under continuing shellfire, the detachment rallied. At one point Mickey took cover under a truck loaded with ammunition, to the laughter of a nearby sergeant and his own embarrassment.[59] That is how Mickey arrived in France, like tens of thousands of other US servicemen: scrambling out of a small boat, wet, miserable, scared, under enemy fire, and dragging heavy gear.

Now on foot, his small group of CA officers made its way across the swamps via Exit 2 off Utah Beach and to the road, where the ten men separated and hitched rides to VII Corps headquarters at Audouville-la-Hubert, situated on the main north-south coast road. Mickey went directly to the war room, where he encountered some friends and got the latest information from Colonel Gerald Higgins, 101st Airborne chief of staff. The colonel stressed safety, reminding the CA officers about mines, snipers, and ambushes, and that he wanted everybody "whole and healthy." That first night was miserable; Mickey and his companions fended for themselves and slept in a loft in a barn.[60]

Mickey and Maginnis were not the first American CA officers to arrive in Normandy. That honor—and the distinction of being the first such unit to participate in an airborne operation—fell to Detachment A1B1, a First Army unit that was slated to govern Cherbourg, the main Normandy port and a principal objective of Overlord. One of the largest G-5 detachments, A1B1 was commanded by reserve officer Lieutenant Colonel (later Senator) J. Strom Thurmond and attached to Eighty-Second Airborne Division for the invasion. Thurmond and his men came in on three separate gliders with the 327th Glider Infantry Regiment at 2200 on June 6, 1944. Each glider crash-landed under enemy small-arms fire, with every team member, including Thurmond, wounded or injured. Other First Army G-5 sections arrived on Omaha Beach the day after Mickey, and a few days later every division and corps ashore had G-5 men at their headquarters.[61]

On June 10, Maginnis's detachment gathered at 101st Airborne headquarters—code name Kangaroo—at Hiesville, about six miles northwest of Carentan. Colonel Moore updated Mickey and other G-5 officers about the progress of the division since D-Day. The countryside around Hiesville and Sainte-Marie-du-Mont gave testimony to the recent fighting. Empty parachutes dangled from trees amid fields strewn with the smashed remains of gliders, blood staining the earth around the still unburied dead, German and American.

That night, the Luftwaffe bombed the 101st's headquarters, hitting the medical company and resulting in twenty-five casualties. The incident inspired a frenzy of foxhole digging. When asked if he would join in, Mickey, who like everyone else at headquarters was still trying to find a place to roll up in a blanket, indoors or out, rubbed his chin thoughtfully and responded, "You know I was just thinking that with so many moving out into foxholes, there might be some attractive bunks available inside. I'm gonna wait and see."[62] Heavy fighting in the paratroop drop zones made travel difficult, and Mickey estimated that it would still be some time before he could begin his mission, including contacting British field marshal Montgomery's Twenty-First Army Group and Lieutenant General Miles Dempsey's British Second Army, operating to the east near Caen.[63]

Carentan, June 11, 1944

The situation facing the 101st Airborne around Carentan was touch and go. Max Taylor's mission was to seize the four exits west of the flooded area behind Utah Beach, protect the southern flank of VII Corps, and move on Carentan as quickly as possible.[64] Opposing his now blooded paratroops was the veteran German Sixth Fallschirmjäger Regiment under Olympic hero and Oxford-educated aristocrat Colonel Friedrich August Freiherr von der Heydte, a talented officer who would continue to bedevil the Allies. His men had already fought a desperate battle at Sainte-Mère-Église early on D-Day, subsequently losing all their vehicles in the first days of the Normandy campaign.

As early as D+1, the brass expressed growing concern about the separate American landing beaches. On his first offshore tour Eisenhower focused attention on the linkage of Omaha and Utah and issued orders making that the top priority. Taking Carentan was the key, but the paratroops remained isolated, exhausted, and could count on little immediate help from the Fourth Infantry Division coming up from the beaches.

In an ironic stroke of fortune, Mickey—gifted but restless staff officer, energetic planner, natural politician, and skillful bureaucrat, taking a breather from a very hectic desk job and hoping to catch a glimpse of the fighting—was standing on the most critical real estate in the whole invasion lodgment. Defeat was possible. If the Germans could prevent a linkup of the separate beachheads, the Allies would lose momentum and the Germans would take the initiative.

Venturing out on a beautiful sunlit Sunday afternoon on June 11, 1944, and getting only so close to the fighting as was prudent, Mickey drove southwest down the hedgerow-lined road that ran from Sainte-Marie-du-Mont southeast to Carentan. Only hours before, it had been the scene of bloody fighting. Before reaching "Dead Man's Corner," a spot just short of the junction of the road to Sainte-Mère-Église, Mickey dismounted, carbine ready. Maginnis, .45 in hand, walked next to him. While the two were walking along the road to get to a better vantage point, Max Taylor drove by and waved in recognition, calling out a hello to Mickey, who turned to Maginnis, noting with a respectful tone, "If he lives long enough, there goes a future Chief of Staff." Years later, Max would preside at Mickey's West Point funeral.[65]

Turning left off the road on foot into a field, Mickey and Maginnis came across the corpse of an American paratrooper. Fighting an impulse to recover the man, they cut a broad swath around the fallen soldier, Higgins's earlier warning about booby traps having registered. Mickey found a spot about a mile from Carentan offering an unobstructed view of the flooded fields, causeway, and bridges where the 502nd Parachute Infantry Regiment had been fighting desperately since D-Day.

Carentan was ablaze, with intense fighting beyond the Madeleine Bridge. Near some buildings to the right and front of the town, the

Germans were trying to push two battalions of the 502nd into the swamps. The extent of the destruction obscured the full irony of Maginnis's observation, "From here it doesn't look as though there'd be much to occupy."[66] After all the preparation and planning for civil affairs and good governance in the wake of liberation, all that would remain was rubble and the dead and wounded. When they returned to 101st Airborne HQ, Marcus and Maginnis were alerted to be ready to move into Carentan in the morning.

Around midnight of June 11, Brigadier General Anthony J. McAuliffe, artillery chief of the 101st Airborne and later hero of Bastogne, coordinated the assault on Carentan. Enjoying massive supporting fires, including from naval guns and air support, the division struck at 0200, driving Colonel von der Heydte's elite paratroopers from the devastated town, then occupying it six hours later.[67] In spite of continued sniper fire, a wild celebration greeted the men moving through the town to take position southwest on its outskirts. Makeshift American and French flags, friendly citizens, and fine wine long hidden from the hated occupiers suddenly appeared.

Three hours later, at 1100, Mickey and the CA detachment entered Carentan and settled into the damaged Hotel de Ville. The merrymaking accompanying liberation was short-lived. The town lay in ruins. Fires. The bodies of dead Germans lying about. Shattered equipment. Rubble. No water, electricity, or food; garbage rotting in the streets, and the whole region covered with the decaying corpses of cattle. Many soldiers, especially the farmers among them, would remember the ghastly scene for years. Worse still, enemy probes, harassing shellfire, and local counterattacks had begun almost immediately after the Allies had taken the town, as per the typical Wehrmacht reaction.

Mickey, his carbine still slung over a shoulder, volunteered to make a jeep tour to assess overall conditions, taking with him Larry LeSueur of *Yank* magazine and an armed driver. Even after, he couldn't tell how many civilians were left in Carentan, or how badly their lives had been disrupted by the bombing and shelling. Maginnis was operating out of a temporary office connected to the radio net through the 506th

Infantry Regiment headquarters. The commander, Colonel Robert F. Sink '27, had been a plebe the year Mickey won the intercollegiate boxing championship, and the two men knew each other.

Things around Carentan were heating up. The detachment wouldn't be settling into town quite yet.[68] That evening on the steps of city hall, Mickey built a fire to make coffee and shared K rations with Maginnis to the increasing crescendo of small-arms fire and intermittent shelling by German 88-millimeter guns, or "88s." At 2200 hours the detachment loaded up the jeep and headed back to Sainte-Marie-du Mont for the night. The officers billeted near the fourteenth-century village church.[69]

The 101st Airborne planned a further advance to secure Carentan on the morning of June 13 and extend their control west of the town.[70] The Germans hit first. Early that morning, the Seventeenth SS Panzergrenadier Division, supported by heavy guns, struck along the Carentan-Baupte-Périers road, the same route the Americans had moved down the previous day. Maintenance of a continuous beachhead with strong internal lines now depended on holding Carentan and forcing a German withdrawal.

Daybreak came cool and cloudy, with enough rain to dampen, but not extinguish, the dozens of still-smoldering fires of the soldiers. The junction of the beachheads and the narrowest stretch of terrain in the whole invasion was still in peril. Enemy infantry with self-propelled guns overran the forward American positions and drove to within a few hundred yards of the town. [71]

Mickey wanted to get back to Carentan as early as possible that morning, but as he was approaching the causeway in a jeep, the sounds of artillery and small-arms fire grew louder, getting closer. Maginnis turned to Mickey: "This firing seems close by, what do you make of it?"

"Seems like it's right in town. What you'd call 'front line stuff.' "

Still driving on the rue Sebline, they turned right into the cattle market, where rifle, machine gun, and mortar fire was audible just yards ahead. Turning onto the rue Holgate, they noticed paratroopers under cover in doorways signaling, warning them that they were heading down a road under fire. The enemy had counterattacked, and things didn't look good. Recalling Higgins's first briefing and his admonition to "stay healthy," Mickey circled past the Hotel de Ville, going out the way he and Maginnis had come in. He wasn't looking for a fight.[72]

At Carentan things remained touch and go on June 13, but the 506th Parachute Infantry held until CCA, Second Armored Division, a brigade-size tank and mechanized infantry formation, entered the battle. Alerted by Ultra and acting quickly, Lieutenant General Omar Bradley, commanding US First Army, dispatched the dashing and successful armor veteran of North Africa and Sicily, Brigadier General Maurice Rose, and his armored infantry, M3 half-tracks, M4 Shermans, M5 Stewarts, and M7 105-millimeter Priest guns. Rose and company, the proverbial cavalry, arrived just in time to spearhead the paratroopers in a counterattack that secured the seam of the beachhead.

The 101st Airborne lost one thousand men during the Normandy campaign, and many times more wounded. Trafford Leigh Mallory's warning of a casualty rate of 80 to 90 percent proved wrong, but the bloody tally was horrendous enough, topping 30 percent. Casualties of CCA, Second Armored, during the fighting at Carentan totaled one hundred men and four tanks. Nevertheless, Carentan was secured, and the junction of VII Corps and V Corps was complete. The enemy lost five hundred men. The cost was also heavy to the citizens of Carentan, who were devastated before the attack and had remained in range of German 88mm guns ("88s") for many weeks. More than sixty citizens lost their lives in the fighting, and many hundreds more were wounded.[73]

Setting Up Civil Affairs Operations in the Beachhead, Mid-June 1944

During the next ten days Mickey worked out of Carentan's city hall, in close association with Maginnis's detachment. An Augustinian convent until it was despoiled during the French Revolution's Reign of Terror, the surviving southwest section of the city hall housed the municipal offices, which were tied into higher headquarters through the telephone net at Kangaroo (101st Airborne HQ), also in the building. It was a beehive of activity, and Mickey encountered a few top officers during conferences about CA affairs.

One such meeting took place late in the afternoon just a few days after the occupation of Carentan. An officer entered, stopping in a spot where the sunlight passed through the window blinds, streaming into his face and slowing his ability to focus. Mickey, sitting nearby, bolted up and, putting his head down like a bull in the arena, charged straight for the visitor, grabbing him around the middle. The well-built adversary was completely stunned, his shock registering in the startled look on his face. One clear-eyed gaze at his assailant, though, and his recognition was instantaneous.

After Colonel John F. Williams, '24 senior artillery supply officer, SHAEF, had been subdued by classmate Mickey, the two adjourned down the square to the Hotel de Commerce et Gare, whose owner they "persuaded" to provide them with table, chairs, and cognac. With the sound of the 88s still working over the Madeleine Bridge as accompaniment, they held an impromptu twentieth-year class reunion on June 17, 1944—the same day as the "official" West Point gathering of the Thundering Herd in New York—reminiscing about friends and classmates and where the latest news placed them. They also talked sports—Williams had been a wrestling champion with Mickey—and finished the hour-long break from reality by renaming the venue "Hotel Thayer."[74]

Through the rest of the month of June, elements of a dozen G-5 detachments attached to the various units arrived.[75] During the day Mickey drove around the First Army area from Carentan east along the line of invasion beaches and villages just inland, visiting the Fourth Infantry one day, and VII Corps headquarters the next. Conscious of protocol, and as a representative of the Allied high command, he also paid his respects to the CA officers at the HQ of the British Second Army and Montgomery's Twenty-First Army Group.

Mickey's focus remained on the unforeseen requirements that cropped up immediately after battle, among them the need to treat diseases, remove and dispose of corpses, tend to all manner of cleanup, and consider compensation claims. Two concrete examples were the need to dispose of the great many dead animals in and around the town and the number and scale of civilian property claims to process. The sheer scale of civilian claims far exceeded the forecasts of CAD's economic planning sessions. Those kinds of issues—as well as overstaffing in some areas, and under allocation of resources for others—were common at every level of command in varying detail and intensity.[76]

Each night Mickey returned to the mess at the Hotel de Ville. The officers stayed in the eastern sector, on the rue Sivard, in what had once been an upscale neighborhood. Mickey shared a room with Maginnis, each man bunking on a narrow, ancient monk's cot. Their quarters boasted a huge, ornate bathtub placed on a raised platform, unconnected to any plumbing. The roommates drew water from a public hand pump across the street; there was a latrine in the once-landscaped palm garden in the rear.[77]

Mickey had been at Taylor's headquarters several times during awards ceremonies. One such event, on June 23, 1944, at the Place de La Republique, the central square of Carentan, was interrupted by the well-timed delivery of a concentration of 88s, which hurled Mickey and Maginnis against the north wall of the square. Given the targeting of civilians, and the location and duration of the concentration, it was clear that internal security had been breached. Even miles behind the front line, the enemy was still too close—and dangerous.[78]

Back in Washington, excitement about the invasion had swept over everyone, and Hilldring realized that he had not heard directly from Marcus since the end of May. By the second week of June both he and his deputy Chanler had begun to make discreet inquiries about where Mickey was, hoping to get him back to Washington and his real job.[79] A few days later, on June 25, 1944, Mickey received the inevitable recall order. General de Gaulle was coming to Washington, and Hilldring needed his report on the political situation.[80] A week earlier, officials supporting de Gaulle had assumed authority in Bayeux, deposing the previous *souprefect*. In that case it was strictly a British Second Army matter, but the French issue was rapidly becoming a front-burner Allied political problem, one requiring Mickey's special skills.[81]

Maginnis, who once regarded the War Department observer with suspicion, now thought that meeting him had been "a very fortuitous circumstance both for the assistance that he gave us and for the leavening quality of his personality in our day-to-day lives."

As they said goodbye, Mickey turned to his wartime roommate. "These days that we were together were American history."

"Yes," Maginnis responded, "and there will be many more. I hope that I will see you again before they are finally over."[82]

He would, Mickey said. At noon, he left Carentan. He took a lot more time going than coming, arriving back at the office four days later. The whole interlude in the ETO had lasted less than fifty days.

War Department, Pentagon, Washington, July 1944

Even before Marcus was back at his desk at the Pentagon, a heroic saga of martial deeds was germinating. Tracking his paper trail from SHAEF to 101st Airborne, Chanler and Hilldring had gone up the chain as far as Major General Walter "Bedell" Smith, chief of staff, SHAEF, to find Marcus and get him back to Washington. Of course, Mickey was never really "lost," and the urgency was more a matter of the growing concern over what to do about de Gaulle, but that kind of special intervention had set people talking.

It started going around that Mickey, loosely interpreting his orders, got transferred to a parachute unit, hopped onto a transport, and made the D-Day night airborne drop, then fought heroically, hand-to-hand, personally killing enemy soldiers. There he crossed paths with the division commander (Taylor), who unceremoniously shipped him home, clad in filthy battle dress and muddy jump boots. Edward Berkman dedicated several dozen pages of *Cast a Giant Shadow* to this fiction. It was a great story, and Hollywood adapted it brilliantly into a movie, with John Wayne as Max Taylor. Emma went along with the script, along with every fiction.

Further exaggerations and vaguely attributed details were quick to appear. Everybody—colleagues, friends, casual acquaintances—had a favorite story. A Regular Army buddy serving in the 101st Airborne told Chanler that "the Civil Affairs officer we had sent over to help them organize a military government, had instead organized a machine-gun nest and held off the enemy for quite an appreciable time until help could come."[83] Walter Winchell, touting the New York connection and untroubled by the truth, claimed that Mickey was "the sixth allied soldier to set foot in France."[84]

West Point proved to be an especially colorful source of tales. One *Assembly* class note claimed that during Mickey's trip to France, "they borrowed him during a hot fight and made him G-2 of a Corps engaged in combat. During the fracas he got far enough forward to kill four Germans personally. He knocked off the Heine [*sic*] quartet while engaged in showing a patrol how to surround a culvert in which they were hiding."[85] Another told Steve Stevenson that he discovered Mickey, "submachine gun close by, behind a jug of fine old cognac at a freedom celebration near Isigny," while "almost simultaneously, a war correspondent claimed to have spotted the CA colonel diagramming a reconnaissance raid in a forward post on the other side of the peninsula."[86] Limpus's *Saturday Evening Post* profile of Mickey included a vignette in which a classmate "met him up in the front lines, showing a bogged-down patrol how to wipe out a Nazi machine-gun-nest. He demonstrated the procedure with an automatic rifle, and when he finally waved them forward, they found six dead Germans beside the machine gun."[87]

This, of course, went way beyond colorful exaggeration, especially from a journalist of Limpus's reputation, who had reported on Mickey's career from the start and spent many long nights with him, drinking and talking about sports, careers, and family matters, as well as military strategy and history.[88] During the war Limpus served as the military affairs correspondent of the *New York Daily News*, and thus on many levels his amplification of the story of Mickey as intrepid frontline warrior was worse than sloppy. He knew how important Mickey's actual work as a pioneer of modern civil affairs and military governance really was, and wartime nation-building, to use a recent term, was a passion shared by both men.

Maginnis forwarded Limpus the details of Mickey's adventures in the ETO soon after Mickey's death in 1948, and the college friends had discussed their wartime experiences after 1944, but the *Cast a Giant Shadow* image became a cultural icon. Limpus never published his manuscript about Mickey, although writers, most notably Berkman, used the D-Day adventure and other fictions in works on Marcus. The heroic Normandy story was a good yarn and had some very important backers, especially West Point classmates, who continued trading Mickey stories among themselves for many years.

John Hilldring and Max Taylor had their own accounts of that period, but neither claimed outright that Mickey jumped on D-Day. Taylor's recollections stressed the critical importance of Carentan and that he had encountered Mickey there just after the area was secure. Years later he still felt a "sneaking admiration for a guy who went so far out of his way to be where the war was, when he could been parked in a comfortable hotel room in London."[89] His recounting of seeing Mickey "stacking sandbags and singing at the top of his lungs" at Carentan rings true, and Maginnis documents several meetings, encounters, and events where Taylor and Mickey were present, including the Silver Star awards incident on June 23, when the entire division staff and all the regimental commanders were caught unawares by German 88s in the open. Whatever may have occurred during Mickey's time attached to his outfit, Taylor felt genuine warmth toward him as an officer and a man.

Of all those who spread disinformation about Marcus during the period, Hilldring was the least restrained. He passed along the D-Day parachute myth in its entirety, though he was careful not to attribute it directly to Mickey. His version of his aide's responses to questions about Marcus's time in the ETO is consistent with the words of a skilled lawyer who neither admits nor denies anything. None of it was malicious. Hilldring esteemed Mickey as a valued colleague, an excellent staff officer, and the damn smartest guy in G-5. He was the most important personal influence on the military career of Colonel David Marcus.

Neither Emma nor Mickey ever publicly challenged the stories, no doubt appreciating the positive effects of the retelling of a tall tale by others, but it was the movie *Cast a Giant Shadow* and the earlier biography of the same name that fixed the Normandy part of Mickey's myth. That entire narrative, based on an extended and very detailed episodic description, a paean to frontline combat heroics, is pure fiction.[90] It undermines the actual significance of Mickey's contribution to his country and yet the fiction persists, and is repeated even by serious historians.

There was no night parachute jump for Mickey, no fighting through fields or hedgerows with 101st Airborne troops, or any of the other fanciful tales of personal heroism (or recklessness) attributed to Mickey by Berkman, Limpus, Hilldring, or anyone else. None of the accounts based on army sources describing this period claim in any way that Marcus made a D-Day jump or engaged the enemy in close-quarters combat. Official documents and historians credit Mickey with "accompanying the 101st Airborne Division in the invasion of Normandy," just one of tens of thousands of ordinary stories on D+2.[91]

Is it possible that Mickey's adventures went beyond the verifiable incidents recounted by Maginnis? Certainly Mickey's orders gave him the latitude to move around the lodgment area. There were elements of at least half a dozen large army units on the continent, a dozen G-5 detachments were in place during the first three weeks of the invasion, and Mickey was able to travel freely. For example, Mickey did visit a detachment at Isigny; and that he drank cognac at some point during the visit, as he did with the CA detachments at VII Corps and V Corps and with combat divisions in the field, was certainly not implausible.

There were times during the period in question when Marcus might very well have been under desultory shellfire, or possibly within earshot of the front line, or in the vicinity of recent skirmishing, maybe with bullets fired nearby. He certainly bumped into, socialized, and drank with combat soldiers. But the suggestion that he fought as an infantryman, or that he wanted to, is unsupported by credible evidence and highly unlikely. That was not why he was there; he knew his own value, and he knew the dangers of straying off the mission. Mickey's actual actions were valued by superiors and colleagues, who (rightly) credited him with having helped to shape the successes of the civil affairs efforts of the army.

Mickey's Image and Civil Affairs Policy

Was Mickey a hero in World War II? Not in the common understanding of the word— "courage on the battlefield," with bullets flying all around; but one should view his contributions in context. In modern wars waged by democracies fielding volunteers wielding technology, rather than large bodies of citizen soldiers firing rifles, few are called to engage in close combat, though it remains essential to victory. Beginning with World War II, large numbers of noncombatant soldiers far from the front line have been exposed to violence and killed. For a few weeks Mickey took the same chances of random death as did tens of thousands of other such men landing in Normandy those first few days. Not the risks on the magnitude of those faced by a first-wave rifleman, tank crewman, or gunner, but the risks of older men on staffs in rear-area headquarters.

What's more, Marcus volunteered to get closer, indeed went out of his way, against some resistance, to be there. Ernie Pyle, not known as a yes man or an apologist for the high command but the voice of "the common soldier—the well-known GI," paid tribute to the "thousands of men of high rank who labored endlessly, woke up early, worked all day, and after supper went back to work far into the night to run the war."[92] These men's stories remain mostly unsung and are not generally included in "the Greatest Generation"—and that is no historian's exaggeration.

Sometimes officers of high rank die in war zones in a myriad of ordinary ways, like any GI, Tommy, or *Landwehr*. A month after Mickey's return to Washington, on July 25, 1944, Lieutenant General Lesley McNair, another genius of organization and the highest-ranking World War II casualty, was killed by an American bomb while observing the preparatory bombing to Operation Cobra. During the last week of March 1945, when most people believed the war already won and over, the Third US Armored Division lost its commanding general, Major General Maurice Rose, killed in action near Paderborn, Germany, on March 30, 1945. The elements of Rose's forward HQ echelon, including the division G-1 and G-3, both wounded, were captured, along with all the signal corps men in the accompanying M20 armored car.[93]

As an eyewitness to the fighting around Carentan, Mickey traveled the front, saw the dead on the battlefield, and experienced the terror of air attack and the paralyzing scream of the deadly 88. He was fortunate, along with John Maginnis and few others in wartime, to also witness some of the results, planned and unfathomable, of all their work, from War Department to the beach to the capture of an important—as it turned out, crucial—provincial city. Once home from the front, Mickey incorporated what he had learned there into the next stage in his mission as a CA officer: tweaking the plans for ruling liberated peoples and refocusing on the surrender of Germany and Japan and the war's aftermath. As it turned out, the trip revealed a few problems, a testament to the quality of the planning. If you believe that civil affairs is as essential to warfare as are weapons, as Eisenhower said on the eve of invasion of Normandy, or that the Monuments Men are heroes for saving priceless symbols of civilization, then Mickey is a hero for his role in establishing American civil affairs doctrine.

Dumbarton Oaks Conference, The War to End All Wars, Aug.—Oct. 1944

In the summer of 1944 at a pivotal gathering at Dumbarton Oaks, a Harvard-owned mansion in Georgetown, diplomats from China, the Soviet Union, the United Kingdom, the United States, and thirty-five other nations gathered to talk about an organization to enforce global security. This conference eventually resulted in the United Nations charter, approved in San Francisco in 1945, which established the institutions and powers of that organization. The US and British delegations benefited from insights gained about Allied civil administration of war-torn countries and military governance during World War II. Many of those contributions were provided by Colonel Marcus, who attended the conference as the G-5 representative of John Hilldring and who drew from his direct experience in the negotiations of the Allied Control Council and its predecessor organizations.[94]

The discussions proceeded in two phases over the course of a month between late August and early October 1944. Since the Soviets were at peace with Japan at that point, diplomatic necessity prevented the USSR and Chinese delegations from meeting, so two rounds of discussions, one without the Soviets, were held at the estate. It was an adaptation of the format used at the 1943 Cairo Conference, but this time with the diplomats moving in and out of a single location.[95]

The primary objective was to correct the mistakes of the post–World War I League of Nations, which did not prevent a repeat of global war. The organization they envisioned would, they thought, provide actual mechanisms with teeth for controlling conflicts, to promote friendly relations between nations, and to support economic, social, and other humanitarian endeavors, where possible. The diplomatic term for the entire endeavor was the well-used idea of fashioning a "framework," or foundation, based on broadly shared objectives. While talks on the shape of postwar peacekeeping institutions were mostly successful, two structural problems remained: voting and veto rules for the Security Council, and the Soviet insistence that all sixteen of its republics be admitted to the UN's General Assembly as separate countries.[96]

In the meantime, Roosevelt and Churchill, along with their military chiefs of staff, reached a consensus on the British and American occupation zones in postwar Germany in the bilateral US-UK Second Quebec Conference, held September 12–16, 1944. They also endorsed the Morgenthau Plan, which outlined the policy of deindustrialization of Germany after the war. Mickey, once again representing G-5, was intensely involved in these negotiations. Decisions made in Quebec also affected the war in the Pacific Theater, including the US invasion of the Philippines at Leyte Gulf scheduled for mid-to late October and plans for the British fleet's involvement in the concluding campaigns against Japan.[97]

A final wartime meeting before the defeat of Germany and Japan, code name Argonaut, convened in the picturesque Crimean resort of Yalta on the Black Sea coast February 4–11, 1945, with Roosevelt, Churchill, and Stalin attending. It would be the last meeting of the Big Three. Once again Mickey sat in Hilldring's seat. With Allied forces driving steadily toward the heart of Germany from east and west, and victory in Europe all but certain after the Bulge and the Soviet offensive into Germany, the leaders shifted their attention to the Pacific, where victory seemed much less certain. Stalin reaffirmed his commitment to join the war against Japan after victory in Europe.[98]

While the governance of postwar Germany and destiny of Eastern Europe were subjects of earlier wartime conferences, the foundational structure of the proposed United Nations remained rickety. Analyzing and creating approaches—if not solutions—to these concerns constituted Marcus's main priority during the Yalta conference, which he attended as the principal military government adviser to the US delegation. His experience in combined operations through his participation in Allied coordinating committees sharpened his natural affinity for people and openness to their diverse points of view. His field experience in the immediate aftermath of the invasion informed his advice about joint government policies, especially about the role of France. His earlier work with high officials of de Gaulle's Free French in Washington and London, combined with his experience at Carentan, now proved useful in diplomacy. The Allies agreed that France would be an occupying party in the joint government, with their sector carved from the western part of Germany (previously reserved for the United States and UK), and that they would receive reparations from Germany. The three main powers also endorsed a US proposal expanding the United Nations Security Council's permanent membership to five member nations, including France and China, with each Security Council member possessing veto authority.

At first Yalta was hailed as a success, not least by Roosevelt, who saw it as a testament to the enduring US-Soviet wartime alliance. That alliance lasted less than two months. With Roosevelt's death in April 1945 and Truman's ascension to the presidency, US-Soviet relations grew tense, especially over Eastern Europe's fate and the actual role of the United Nations.[99]

For Mickey, FDR's death was a blow, but he soon settled back into the routine of his work. The recent conferences had laid out the parameters of his postwar work at the Pentagon, where he remained the principal CA planner. More of his time was focused on the Pacific theater and the surrender documents for Germany and Japan, building on his experience with Sicily and Italy. At that time one of a handful of top American legal experts on the laws and conventions of surrender, he had dealt with the top command of every Allied army, held his own against the Russians and British, and won praise, promotion, and decorations. Now he was looking forward, like every other GI, to getting back to his real life and practicing law. But the high and mighty in the US Army had other ideas.

CHAPTER 3

The Occupation of Germany

> The stink of the camp was like no other smell—as though the odors of all deaths, diseases, and decays in that frightful establishment had been distilled into one distinctive essence that shocked and revolted all the senses.
>
> —Lieutenant Colonel John Maginnis, April 29, 1945, after visiting Buchenwald

Office of the Deputy Commanding General, US Occupation Forces, Berlin, Spring 1945

Just weeks before his death on April 12, 1945, President Roosevelt summoned General Lucius D. Clay, the de facto head of US Army procurement during the war, to the White House. FDR planned to name Clay deputy military governor for the American occupation zone of Germany, reporting to General Eisenhower and responsible for ruling and sustaining the civilian population, punishing war criminals, and caring for refugees in the American zone. Execution of US postwar policy, including the degree of German reconstruction, reparations, and punishment—as well as coordination with the other Allies—would be based in Berlin. Eisenhower's wartime SHAEF headquarters would become US Forces European Theater (USFET), an American-only command, also with a traditional G-5 structure. The celebrated general would assume the job of military governor of Germany under the Office of Military Government of the United States (OMGUS) with his own staff, including traditional G-5 military government responsibilities, after the formal German surrender. Each of the other wartime allies—Britain, France, and the Soviet Union—had their own arrangements for governing the German territory assigned to that state by the various wartime conferences.[1]

Accompanying Clay to the White House was his mentor and wartime boss James F. Byrnes, who gave him a quick rundown on what to expect. Byrnes, a former South Carolina governor, senator, and US Supreme Court justice (serving the shortest term in history), was the director of the Office of War Mobilization. He was close to Vice President Truman and would soon become his secretary of state. Truman was a neophyte in international affairs and would come to heavily rely on his friend. Byrnes warned Clay that, as victory in Europe neared, the White House was preoccupied with the possibility of postwar armed guerilla resistance by die-hard Nazis in an Alpine redoubt. He did not inform him about the rapid deterioration of Roosevelt's health over the past months. During Clay's visit, the president said little about the new assignment. Instead, he drifted into reminiscences about his youthful observations of the Germans, whom he described as "arrogant and provincial," and his idea that better education and harnessing hydroelectric power could temper their aggressive national character. Clay was grateful that FDR was doing all the talking, saying that he was "so shocked at his physical appearance that I felt it difficult to say anything." Clay left the meeting with great foreboding and even more trepidation about his new job. Two weeks later FDR was dead.[2]

Lucius D. Clay, a Georgian born to a sitting US senator and descendant of the Great Compromiser Henry Clay, graduated from West Point in June 1918 as an engineer, the Regular Army branch into which the best students were commissioned at that time. Too late for the Great War, he made his reputation building major national infrastructure, including the prewar domestic airport system, and was credited with restoring the shattered Normandy port of Cherbourg in November 1944, months after its capture. The army's best logistician and a hard-nosed administrator, he was not averse to using pressure, and was among a small group of US generals to earn four stars during

World War II without holding a combat command. He was a man who knew how to do difficult things quickly and, if necessary, ruthlessly.[3]

Fig. 10. Major General Lucius D. Clay, deputy military governor of Germany, 1945. National Archives, credit Harris and Ewing

After the meeting at the White House, Clay headed to the Pentagon to consult with his longtime friend Major General John Hilldring, head of the Civil Affairs Division (CAD) in the War Department. They were quickly joined by Colonel David Marcus, an officer Clay knew from meetings and conferences convened when army production policy intersected with civil affairs responsibilities.[4] Sharing with Hilldring and Marcus his candid observations of the clearly failing president, Clay expressed surprise at his own appointment as a direct subordinate to Eisenhower rather than in a traditional general staff role. Clay sought a realistic appraisal of the problems he would face, especially issues of divided responsibility between the civil affairs officers at USFET and his forming OMGUS staff, as well as recommendations for appointments to the key positions in the latter. Political sensitivity and experience with combined operations would be crucial, as it was increasingly clear that success in defeating Hitler would soon strain wartime alliances, which rested on little else by the end. Each of the major powers—the United States, the United Kingdom, the Soviet Union, and China—would return to its own geographic, political, and ethnic realities, aggravated by historic fears recently realized in an ocean of blood and tens of millions of dead. Clay would remain in Germany from 1945 to 1949 and participate in the dangerous early skirmishes of the Cold War, before that decades-long undeclared conflict had taken that name.[5]

Impressed anew by his familiarity with the policy issues, personalities, and politics involved, soon after arriving at SHAEF Clay made a by-name request that Mickey Marcus be transferred to his office.[6] Mickey arrived in Europe just days after Hilldring, on May 18, 1945, in Washington, pinned the Distinguished Service Medal (DSM) on his blouse for his contributions to the establishment and success of Civil Affairs Division in all theaters of the war. He didn't get a chance to see Emma before leaving for Germany, with just enough time to mail the medal and citation to her before boarding a C-47 for the long flight. A rare decoration for a noncombat field grade staff officer, the DSM citation is evidence that the top Army brass agreed on the scope and depth of Mickey's responsibilities as a founder of wartime civil affairs doctrine and practice.

> "Colonel Marcus . . . represented the Director of the Division in the negotiation of important international agreements and, with representatives of civilian agencies, in the formulation of basic United States policy with respect to civil affairs and military government. As a result of firsthand experience gained by him in carrying out an important mission in Sicily and Italy, and through that acquired in accompanying the 101st Airborne Division in the invasion of Normandy, he was able to recommend and to see instituted important modifications of policies and procedures

concerning military government in the occupied areas and basic improvements in administration in civil affairs in France. He assisted in the negotiation and drafting of the Italian Surrender Instrument, The Instrument of Unconditional Surrender of Germany, and the international agreement concerning the machinery used for the control of Germany after her total defeat. His efforts in every case contributed to the successes attained by the Civil Affairs Division."[7]

Fig. 11. General Hilldring decorates Mickey with the Distinguished Service Medal at the Pentagon, May 18, 1945. Military History Institute

That last reference to postwar "machinery" meant the central military government executive agency, the Allied Control Council, sometimes referred to as the Control Commission, which ran the postwar occupation government. As an architect of that machinery, and participant as US representative in many of its meetings, Mickey was well positioned to shape the bureaucratic structures that would control the most immediate security-related issues at the local, regional, and national level. In this, he drew heavily on his New York City and Hawaii experience in police, prisons, and law enforcement as well as his many contacts with other agencies of government. He was the secretary of the US Group Control Council, directly under General Lucius Clay and the US representative on the Allied Group Control Council Staff. Paramount among all priorities and concerns stood the security of US occupation forces and the maintenance of peace and order in the streets.[8]

Clay arrived at SHAEF headquarters at Reims before the end of the fighting to sort out the lines of authority between the existing CA operation and the new military governor's office. Early professional and personal friction between the two groups added to Clay's difficulties in gathering his own experienced staff for the military government structure that would rule the American zone of Germany from its divided capital of Berlin. Clay continued to build out his new command, and in May he received a welcome new deputy, Major General Oliver Patton Echols, to direct all communications and external relations, a growing problem with the Soviets. The Army Air Force's procurement genius, and responsible only to its chief Hap Arnold, Echols had run development, acquisition, and deployment of all US Army Air Force aircraft and related equipment during the war. The numbers reflecting his wartime industrial achievements are staggering by any historical, or contemporary, standard for expansion of heavy manufacturing capacity and output. In 1940 the United States produced just over 6,000 airplanes and 12,300 tons of support material. At the peak of the buildup in 1944, American factories, now fully mobilized, produced just over 96,000 airplanes of all types and a staggering 550,000 tons of support equipment, sixteen and forty-five times more, relatively, than just four years earlier.[9]

The paths of Clay and Echols had crossed many times, and they spoke the same language. Clay quickly found a way to shorten Echols's learning curve by assigning Mickey as his deputy. By mid-August 1945, their office in Berlin bore the bold title "Deputy Commanding General, Headquarters US Control Council." Echols was Clay's number two, and Mickey was Echols's number two. Clay and Echols dealt with the top Allied officers and civilian officials, including the Soviets, and Mickey assumed his familiar role as chief staff officer, planner, behind-the-scenes operator, and general troubleshooter.[10]

Oliver Echols was at the end of a distinguished career and was already planning for his future business interests in aviation. More immediately pressing was his severe, chronic neck pain, which sidelined him and eventually led to a medical retirement. In a well-practiced role, Mickey stood in for his boss frequently, as well as for members of staff, planning and performing options analysis for governing the American zone of Germany. He coordinated with CAD in Washington, USFET in Europe while it was a player, and the British and French. In the vortex of the war's aftermath stood the basic questions applicable to every war that ends with the surrender of one side: What kind and how much reconstruction should be allowed for the defeated nation? How severely should the defeated people be treated? How to define, prosecute, and punish those guilty of war crimes, and how deep down the chain of command should justice be pursued? And what economic reparations should, or could, the Allies impose on Germany, especially considering the aftermath of Versailles and the immediate postwar Soviet actions?

Clay had a basic understanding of the mission of OMGUS, but it did not yet reflect the hard realities defined by the battlefield or the emerging character of Soviet rule. In a meeting with his staff soon after taking command, Clay offered a slightly softened statement of the so-called Morgenthau Plan, embodied originally in Joint Chiefs of Staff Memorandum 1067. This was aimed at destroying the military capability of Germany but not its long-term viability. The plan as developed by Henry Morgenthau, FDR's secretary of treasury, and the only Jew in his cabinet, was intended to be hard-edged to the conquered Germans and indifferent to their suffering. It would have reduced a permanently divided Germany to a low-tech agricultural producer for Western Europe and Russia's new dominions. The Office of the Military Governor, most crucially during those first months, would have extraordinary latitude in guiding the actual policies that gave meaning to Clay's words.[11]

Mickey may have had legal reservations about some aspects of the plan, according to Maginnis, but he was a key agent in implementing Clay's policies and never expressed such reservations. Clay's initial guidance was severe: "Let this much be clear: The Germans will know we are running a military government. We are not concerned . . . with how they will manage their economy or their government in the years to come. We are determined first to smash completely the German capacity to make war. Nazis will be driven from power and will be kept down and out. The war criminals will pay for their savagery with their lives and liberties, with their sweat and blood. When these aims are accomplished, there will be time enough to consider the regeneration of the German people."[12]

Stalin's vision for occupied Germany, though, went well beyond Clay's language: looting, forced relocations, repression of human rights, ubiquitous secret police, arbitrary arrest, and violent abuse of the population to force acquiescence.

Dachau Concentration Camp, Munich, American Zone, Occupied Germany, May 1945

Mickey arrived at Clay's headquarters in Frankfurt just after the DSM ceremony. The recent occupants of his executive suite at the chemical giant IG Farben main building, the manufacturers of the gas Zyklon-B used in the extermination camp at Birkenau-Auschwitz, would soon face war crimes charges. By that time, Lt. Colonel John Maginnis was serving as executive officer of Detachment A1B1, at the top of the Civil Affairs Regiment, and led the first civil affairs field unit to enter Berlin. By the time he arrived in the German capital, the Allied Kommandatura, the governing body for the city and a key instrument of American policy, was already being organized, and Maginnis was quickly appointed the US chief of staff. Since there were no precedents for what lay ahead, and victory brought the prospect of a humanitarian disaster beyond anything seen before, practical and political questions had to be resolved quickly. Sometimes that required the authority of the highest level of the occupation authorities.

On a late July day, as Clay was setting up his headquarters in Berlin, Maginnis headed over there. Making his way among the buckets, tarps, scaffolding, and workers, he recounted, "I heard a loud shout behind me and turned to stare into a familiar face with an ear-to-ear grin on it—none other than Colonel Marcus! We had a brief but joyful reunion amidst the ladders and paint buckets. He was the Secretary of the US Control Council for Germany, a most consequential and strategically important assignment."[13]

Over the succeeding months, the friends met a half dozen times on social occasions and crossed paths during official duties. They talked about their work, and about specific issues of personal interest, including Jewish refugee affairs, and what they had seen of the Nazi evil. Maginnis had commanded civil affairs units from Normandy to Berlin but the impact on him of a visit to one of the most notorious of the concentration camps is plain in Maginnis's written account. He had seen Buchenwald on April 29, 1945, only days after its liberation by units of George Patton's US Third Army. Maginnis's old friend Lieutenant Colonel Carroll Lewis was the displaced persons officer at First Army G-5 and arranged a tour of the recently liberated concentration camp. Lieutenant Peter Ball, also in G-5, was the American officer in charge of the camp and showed Maginnis around. "It was a real hellhole," Maginnis would write, "even though some cleaning up had been accomplished. The inmates were mostly political prisoners, and there were still over twenty thousand there at this time. There had been at times as many as fifty to sixty thousand people there. Many were dying every day; they were just too far gone to be saved. The stink of the camp was like no other smell—as though the odors of all the deaths, diseases, and decays in that frightful establishment had been distilled into one distinctive essence that shocked and revolted the senses."[14]

Only a few weeks later, under standing orders at Clay's headquarters that all general staff officers assigned to his command visit Dachau on arrival, Mickey arranged a tour two weeks after that camp's liberation by elements of Courtney Hodges's US First Army. What Mickey saw and learned at Dachau was a life-changing experience, and a central hinge point for understanding his later decision to work for David Ben-Gurion and the independence of Israel. This is where Mickey's conversion to Zionism began, not just as a national liberation movement for the Jews as originally envisioned by Herzl and others, but as their only possible hope of refuge and survival after the Holocaust.[15]

As with other elements of the Mickey Marcus image stretched by inconceivable exaggeration—New York gossip Leonard Lyons's "Lyons Den" *New York Post* column on June 15, 1948, claimed that Mickey was the first American in the first tank to liberate Dachau—and Lyons was not the only one to make that claim. There are few direct or detached sources for Mickey's actual experience. Maginnis's account offers clues, but no account disputes the centrality of the Dachau visit in Mickey's complete conversion to hard-core militant Zionism by his last two hundred days. No less relevant is the range of the versions of that experience and its uses, often political, as reported by those who claimed knowledge of Mickey's true feelings. Even without considering the impact of visiting Dachau on the evolution of Mickey's thinking on a Jewish homeland and the need for professional self-defense, Maginnis's account of their discussions has a broad historic reach. They touch the plight of the Holocaust survivors and other victims of oppression, punishment of the war criminals, and the practical problems of ruling a conquered country.[16]

Although Mickey and Maginnis were not official liberators, they were witnesses to the immediate aftermath of the liberation of the camps at a time when the physical evidence of the atrocities committed there still overwhelmed the senses. The experience was not unique; it was shared by frontline GIs of the thirty-six officially recognized American liberator divisions. [17] They had overrun literally thousands of SS installations of murder, torture, and the master-slave economic empire spread out along the Allied routes of advance into Germany. These places include the large well-known concentration camps and thousands of subcamps, which included extensive and permanent facilities as well as small, temporary places, some of which comprised only a single building filled with slaves and a few guards. The images of the Holocaust in people's minds right after the war did not come from the sources that pervade our culture—TV miniseries, movies, comic, memes, and YouTube videos. In the mid-1940s it took some time for the still and video images taken in the final days of the war and right after it to reach rightly horrified viewers around the world. Then as now, many did not believe that these images were real, dismissing them as Allied or Jewish—lately Zionist—propaganda.

Only as the victors returned home did Americans and Britons get some hint of the horror of the SS crimes, and even then only at a distance, informed by weekend movie newsreels and mass syndicated columns in the papers. Radio broadcasts by trusted war correspondents embedded with the first liberators narrowed the distance. Tens of thousands of frontline American soldiers passed through the camps, either in haste toward the next battle or slowly to provide aid to the survivors. American GIs saw the horror for themselves, some spoke to the survivors in Yiddish, they took pictures, wrote letters, and recorded their thoughts in diaries and memoirs. But the reactions of the GIs were nondenominational and independent of faith. Except among each other, most spoke of it sparingly, or not at all, their roles in the actions revealed only after their deaths, but as long as they lived, what they had experienced never left them, as historians of liberator units know from personal interviews with veterans.[18]

The same experience was true on the eastern front, beginning with the liberation of the extermination camp of Majdanek in eastern Poland on July 23, 1944 and including Auschwitz-Birkenau on January 27, 1945. Everywhere, the captured guards, administrators, and collaborators denied everything, but to no avail. The Allies forced them and the local populations, who knew very well what was going on in the camps, to personally bury the slaughtered and confront the evil they had supported, cheered, and now wished to disavow, deny, and forget.[19]

Terminal Conference,
Potsdam, Germany, mid-July to early August 1945

In the last major wartime meeting of World War II, and by acts of sovereignty and providence, new leaders of the West faced Stalin in Potsdam, a suburb of Berlin. Flushed with victory, the Generalissimo aimed to exact massive tribute from the conquered and liberated peoples alike, ruling and plundering the latter under the doctrine of "spheres of influence." President Harry S. Truman, who found himself thrust into the presidency upon Roosevelt's death, was untested on the world stage, and Clement Atlee replaced Churchill as prime minister midway through the conference, a potent display to Stalin of political instability among the western allies. The agenda was twofold: as discussed at Yalta, now that the war in Europe had ended, the Allies would agree on surrender terms for Japan and finalize the borders and terms of peace in Europe, including the fate of Poland and the nature of military rule over Germany. Regarding the latter point, Mickey attended the meeting as the US expert on American military government.

The final Potsdam Declaration repeated the demand for Japan's unconditional surrender, without input from the Soviets, who were at that point still not at war with Japan. It called for the dismantling of the Japanese empire but reaffirmed the Allies' commitment to the human rights of the Japanese people. In its declarations about postwar Germany, all three allies outlined a sweeping and ambitious project to recast Nazi society into a democratic nation, complete with all the protections of minorities and balance of powers. Every law from the Nazi era would be stricken from the books, every war criminal would face true justice, and every trace of authoritarianism would be purged from schools and the judiciary, with robust monitoring and sanctions put in place at the local and regional level. A unified German government lay decades in the future, and the Allied Control Council would rule the country, with each of the occupying forces—the United States, Britain, the Soviet Union, and now France—ruling a sector of Germany and assuming the reins of the defeated Reich. Mickey had played a key role all throughout the war in the planning of the Allied Control Council, particularly in concert with the British.

Delineating the final borders between Germany, the Soviet Union, and Poland was the last major issue at Potsdam. In the aftermath of the agreements, which stirred further unrest, and with Soviet support, Poland, Czechoslovakia, and Hungary began to deport their minority populations of ethnic German Christians who lived in their countries and were viewed as Nazis by their neighbors. This was in addition to the Jewish survivors of the Holocaust already sheltering in the west. Concerns grew about a mass influx of ethnic Germans into zones ruled by the western allies already facing large demands on their resources. The weak diplomacy of the western allies, merely insisting that such transfers be orderly and humane and asking Poland, Czechoslovakia, and Hungary to pause further deportations temporarily, was more than cowardly, it was ineffective. The ethnic German refugees were targeted for forced deportation, and thus the victims of a war crime under the laws soon to be established, and at the least the official indifference in the west, and open hatred in the east, masked the desire for vengeance by east and west. The millions of expelled ethnic Germans moved slowly through their home countries without resources, stalled, suffered, and many lost their lives, mostly women and children.[20]

In a private meeting between Truman and Stalin on July 24, Truman told the dictator about a new American "super bomb," thinking that the successful atomic explosion south of Los Alamos just eight days earlier, on July 16, would underline the hard line the Americans were taking in Stalin's eyes. Truman's new team considered FDR's approach earlier at Yalta too conciliatory and too sympathetic toward the enormous cost—with estimated military and civilian losses of over 25 million people, or more than 10 percent of the prewar population—of the war the Soviets had borne on the eastern front. But Truman's diplomatic muscle-flexing proved ineffective. Stalin already knew about the successful nuclear test through his British and American espionage agents, who had penetrated the American A-bomb program, and Soviet scientists, now assisted by captured German scientists, were already at work on their own nuclear bomb. Instead of capitulating, Stalin held firm and waited, expecting the western allies to fragment as domestic matters, such as the rebuilding of their economies, claimed their attention. The victors of World War II, who had stayed together grudgingly throughout the war, never met again after the Japanese surrendered, and they abandoned high-level meetings and personal diplomacy as a tool to fashion the postwar world.[21]

Victory Parade, Occupied Berlin, Soviet Sector, September 7, 1945

Mickey and Maginnis stayed connected by phone for the next couple of months but were unable to meet face-to-face until the Victory Parade held on September 7, 1945, in the Tiergarten park in the Soviet sector of Berlin. This grand spectacle featured top generals and combat units from the four ruling powers, including the constabulary US Second Armored Division, completing its Benning-to-Berlin odyssey despite the fact that few of the soldiers in the fighting regiments who had started at Fort Benning in 1941 made it to the parade.

Marching bands and a thoroughly bemedaled Marshal Georgy Zhukov and grinning General Patton held center stage, competing for the attention of photographers. Lucius Clay, Ike's deputy, hovered close to Patton. Also on the reviewing stand, lost in the mass of Control Council officers, stood the tanned and unusually fit Colonel Marcus, who greeted Maginnis with his usual broad grin and "Cheerio." After the victory celebration, the two friends met again socially, as well as during several office visits, but three events stood out to Maginnis as indicative of what Mickey thought about the Germans, the plight of the Jewish survivors, and who he was at the core. [22]

The first came as the hard winter of 1944–45 descended on the bomb- and shell-shattered occupied city of Berlin, with the prospect of a severe fuel shortage, among other humanitarian crises, almost certain. In response, the Kommandatura allowed wood gathering in the Grunewald forest if the Berliners made their own arrangements for chopping and cartage. On a very sunny morning in late fall, Maginnis invited Mickey to accompany him to the forest to observe the operation.

Walking among the destitute civilians, Maginnis engaged individuals and families in his basic German, while Mickey intensely watched the interactions. The Germans, some with small children in tow, collected wood as quickly as they could in order to make it back home before the nightly curfew, only to wake up the next morning and do it again. The common goal was basic: survival. As the two officers headed back to their quarters, Mickey expressed his gratitude for the opportunity to see for himself what the Berliners faced. Curious what he thought, Maginnis asked, "Well, what do you think of these Germans now?"

"The question is," Mickey responded, "which of these people that we have just been talking with are the guilty ones and which are the innocent? I can't tell and I really wonder if they know themselves. Anyway, there they are, innocent or guilty, pitifully grubbing around there in the forest for enough warmth to keep themselves alive. Innocent or guilty, they are now paying the piper and if they have really learned their lesson, perhaps this is punishment enough." In this one observation Mickey gets to the basic issues of the moral conflicts between collective punishment, individual rights, and the need to hold accountable occupied enemy populations for their large-scale political support and mass participation in horrendous war crimes and crimes against humanity.[23]

During this same period, Maginnis observed Mickey during a second event, a tragic refugee crisis that reflected the tensions between the Soviets and the West over events in Poland in the immediate aftermath of Potsdam. Maginnis describes postwar Berlin as permeated by an atmosphere of continuous urgency punctuated by real emergencies, what the British called "flaps." One such flap happened right after the wood-gathering episode, when the Kommandatura reached an agreement on the Central Berlin Trade Union Committee elections after months of heated discussion. Everyone hoped for a quiet holiday season and a respite, however brief, of the growing hostility among wartime colleagues.

A large influx of Polish and other Jewish survivors broke the apparent calm. On December 28, Maginnis wrote in his journal, "the Polish Jewish refugee situation in Berlin was the critical issue. Everyone seemed to talk around the issue, apart from the British who made it clear that they would not accept these refugees in their sector and if they did come in, they would not be fed or housed."[24]

In the immediate aftermath of the war, sixty thousand displaced Jewish Holocaust survivors from all over Europe languished in camps in the western sectors of Germany, some still fenced off in the same places used for their torture and destruction, and often housed alongside collaborating anti-Semites also displaced from the same countries or caught up in the refugee migrations. At first the Jews were not recognized as a separate group in the displaced persons (DP) camps, even though they composed the majority in some facilities, and they received no direct occupation support though they faced problems many others did not. Those included ongoing violent anti-Semitism both in their former countries and among their fellow DPs, now stoked by Communist zeal. That, and the same old brands of nationalism and Jew hatred, made the prospect of a return to their former homes abhorrent.[25]

In the United States, pressure for aiding Holocaust survivors in Europe came from rabbis serving in the Chaplain Corps, who discovered while visiting the DP camps that US and British military personnel running the facilities were not carrying out the SHEAF-mandated policies. Their complaint that these personnel were "incompetent and disinterested" led to a Department of State inquiry into the needs of DPs in the western zones who were unable or unwilling to return to their homeland. To head the inquiry, President Truman approved the selection of Earl G. Harrison, a distinguished jurist who had been commissioner for immigration and naturalization under FDR.[26]

In his inspection of the DP camps in Europe, Harrison paid special attention to those holding Holocaust survivors. His report was extremely critical of their treatment, comparing it to the same kinds of restrictions and humiliations they had faced under the Nazis. "We appear to be treating the Jews as the Nazis treated them," he said, "except that we do not exterminate them."[27]

The Harrison report led to better treatment for Jewish DPs and built support for the immigration of Jewish refugees to Palestine, even though British officials and Arabs in and surrounding Palestine resisted that idea bitterly. The issue remained a major concern of the Control Council for the remainder of Mickey's tenure as Echols's deputy.

On January 10, 1946, Maginnis wrote, "A finish was put to our biggest current issue when General Clay ordered all Polish Jews in the U.S. sector to be cared for. Everyone was relieved, and we went to work on the 3rd Battalion, 30th Infantry Regiment camp. A military camp was more quickly adaptable for a large influx of refugees than were the DP camps now in preparation."[28] Within a week the Jewish refugees were in a temporary camp at the regiments base. Mickey, already known for his empathetic and upbeat attitude, appeared deeply moved by these events. Maginnis and others detected an uncharacteristic solemnity descend on him, the crisis clearly resonating, Maginnis thought later, due to his Jewish origins. Mickey never alluded to those origins directly except through humorous cultural references, but after this episode he remarked, "These events underscore that the war's shadows linger long after its end, particularly for its most tormented victims." It was what Maginnis called a "Marcusism," or a reflection on the moment that conjures the universal truth underneath. The use of the word *shadow* is also more than striking. And while the sentiment reflects Mickey's passion about universal human rights, having seen firsthand a new round of misery for the Jewish people postwar must have played a part in what happened later.[29]

As Mickey prepared for a new assignment, his conversations with Maginnis turned again to justice for the victims they had both seen up close. While hot anger and a desire for vengeance against Germany might naturally result from such experiences, Mickey looked beyond the punishment of war criminals. His focus remained on the postwar relations of the wartime Allies, knowing that what they did in the next months would shape the future, either away from the horrors they had just seen, or toward continued instability, violence, and war. He would frequently ask Maginnis, "How are you getting along in the *Kommandatura?* or 'How are you getting along with the Russians and never about the Germans." He was not only intent on punishing the guilty but rather championed a vision that secured the rights of those who had suffered to make sure it never happened again.[30]

A month after Christmas, January 1946, it was clear that the first phase of the occupation was ending, the demobilization had gained momentum, and conversations had discreetly turned toward commendations for the departing personnel. During this time, Maginnis marked a final meeting that captured Mickey's essence. Maginnis asked him why he hadn't received recognition for his services.

"Like what?" asked Mickey.

Maginnis clarified, "Like a promotion or a decoration."

"Oh, but I have. I have the DSM [Distinguished Service Medal]."

Maginnis said he had never seen Mickey wear a DSM. Grinning, Mickey produced the DSM medal from his drawer.

Maginnis spotted another ribbon. "What's that?"

"The British gave it to me. It's the OBE [Order of the British Empire]."[31] Mickey's face lit up at the sight of Maginnis's surprise.

"For God's sake, Mickey," Maginnis asked, "why the hell don't you ever wear these decorations?"

It was too much trouble trying to keep the ribbons clean, Mickey said, which Maginnis characterized as a typical response.

Turning the tables, Mickey asked Maginnis, "Now, what are we going to do about getting a decoration for you?"

On February 1 Maginnis visited Mickey in the hospital, where he'd landed after falling asleep under a sunlamp and burning a big patch on one side of his body. The next day Mickey was at his office when Maginnis came by to say goodbye before he headed back to Washington. Sensing that this was the last time they would see each other, Maginnis tried to tell Mickey how good a friend he had been during their time together in Normandy and in Berlin. During their half-hour conversation, Maginnis thanked him for endorsing his promotion to full colonel, and Mickey responded by noting that he had recommended his Normandy bunkmate for a Legion of Merit—a final gesture of a generous spirit. The friends would speak on the phone but would indeed never see each other again. Three decades after the death of his battlefield buddy, Maginnis remembered, "He had a quick and keen mind, a healthy, well-developed body, an innate belief in the virtues of honor and patriotism, and a compassionate heart. These qualities united to turn his thought and spirit outwards away from himself. He gave more than he received and was all the happier because of it. It was his natural way of life. Unselfish was the word for Mickey Marcus."[32]

War Crimes Branch, Civil Affairs Division, Pentagon, Washington, DC, April 1946

The US Army had been preparing for the punishment of Nazi and Japanese war criminals well before the end of the war. Under varying authorities and offices, and in coordination with the US State Department and other US agencies, other allies, and the UN War Crimes Commission, in October 1944 the judge advocate general Major General Myron C. Cramer, set up the War Crimes Division in the US Army under career judge advocate Brigadier General John M. Weir. His office collected reports of atrocities and lists of suspected criminals and established liaison with the commission. At the end of the war, this evidence and documentation passed to Allied officers and occupation authorities as the momentum for punishing the guilty—one thing they all theoretically agreed upon—replaced the drive for victory.[33]

On December 20, 1945, the Allied Control Council enacted Law No. 10, establishing a "uniform legal basis in Germany for the prosecution of war criminals and other similar offenders other than those dealt with by the International Military Tribunal." The International Military Tribunal case famously tried twenty-two top Nazis for war crimes, crimes against humanity, and crimes against peace. Brigadier General Telford Taylor was the chief prosecutor for what are commonly called the Subsequent Nuremberg Trials, all held under the authority of Law No. 10. These trials were conducted under the monitoring of the US Office of Military Government to mete out justice to persons charged with offenses recognized as crimes in Law No. 10. These are the definitions that have guided war crimes trials ever since:

> **Paragraph 1A. Each of the following acts is recognized as a crime:**
>
> (a) Crimes against Peace. Initiation of invasions of other countries and wars of aggression in violation of international laws and treaties, including but not limited to planning, preparation, initiation or waging a war of aggression, or a war of violation of international treaties, agreements or assurances, or participation

in a common plan or conspiracy for the accomplishment of any of the foregoing.

(b) War Crimes. Atrocities or offenses against persons or property constituting violations of the laws or customs of war, including but not limited to, murder, ill treatment or deportation to slave labor or for any other purpose, of civilian population from occupied territory, murder or ill treatment of prisoners of war or persons on the seas, killing of hostages, plunder of public or private property, wanton destruction of cities, towns or villages, or devastation not justified by military necessity.

(c) Crimes against Humanity. Atrocities and offenses, including but not limited to murder, extermination, enslavement, deportation, imprisonment, torture, rape, or other inhumane acts committed against any civilian population, or persecutions on political, racial, or religious grounds whether in violation of the domestic laws of the country where perpetrated, or not.

(d) Membership in categories of a criminal group or organization declared criminal by the International Military Tribunal.[34]

The Army's early prosecution efforts were held under the US War Department's Judge Advocate General authority, in coordination with Jackson's staff and all still under the assistant secretary of war at the Pentagon. The new projected trials would require more resources and staff attention, and the War Department began planning for the transfer of the War Crimes Office from the Judge Advocate General (JAG) Division (Special Staff) to the Civil Affairs Division (General Staff), a higher level in the bureaucracy. With the formal establishment of the lines of authority scheduled for March 1946, War Crimes would then be under the command of John Hilldring. Faced with the demands of the postwar government and the new trials situation, Hilldring began his own recruitment efforts and wrote to his good friend Lucius Clay, asking for Mickey to be released back to him for a new job. Hilldring assured Clay he would never ask, "except for the fact that I understand General Gailey is scheduled to take over Marcus' job. I would under no circumstances ask you to release him but believe me, I have an important assignment for him and would rest easier at night if I knew he was on the job."[35]

It was a double homecoming for Mickey, personally and professionally if not geographically directly to Brooklyn, but not a respite from his wartime pace, nor a divergence from his range of responsibilities. The workload was intense and covered both theaters of the war. While closer to Emma, especially on weekends, he still found himself squarely in the middle of frantic activity, and the nature of the material under his review would weigh as heavily upon him as anything he had seen before

Mickey was responsible for recruiting the trial lawyers and judges and staff for the Allied war crimes trials that followed the high-profile International Military Tribunal (IMT) High Command trial at Nuremberg. He had been involved in the early debates and planning for prosecution of war crimes and crimes against humanity at the major conferences dealing with that issue. Then, as one of the American architects and executors of the postwar administration, he helped shape the Allied Control Council governing rules, including Law No. 10, the authority governing the actual prosecution of war crimes.[36]

One of the key underlying issues in the war crimes legal structure was the definition of genocide. Fully engaged in the debates, Mickey had passed along an advanced copy of Raphael Lemkin's groundbreaking book *Axis Rule in Occupied Europe* (1944) to Colonel Murray Bernays as the latter was preparing for one of the first Law No. 10 trials in mid-1945. Mickey was briefed on war crimes activities during the war in connection with the major conferences and knew Lemkin's work from the War Crimes Office at JAG in the War Department, especially his deep analysis of the structure of the German occupational authorities across Europe as evidence that they organized the crimes that define genocide.[37] This provided the documentary evidential and intellectual basis for declaring that members of a particular state organization, for example, the Security Service of the SS (Sichersheitsdienst, or SD), the Gestapo (Geheime Staats Polizei), or the Reich Security Main Office

(Reichsicherheitshauptamt, or RSHA) were de jure criminals, per section (d) in paragraph 2 of the law.[38]

Josiah DuBois, an expert at Treasury on the interactions between American and German corporations, focused on the IG Farben chemical cartel. Before he left for Nurenberg, DuBois recalled, he had a conversation with Mickey at the War Department, where they pondered whether and under what circumstances a private enterprise should be held responsible for its involvement in a country's war effort. Mickey candidly shared the prevailing view around CAD: "A lot of people in this Department are scared of pinning a war plot on these men. There's no law by which we can force industrialists to make war equipment for us right now. A few American manufacturers were Farben stooges. And those who weren't, can say, 'Hell, if participating in a rearmament program is criminal, we want no part of it.' " Top American business leaders might well conclude that if it happened to the Germans, it could happen to them.

This dilemma of the nation-state also raised both legal and political questions at the foundation of the wartime conferences, agreements, and structures for the postwar order that Mickey helped construct touching international law and standards of behavior in conflicts. Now the effort has crossed into a theory of the modern state by defining its moral obligations against the limitations of its institutions and ability to govern its economy. Slavery, rape, torture, and deportation are abhorrent. But codifying them as genocide is difficult to define in actual law. Mickey had closely followed the work of the exiled Jewish scholars shaping the legal theory, including Franz Neumann, Otto Kirchheimer, and Herbert Marcuse, all employed by the Research and Analysis Branch of the Office of Strategic Services (OSS) in the Central European Section. Crucial to their efforts was Neumann's study of the German Nazi regime, titled *Behemoth*.[39]

At the conclusion of the High Command Nuremberg trial before the IMT, US Justice Jackson resigned as chief of counsel and then Colonel Telford Taylor took over responsibility for the Allied Control Council Law No. 10 trials. Taylor needed to recruit people quickly for a projected dozen broad-scope prosecutions in Europe like the IG Farben case. That would involve hundreds of defendants and span every aspect of the newly born policy of prosecuting large numbers of war criminals in the modern age. Taylor had arrived back in Washington in February 1946 and established contact with John Hilldring at CAD for administrative support.

As in so many previous cases, that meant dealing with Mickey, who was already in the office of the newly organized War Crimes Branch. "I was very lucky," Taylor wrote. "Mickey was a heart-and-soul supporter of the war crimes trials, intelligent, energetic, and a skilled 'operator,' with many contacts and friends in legal, military, and New York political circles. In recruiting and in ensuring a logistical base for our enterprise, Mickey played the leading part."[40] By the end of March, Mickey alerted the OMGUS, his old haunting ground, to prepare for the arrival of forty-five attorneys, and twenty to thirty each of administrators, court reporters, translators, stenographers, and typists.[41]

Among those Mickey recruited was Arthur L. Petersen, a 1942 graduate of Columbia Law, attractive because of his expertise in documentary evidence and fluency in German. It was clear early on that Germany at every level, in every organization, civil and military, had maintained meticulous records of their own criminality, documents bearing the signatures of hundreds of thousands of officers and officials, initialing transport orders to extermination camps, reporting on their murder operations, detailing production figures of the SS economic empire and the daily, weekly, and monthly death rates of slaves in the tens of thousands of installations. Files were uncovered by the truckload by the advancing Allies, many of them dispersed among the stolen art treasures of Europe that the Nazis had buried underground.

Mickey eyed Petersen for the prosecution of SS General Gottlob Berger—head of the RSHA, the centralized Reich main security office, and architect of the Waffen SS—in the so-called Ministries Trials for a range of war crimes and crimes against humanity. The court found evidence of direct participation in crimes and sentenced him to twenty-five years. John McCloy, who succeeded Lucius Clay as governor, reduced the sentence to ten years in line with a policy of leniency for the few actual convicted war criminals. The high-minded and stirring rhetorical calls for prosecuting the criminals and justice for the millions slaughtered had given way to the Cold War. Gottlob Berger was released in 1951, after serving less than seven years. He died in 1975, well into old age, a free and rehabilitated citizen.[42] Hundreds of thousands of genocidal murderers, torturers, and rapists never faced accountability. The record of war crimes prosecutions in Asia was even worse.

Among the prosecutors recruited for these later Nuremberg Trials was a combat veteran and lawyer, later human rights advocate Ben Ferencz, then a 25-year-old Harvard Law grad. He became a titan of international law active to his last days in 2023. He would lead the prosecution of the top 24 commanders of the four mobile killing units known as the SS Einsatzgruppen (German for "operations groups"), many of whom held advanced degrees, including doctors, lawyers, judges, architects, and social scientists, and who killed Jews all over the conquered Soviet areas.[43]

After the locally assigned SS, police, other German units, and their collaborators brutally rounded up, ghettoized, enslaved, raped, tortured, and killed the local Jewish population immediately after conquest, the four Einsatzgruppen later went systematically from place to place, assisted by locals, and methodically murdered in cold blood, up close, more than two million Jews in the Holocaust by Bullets. The victims' bodies were dumped in countless mass graves they often dug themselves. Their murderers, well-oiled by alcohol, often committed these atrocious acts in full view of the victims' neighbors, who looked on with indifference or pleasure before proceeding to loot their dead neighbors' homes.[44]

After a chance encounter with a Harvard classmate on Fifth Avenue in which Ferencz mentioned his early postwar work investigating war crimes for his division, his classmate relayed that Telford Taylor was looking for help in the prosecution of war criminals. Ferencz came to Washington in March 1946 to meet the now-famous prosecutor, also a Harvard Law graduate.[45] Taylor had asked Mickey for advice and help on recruitment after receiving his new assignment, and when he came back to Washington, he invited Mickey to interview the New Yorker. Mickey, described by Ferencz as "a shrewd and tough cookie, my kind of guy," leaned hard on the young veteran's moral responsibility. Opening with his typically disarming "Call me Mickey," in Ferencz's telling he explained that there was a dearth of lawyers with any experience with war crimes trials, and the army was scrambling:

> "Benny," he said earnestly, "we want you to go back to Germany. We'll make you a Colonel." I thought he was kidding. I replied that the only time I would go back under military command would be if our country declared war on Germany again and we were losing. Mickey made a counteroffer. He offered me a simulated rank equivalent to a full Colonel with all its privileges, yet I could remain a civilian employee who could quit at any time. He was a good salesman and suggested I finish with Taylor.[46]

Then Taylor made his pitch:

> "Look, I'm going back to Nuremberg, I've been over there, the International Military Tribunal is already in process, Justice Jackson is there, we're winding up that trial but I'm going to take over after him, and we're going to set up a whole series of subsequent trials. We will reveal the full range of Nazi depravity at every level of the German *Reich*, and I'm going to be in charge, I need staff, I've heard about you, and I'd like you to come with me."
>
> "What have you heard about me?"
>
> "I heard that you're occasionally insubordinate."
>
> And I said, "That's not correct. I'm usually insubordinate because I will not follow orders that I know are stupid. But I've also been checking up on you, and I know you're a Harvard man, I know your background, and I don't think you're going to give me stupid orders, and if you don't you couldn't get a better man."
>
> He said, "You come with me."

So, I said, "Fine," and later called up Mickey, "I'm off to that army junket. I'm going out there with Telford Taylor."

Ben won convictions against the leaders of the SS Einsatzgruppen, proving that the defendants had murdered at least a million innocent noncombatants, the largest mass murder trial in history. Years later, when asked why he didn't go for the full legal establishment of the tally of those slaughtered, more than two million by most estimates, Ferencz responded that he stopped when he had proved his case beyond doubt.[47]

As part of his ongoing supervision of the war crimes courts, Mickey made inspection trips to Germany, and on July 22, 1946, judge advocate general Major General Thomas L. Greene dispatched him on a major inspection tour to East Asia with stops in the Philippines, South Korea, occupied Japan, and Nationalist China. His mission was to deal with "numerous problems confronting the prosecution of war criminals in the Far East" and respond to concerns expressed by the senior UN liaison with American war crimes efforts in the Pacific Theater of Operations. Operating under the authority of General MacArthur as Supreme Commander for the Allied Powers, Mickey focused on inter-Allied cooperation. Because numerous Allied nations had experienced Japanese atrocities against their soldiers and civilians, there were some disagreements about who had authority where. The Joint Chiefs of Staff assigned responsibility for the trial of war criminals in the India-Burma theater to the government of India (then under British rule) and the British South Asia Command. The same applied to the central Chinese government, with US support for fourteen cases involving offenses committed against US forces and nationals in China.

The army's War Crimes Branch worked on a joint basis with the navy on war crimes in the Mid-Pacific Area, limiting turf skirmishing. Eventually these trials also fell victim to Cold War politics, with the result that very few Japanese war criminals were held to account even after the high-profile trial of that nation's top military leaders. During that Pacific Theater trip Mickey exercised his well-honed talents in inter-Allied operations, as well as his knack for smoothing out bureaucratic roadblocks on the path to the rapid resolution of high-profile and complex legal problems.[48]

A year later, Mickey received notification of another nomination for the rank of brigadier general, this time a near certainty, and pushed through by Hilldring and Clay. But the star came with a specific job: military attaché at the US Embassy in Moscow.[49] No doubt the Russian officers who had served with Mickey in Berlin, and the intelligence services keeping track of him, would have welcomed the chance to drink his scotch, but he was done. Once again, he didn't discuss his decision with Emma, but after months of frustration in dealing with the fractious Allies as their wartime amity quickly dissipated into bitterness and hostility, and finally having had enough of army life even at the highest levels, he decided instead to walk away from every professional soldier's dream, the flag officer title of general. He would finally put his ambitions and high responsibilities aside and, as he had promised her so often in so many letters, return to Emma and begin a private law practice. Once again, having achieved public recognition, prestigious awards, and personal success in his job, Mickey Marcus walked away from those momentous achievements—on his own terms.[50]

CHAPTER 4

"Code Name: Michael Stone"

> This strange American who, not only came to observe, to look, to comment and advise, but stayed with them, braved the bullets, participated in the raids, and lived with them in the same primitive conditions. The magic word "Stone," which was his pseudonym, soon spread throughout the Army and everywhere you went you could hear, "Stone is here, Stone has been here, Stone fought with us."
>
> —Colonel Chaim Herzog, Israeli military attaché to the United States, June 8, 1950

Shlomo Shamir

In the summer of 1946, the chief of Haganah operations in North America, the perennially ailing Yaacov Dori, was recalled to Palestine to assume his earlier post as chief of staff of the Haganah. To replace Dori, David Ben-Gurion named Shlomo Shamir, who had recently been discharged from the Jewish Brigade and completed his assignment in Europe. Arriving in the United States on December 5, 1946, Shamir took over Haganah operations in the safe house on the thirteenth floor of Hotel Fourteen, located above the Copacabana nightclub in midtown Manhattan.

Ex-major of the British army Shlomo Shamir (Rabinowicz) was exactly the kind of officer Ben-Gurion wanted to lead the Jewish army.[1] Born in Berdichev, Ukraine, at the start of World War I, Shamir escaped as a child from Kyiv aboard Leon Trotsky's armored train during the civil war sparked by the Bolshevik Revolution. Shamir's secret flight cost the lives of his mother and a sister, and only after four years in Poland did the boy and surviving family finally reach Jaffa port in April 1925.

Shlomo joined the Haganah in his teens, undertaking Paul Revere–type missions on his bicycle, a prize possession from his bar mitzvah, avoiding British police to alert underground leaders of clandestine meetings. Years later, during the anti-Jewish riots of the 1936–39 Arab Revolt against the British mandate, he commanded the Haganah's Jerusalem Field Forces. During the revolt, in a rare instance of converging interests with the Mandatory police, Shamir led two famous retaliation operations against the well-known terrorist village strongholds of Yarda and Lubiya, earning an official rebuke by the Haganah followed by immediate forgiveness.

Despite his Hebrew nickname Fistuk ("Peanut"), Shamir was well-built, though not tall, and displayed early natural leadership. He personally trained Haganah members as well as some who also belonged to the Palmach, its permanently mobilized fighting force, in the use of hand grenades and wrote the first manual for grenade operations, *Ha'Rimon*. In January 1940 Shamir earned a civilian pilot's license for light airplanes, took some time off from the Haganah, and headed north to the Galilee to gain experience farming.[2]

Later that year, on September 30, 1940, under Haganah orders to gain professional training, he enlisted in the British Army, making him among the very first of the more than thirty thousand Palestinian Jews who eventually served in the British Allied Forces. This was two years before Erwin Rommel's drive to Alexandria in October 1942. As a group, with diverse personal motivations and political leanings, it was the British-trained World War II veterans who would become the professional backbone of the Jewish army, some of that cadre going on to be prominent military, political, diplomatic, and business leaders in the early history of the state.

The British, not anxious to support establishment of a Jewish army under the aegis of their mandate in Palestine, at first limited the opportunities for Palestinian Jews to serve in combat, although some served in infantry companies that operated in combat zones. This included the fight in Greece, where large numbers of noncombat Pioneers (support) troops were engaged, with one hundred killed and twelve hundred captured. When the danger from German forces to British interests was greatest, especially in their drive to the Suez Canal, their SOE (Special Operation Executive) trained some Haganah personnel for special operations, but it was not until 1942 that the British Army formed the Palestine Regiment of infantry. Other large groups of Palestinian Jewish volunteers served with the Royal Pioneers, Royal Engineers (RE), and Royal Army Service Corps (RASC).[3]

Shamir served in Palestine and Cyrenaica as an officer in the Second Battalion, Palestine Regiment, and later saw combat. A part of the original cadre when the British Army finally formed the Jewish Infantry Brigade Group (Jewish Brigade) in September 1944, he rose to adjutant of the Second Battalion of the brigade during the Italian Senio river crossing campaign in the closing days of the war. Ben-Gurion and political leader Moshe Sneh appointed him "commander of the Brigade on behalf of the Haganah and national institution in Palestine," a covert parallel authority that had responsibility to protect the interests of the Yishuv (from the Hebrew *ha-yishuv ha-ivri*, "settlement of the Jews") during the war and coordinate Jewish concentration camp survivor side efforts in Europe after the war.[4]

Shamir visited the Mauthausen concentration camp in July 1945 and Bergen-Belsen in September 1945, and he had close and continuing contact with Holocaust survivors and the Allied-controlled camp administrations. Belsen was liberated by the British Eleventh Armoured Division, and newsreels of British soldiers in tears bulldozing the dead into mass graves are seared into the national consciousness. Shamir attended the war-crimes trial of the Belsen commanders and functionaries and got to know the witnesses who had miraculously survived the camps.[5]

Even after the British redeployed the Jewish Brigade from Central Europe/Austria to the Low Countries to stifle the Holocaust survivors' rescue efforts, the soldiers managed to perform their official duties and continue the strategic mission of getting the survivors ready for immigration to Palestine. Some individuals engaged in direct acts of revenge against the Germans, but that was not the policy of the Haganah, and Shamir did not provide support for such efforts. He was well informed about the Allied occupation policies overall, and he had contact with American officers, though at that time he was unaware that Mickey Marcus was a guiding hand in executing Allied occupation policy in Germany, including that regarding Jewish refugees.[6]

During its existence, the Jewish Brigade was the largest single factor in finding and gathering Jewish refugees that had been scattered across Europe into separate camps, and then moving them to Mediterranean ports for emigration to Palestine, or *aliyah* ("going up"). They also undertook organizing, educating, and preparing the refugees for life in a post-mandate Jewish state. That operation created political and diplomatic facts on the ground and public pressure that stood in dialectical opposition to the desired policies of Britain and the US State Department, regardless of public statements by both nations' politicians and diplomats.[7]

Even among the Americans, only the Jews consistently and by a large majority favored large-scale immigration of the survivors of the Shoah into Palestine. The occasional pushback against British emigration restrictions, and President Harry S. Truman's open support for allowing immediate entry of a hundred thousand Jews into Palestine, yielded to direct diplomatic appeals by the British, still America's closest ally, to back off. Facing increasing hostility from the Arabs and with their forces stretched thin across a disappearing empire, the British contemplated the very real prospect that the end of their long-troubled mandate would descend into civil war. Having grown weary, the British began to withdraw, in some cases handing control of their military installations to local Arabs.

Beginning in December 1946 and during the entire run-up to the vote on the UN partition Plan for Palestine on November 29, 1947, Shamir headed the underground North America Haganah operations, based in New York City. One of his missions, given to him face-to-face by David Ben-Gurion in October 1947, was to recruit a combat general and a few assistants to help organize the top-level general staff of a modern Jewish army. Very soon, Shamir's search would lead to onetime US Army colonel David Marcus, who everybody seemed to know.[8] Shamir's recruitment of Marcus marked the start of Mickey's last two hundred days. The relationship that followed their initial encounter would prove to be a profound and formative experience in Shamir's life.[9]

Shlomo Shamir was the catalyst for Mickey's association with Israel and is the crucial witness who brackets the last two hundred days of Mickey Marcus. Shamir's files contain his account in documents, letters, and notes, and remain remarkably consistent about what he did and saw with Mickey Marcus. Without Shamir, as much as possible in his own recollections, there is no full story or context for uncovering the substance and the imagery of Mickey's enduring appeal.

As a citizen-soldier exemplar of the American Jewish military experience in the first half of the twentieth century, a founder of US Army civil affairs and psychological operations, and a founder of American war crimes doctrine and practice, David Daniel Marcus, West Point '24, racket-busting prison commissioner, and citizen-soldier, would have been an interesting character in army institutional history. But it was Shamir's judgment and the high regard in which longtime Zionist leader David Ben-Gurion held him that started the legend of the man code-named Michael Stone. Mickey's personal spell captivated Ben-Gurion in time; his diary stands as testimony to the American's influence on him. Mickey's death, simultaneous with the first UN ceasefire in June 1948 and the opening of a supply route to Jerusalem, created the political atmosphere and context for the legend—and a compelling and lasting military and political symbol.

Club "Copa Haganah," Hotel Fourteen, 14 East Sixtieth Street, New York, October 1947

Shamir operated out of the principal New York safe house, Hotel Fourteen, under his own name (itself a cover name), with the employment papers, including work permit and other documents, of a "commercial exhibition specialist" for the Jewish Agency, the central Zionist organization in Mandatory Palestine. The agency represented Jewish interests with the British and facilitated immigration there, legal and illegal, for the Jewish survivors of the Holocaust still displaced in Europe, particularly in the year before the establishment of the State of Israel.[10]

Hotel Fourteen, an establishment that "befitted its location, genteel and sheltering, and was attractive to elderly widows of means and breeding," ran as a legitimate business under the watchful eyes of Rudy and Fannie Barnett, a pleasant, unassuming couple in their sixties. Fierce Zionists, they had known Ben-Gurion for more than a decade, and the hotel was a Haganah front for meetings, mail drops, and recruitment, as well as a safe place for agents to stay. Rudy was the lookout and Fannie kept the books, giving her own code names to Haganah guests, in case of inquiries from police or federal agents.

The hotel proved an excellent venue for underground work, discreet but on the literal doorstep of a nightclub and favorite gathering spot for leaders in media, entertainment, sports, and NYC politics, as well as characters involved in the smuggling of arms and people. The latter included Teddy Kollek, later mayor of Jerusalem, and diplomat Gideon Raphael, both Haganah and intelligence agents who maintained their links with World War II Office of Strategic Services (OSS) contacts in the United States and Europe. Persistent stories still link Frank Sinatra and other entertainment figures who frequented the Copa to arms smuggling and money transfers to the Jews in the British mandate, whose recipients spanned the political and religious spectrum.[11]

Years before the brand-new UN turned its attention to ending British rule over Palestine, the secret arms agents of the Yishuv, drawing on a postwar global network of arms merchants, were scouring the junkyards of the world looking for World War II surplus weapons to equip a future Jewish army in Palestine. Recruiting stations were active in the States under front organizations like Land and Labor for Palestine and the Committee for a Free Palestine, and others that spanned the ideological Zionist spectrum. The safe house at Hotel

Fig. 12. Haganah plaque at the site of Hotel Fourteen. The *Forward*

Fourteen was the main venue for the recruitment of sailors, mostly, initially to man illegal immigration ships from European ports to Palestine. After a security and psychological screening by Haganah agents at that location, those selected received instructions and travel documents.[12]

The legality of many of the activities run from Hotel Fourteen was questionable under a half dozen statutes, and FBI counterintelligence, the Central Intelligence Group (CIG)— forerunner to the CIA in 1947, during the winding down of the OSS and reorganization of the US Intelligence Community (IC)—Army G-2, the Justice and State Departments, and local police all surveilled the Haganah to varying degrees. Operatives assumed that their communications were being monitored and conducted their business as best as possible. Under agreements that reached back to the origins of the special intelligence relationship between the UK and the United States, the British also tapped the phones of those who opposed their policies in the Middle East. Occasionally those activities ensnared prominent citizens after authorities leaked stories to the press, reminding everyone, especially those in the Jewish community, that these activities skirted the edge of the law and US interests.[13]

Haganah operations caused similar concern among law enforcement and national security officials in Britain, Canada, and South Africa, especially after disclosures that British officers had participated in the Arab cause. The Jews in the Commonwealth who wanted to fight for Israel were set squarely against official British policy, but their position was buttressed by the obvious truth that the Arab Legion of Transjordan, a part of the original Mandatory Palestine that had been splintered off to meet British interests in the oil-rich Middle East was led by serving regular British officers. The situation of Americans who wanted to fight for the Jewish side, many of them recent veterans and beneficiaries of the postwar GI Bill of Rights, varied. Some of them got caught up in a complicated web of international intrigue and shifting interests, and involved elements of wartime cloak-and-dagger tactics, including the occasional narrow escape that would stimulate the imagination of any spy thriller devotee. During the fighting before and after Israel's independence, some foreign volunteers who were apprehended by law enforcement in the United States suffered fines, ended up in jail, or lost the basic rights of US citizenship for violations related to participation in a foreign war. Still others encountered few obstacles and suffered no consequences. Finally, for the 129 North Americans who did not return from Palestine, the application of laws governing foreign agents was moot.[14]

After Shamir settled his family in New York, he began his mission, which remained essentially unchanged from Yaacov Dori's mandate: first, communicating the Haganah message and countering other narratives, including those held out by Christian and other pro-Palestinian groups, right-wing Jewish groups, and even some friends; second, support of open and covert fundraising by American and Canadian sympathizers, including the New York–based Sonneborn Group, a group of wealthy Americans that met with Ben-Gurion in NYC right after the war in 1945, and pledged to raise money for arms acquisitions; and third, securing surplus weapons and other vital equipment, for the most part legally, as well as recruiting specific technical specialists.[15] Shamir frequently addressed of-the-moment specific requirements, like certain radio communications equipment, when specifically directed by Haganah high command. Things heated up as the UN vote on the partition of Palestine approached.[16]

According to a secret CIG report circulated on October 10, 1947, Jewish Agency sources reported that the Haganah initially planned to field a corps-size army of two divisions, each with a table of organization of ten to twelve thousand men and attached combat support and administrative/coordination units. The Jewish provisional government had adequate manpower for that force structure, and CIG knew arrangements had been made for the large-scale importation of heavy equipment, especially fighter, bomber, and transport aircraft, tanks, armored vehicles, towed and tracked artillery, and large quantities of military stores. Agency sources, very possibly Teddy Kolleck himself, had expressed a strong belief "that they will be able to withstand attack until the Haganah is equipped."[17]

The report did not name specific arms suppliers, but earlier intelligence left little doubt that the Soviets were supporting these efforts via Czechoslovakia, including use of an airport complete with facilities for maintenance and training. This shortened the airbridge from Europe and simplified the Yishuv's ability to resupply during the initial stage of a war against Arabs opposed to the formation of any Jewish state of Israel, a conflict that the American intelligence community strongly believed would follow a positive vote on partition.

For their part, the Soviets had a continuing interest in prolonging the pain of Britain's withdrawal from the mandate and embarrassing the United States whenever possible. They were unremitting in their support of Israel in the early years, while still pursuing their interests in the Middle East. The Soviets, who naturally supported labor and left-leaning governments casting off Western colonialism, brushed aside anti-Zionism and other ideological inconsistencies for the moment, muting state-sponsored anti-Semitism for the new Communist Party line. The Soviets also occasionally evoked the Holocaust whenever doing so proved useful. In this crucial moment, the ironic convergence of interests of the world's most powerful states, except for Britain, cast the weight of those with roots in Western liberal democracies on the same side. A Jewish slice of Palestine fit in well with strong constituencies' perception of their postwar interests.[18]

Certain Latin American nations, for various reasons, some related to corruption, were also facilitating arms transfers to the Jews in Palestine. American policy on the matter remained in flux until the aftermath of partition, but eventually led to a boycott of arms shipments to both sides. The CIG report did not mention the efforts by the Haganah or other Jewish groups like the Irgun to acquire arms in America, although that issue had been the subject of earlier FBI reports.[19]

The Red House, Haganah HQ, Ha'yarkon Street, Tel Aviv, October 21, 1947

On the same day the CIG memo began to circulate, Ben-Gurion sent a message to Shamir outlining his new priorities and reflecting the growing pressures preceding the vote on the partition of Palestine and end of the British mandate, now just weeks away. First, all efforts would be concentrated on building the Jewish army, from the top down. Ben-Gurion wanted Shamir to recruit a senior military adviser, along with a small staff. Second, efforts to recruit ex-military pilots and find surplus aircraft, as well as other specialists and ground crew, would accelerate. Third, the Haganah, in anticipation of intensified counterintelligence activity by American and British agents known to be operating in the United States, Ben-Gurion would tighten security around direct involvement with local Zionist groups. Finally, Shamir was to send an accounting of his expenses and transfer some equipment to another agent.[20]

Soon after receiving the message, Shamir was recalled to the Yishuv for face-to-face consultations. He arrived in Tel Aviv on October 21, 1947. Meeting Ben-Gurion at the nondescript two-story Haganah HQ (dubbed "the Red House") near the beach, the longtime leader of the Jewish Agency and de facto head of the Yishuv's defense outlined his estimate of the situation.[21]

David Ben-Gurion (nee Gryn; 1886–1973) was born in Plonsk, now in Poland but at the time part of Russia. He was influenced from an early age by his Zionist father, as well as by the loss of his mother when he was eleven. His activities with Zionist workers' parties led to his arrest during the 1905–1906 uprising, and his immigration to Palestine in 1906. Working as a laborer in its fields and wine cellars,

Fig. 13. The Red House, Haganah HQ, Ha'yarkon Street, Tel Aviv. Israel Government Press Office

he developed a strong belief in developing the land of Israel. In 1910, writing for a Zionist workers' newspaper, he adopted the pen name of Ben-Gurion, Hebrew for "son of a young lion." At the beginning of World War I he supported the Ottoman (or Turkish) Empire, then part of the Central Powers, along with Germany, Austria-Hungary, and Bulgaria, but in 1915 he was exiled by the local government to Egypt. Soon after he ended up in New York, preparing young Jews for eventual immigration to Palestine. There he met and married Paula, his lifelong partner. While he was still in New York, a single piece of paper changed his entire world, and the fate of the Jewish people.

On November 2, 1917, the British foreign secretary Arthur James Balfour wrote a letter to Lionel Walter Rothschild, 2nd Baron Rothschild, a leader of the British Jewish community. In what would be thereafter known as the Balfour Declaration, Balfour proclaimed that "His Majesty's Government view with favour the establishment in Palestine of a national home for the Jewish people." For centuries a poor, agriculture-based, backwater Ottoman Arab province with a small minority of Jews, Palestine was at the time of Balfour's letter under attack by British and Commonwealth troops under General Edmund Allenby, who took Gaza from the Turks on November 7, 1917, a few days after the letter was posted. Then, in a brilliant flanking maneuver from Beersheva, he entered Jerusalem without bloodshed on December 8, 1917.[22]

Commonwealth Jews had contributed to the British war effort economically and even more dramatically through the actions of a small Palestinian spy group called NILI, whose members were tortured and executed by the Ottoman administration. Many people in England and the Commonwealth, and Jews living in the Western Allied nations, viewed the Balfour Declaration as symbolic repayment for Jewish past support and enticement for future backing. America, which had entered the war in April 1917, and its Jewish population also represented an important audience for the declaration. Britain hoped for global Jewish support during the ongoing Great War and its aftermath, including its plans for oil-rich territories it hoped to conquer. The Jews fighting against Britain in the Central Powers had more nuanced reactions.[23]

The Balfour Declaration was the first official and public endorsement by a major world power of the broadest goal of Zionism, the creation of a safe place for Jews in Palestine. What the Zionists leaders wanted was an independent, democratic, sovereign Jewish nation-state with its own government and Jewish army, both rooted in Jewish and Western liberal democratic institutions. In the endorsement itself, the British had a much more limited view of what that endorsement would mean, stopping short of support for a sovereign nation and using the ambiguous phrase "national homeland" for Jews. Further, without naming them, it called for recognition of the rights of "existing non-Jewish communities in Palestine."

That community, the majority Arab population in Palestine and the people in surrounding Ottoman provinces, also had national aspirations and reviled the Balfour Declaration as a betrayal by Britain. For Zionists, however, the declaration was electrifying. Only two decades had passed since Theodor Herzl, an assimilated Austrian journalist outraged by the renewed anti-Semitism in Europe stoked in France by the unjust arrest, trial, and imprisonment of Captain Alfred Dreyfus, organized the first Zionist Congress in Basel, Switzerland, in 1897. There, the basic goal of Zionism was declared: "To create for the Jewish people a home in Palestine secured by public law." The last part of that formulation, the power and protection of law, is a harbinger of the UN's original approval of Israel's sovereignty over that homeland.[24]

The Balfour Declaration inspired Ben-Gurion to join the Zion Mule Corps, a British military unit, but he arrived too late to fight in the war. After returning to Palestine, by then under the British mandate, he quickly became a Zionist leader and head of the Jewish Agency for Palestine. By the end of World War II, he was the de facto leader of the Zionist movement, and through his will and energy the Yishuv had reached the edge of independence. After the state was established, he was revered as a father and founder of his nation, no less than Washington in America. Like the military hero of the American War for Independence, Ben-Gurion would lead his newborn nation during its first decade.[25]

Ben-Gurion told Shamir that a UN vote for partition, if successful, would provoke immediate communal Arab-Jewish civil violence, followed by full-scale conventional war with the surrounding Arab states as soon as the British withdrew. There was active debate about whether the British would support direct intervention by King Abdullah I of Transjordan's Arab Legion to secure Arab Palestine or go further when the Yishuv declared independence upon the British withdrawal. Some in Palestine and the United States were urging a delay until the security situation was clarified. Others viewed the intervention of the Arab Legion as a certainty, a backdoor method for the British to maintain their control of the region.[26]

Everyone agreed that a unilateral declaration of the independence of Israel any time before the formal and inevitable end of the mandate would certainly mean immediate Israeli-Arab war, but no such declaration was at the time forthcoming, at least not from Ben-Gurion. Tacitly confirming the US report of the Jewish Agency estimate,

Ben-Gurion told Shamir he was confident that Jewish forces could hold their territory, but his longtime strategic fixation on building a modern Jewish army had become his most urgent problem. He had to transform the fractious leaders of the underground Haganah and its mix of various elements into a professional force able to withstand the initial onslaught, and eventually counterattack a superior and aggressive coalition of surrounding states. His confidence about a positive outcome in the second part of that scenario, dependent on a modern Jewish army, was much less firm.

The Jewish soldiers in Palestine operated in loosely coordinated, semiautonomous small brigade-size militia units, each with its own commanders, political and ideological objectives, military doctrines, traditions, and organization. These units were not capable at the time of the UN vote in late November of mounting any operations on a larger level than company strength, and even an effort of that size stretched resources and personnel. Complicating matters further, despite Ben-Gurion's attempts to consolidate central command authority, it was more an aspiration than a fixed structural practice. The various Jewish groups managed to cooperate during World War II and on several occasions during the final years of the British mandate, but that was only possible when the shared objective was ending British rule as quickly as possible to establish a Jewish state.

Regardless of the differences of military and political opinion, everyone, right and left, was bound in reverence for the heroism of the Yishuv's first defenders. Josef Trumpeldor, a one-armed decorated veteran of the czar's army who died defending the Tel Hai kibbutz in 1920; the Zion Mule Corps of World War I; and the men of Hashomer ("The Watchmen"), organized to protect the early settlements—these were iconic, revered names. Self-defense became the watchword, with all offensive operations framed as such.[27]

The main Zionist militia, the Haganah, was founded in 1920 with the sponsorship of the Jewish Agency and World Zionist Congress. Its high command represented the various political parties, and professional matters were run by a general staff, but by this time the organization was in effect the militia of Ben-Gurion's dominant left-leaning labor-oriented party Mapai (Workers Party of Israel). At the time of partition, it controlled about twenty thousand mobilized soldiers in ten territorial brigades, including combat veterans of the Jewish Brigade and other Allied units. A similar number of reservists formed the core of various citizen-soldier groups that had protected the Yishuv for decades. Among the advantages enjoyed by the emerging state were internal lines of communication, a long tradition of active self-defense, better training, unit cohesion, and esprit-de-corps than most of their adversaries, excellent battle-proven platoon and company-grade leaders, and a universal no-choice-but-victory attitude intensified by the Holocaust.

The offensive arm of Haganah was the Palmach (Strike Companies), three small brigades of light infantry that were quick to take the initiative, imbued with the spirit of the attack, and skilled in scouting and raiding but openly scornful of traditional military disciple, ranks, and procedures. Formed in 1941 with the blessing of the British, the Palmach numbered just two thousand men and women fully mobilized, with an additional thousand fighters scattered around the country. Rich in legends, heavily linked to far-left politics, and bound to the kibbutz (collective farm) and moshav (cooperative settlement), the men and women of the Palmach had clashed often with Arab irregulars in low-intensity on-and-off warfare since the organization's founding.[28]

Some Haganah were also World War II combat veterans of special operations in Axis-dominated Syrian and Lebanese territory during the darkest days of the German advance into the Western Desert.[29] That wartime comity was short-lived, however, driven on both sides by existential necessity and the human tendency to align with enemies against even greater enemies. And a very high level of tension undermined unity in conflicts between more professional, mostly British-trained officers, including those with service in the Jewish Brigade, and home-grown officers in the highest Haganah ranks. With few exceptions, even when Diaspora Jews were integrated into the Israel

Defense Forces (IDF), all foreigners were suspect, except the legendary Orde Wingate— and Marcus.

Occasionally bound by common interest but outside Haganah command, the Revisionist Irgun (Jewish national army) and the smaller splinter group Lehi (Fighters for the Freedom of Israel), commonly known as the Stern Gang for the name of its executed leader Avraham Stern, mustered six thousand men between them. Ze'ev (Vladimir) Jabotinsky founded Revisionist Zionism in the early 1920s to aggressively pursue Jewish statehood encompassing all of the British Mandate of Palestine, on both sides of the Jordan River. He believed the territory was essential for security and viability and called for immediate and full political sovereignty for Jews in Palestine and control over immigration. Prioritizing military preparedness and self-defense, he formed the Irgun to engage in armed struggle against British colonialism and Arab opposition. Jabotinsky was viewed as an extremist by the dominant labor and socialist elite but recognized as a founder of Jewish active self-defense. His aggressive policy against the British was consistent with the struggle against the colonial occupiers of Palestine, where the Jews had been indigenous since biblical times, and sovereign until the first century AD, and the only place they could be safe by right of self-defense and the strength of their arms. The Irgun called their campaign to eject the British from their homeland "the Revolt."[30]

After Jabotinsky's death in 1940, leadership of the Irgun passed to the charismatic and versatile Menachem Begin, later to be prime minister of Israel. An expert in disguise and survivor of dangerous underground adventures, Begin believed in the early tactics of decolonialization—sabotage, counterintelligence, assassination, and spectacular bombings, mostly with military objectives but with collateral casualties. The Irgun and the Haganah carried out some joint operations, like the late July 1946 destruction of British Mandatory and Army HQ in the southern wing of Jerusalem's King David Hotel and the daring escape of condemned men at Acre Prison in May 1947.[31]

Mickey had little contact with the Irgun, but he knew their politics, as well as some of their American supporters, and he consistently backed integration of all the militias into the IDF, whatever past grievances might come between them. Extremely resistant at first to that idea, Menachem Begin later gave way, and much later he would even come to embrace Marcus as a hero of Israel, meeting with Emma during a state visit.[32] Despite the intense controversies about that time that linger among the modern political descendants of the Revisionist movement's founders, their tactics were effective. The British acknowledged that the Irgun's resistance campaign, which resulted in military, police, and civilian losses during the period from before partition to their withdrawal, was effective, helping to force the grudging retreat of the British from imperial power in the Levant in the aftermath of World War II. After Israeli independence, the Revisionist parties and fighters formed the conservative party Herut (Freedom), which later became the basis for the Likud (Consolidation) Party, founded by Begin in 1973.

Although a few soldiers in the Yishuv had some leadership experience at the battalion level and as division staff, the list of officers with command experience of modern combined arms maneuver warfare at any level was limited. These included veterans of the British Army, especially Shamir, fellow Jewish Brigade veteran Chaim Laskov, who commanded a machine gun mechanized infantry company in the Jewish Brigade, and British Thirtieth Corps intelligence officer Chaim Herzog, among a very few others.[33] Presently engaged in more immediate tasks, in any event, none of them had the breadth of experience required to organize an army at the general staff command level. Further, they were associated with and favored by Ben-Gurion, and that would not go down well politically with some in the local Haganah, especially the Palmach.

Ben-Gurion was running out of time, but not bold ideas. Unfamiliar with military organization, administration, and training at the professional level, he knew that his self-education efforts would not suffice in the circumstances. There wasn't enough time to learn, and he needed advice beyond anything his associates, subordinates, or confidants could provide. They were brave and resolute men, but bound to the tactics, time horizons, and traditional enemies of the quarter-century underground struggle against tribal guerrilla fighters. While they were fully wedded to territorial defense through ideology and personal connections to land and kin, none of them could be considered practitioners of maneuver warfare at any level. He would have to look outside the Yishuv.

Ben-Gurion had no need to explain this to Shamir, who concurred that most of the locally trained Haganah and Palmach would not be much help in the mustering, organizing, training, and commanding of large-unit formations, at least not at the beginning of the war they both knew would come. The men were effective at the squad, platoon, and company level—in fact Shamir knew and had trained some of them personally—but they had never seen a battalion of well-trained, well-equipped mechanized infantry, with artillery and close air support, coming straight at them. They scorned discipline, ranks, and drill, and would have their hands full during the next months and with what was to come after that.[34]

More than any other leader, Ben-Gurion openly opposed the provincialism of the Haganah and Palmach leaders, men devoid of outside professional military training or education. Their most motivated fighters were suspicious of anything British, including their own colleagues from the Jewish Brigade, or anyone with service in any British units. Some believed that the Palestinian Jews who chose to fight for Britain in the war should instead have stayed at home and trained locally with the Haganah.[35] Ben-Gurion's low estimate of the locals' capabilities measured against what would be asked of them in the coming conflict was reciprocated by the Palmach leadership. They viewed him with hostile suspicion due to both his politics and his infuriatingly sincere admiration for his longtime adversary, occasional ally, and sometime enemy, the British Army. Suspicion of Ben-Gurion's military judgment reached to the very top of the Haganah, and included the chief of operations, Yigal Yadin, and other emerging leaders.

One of the rising Palmach stars, Yitzhak Rabin—who would command the Harel El Brigade during the costly first (civil war) stage of the war in the Jerusalem hills, and some thirty years later serve as Israel's fifth prime minister—expressed in his memoir the widely-held Palmach disparagement of the grasp of the military situation of the British-trained officers, and Ben-Gurion in particular. After the latter took over the defense portfolio at the Jewish Agency Executive in 1947, Rabin wrote, "My feelings about Ben-Gurion could only be described as ambivalent. Though I respected his breadth of vision, I could not help objecting to his attitude towards the Palmach. Between 1942 and 1947 he showed little regard for the idea of fostering an independent Jewish force and placed an exaggerated stress on enlistment in the British Army. Then, upon assuming the defense portfolio, he gave preference to British Army veterans over 'homegrown commanders.'"[36]

That attitude lingered for decades. One notable outlier among Palmach leadership was Yigal Allon, one of its founding commanders, who found a mean between the British professionals and his closest comrades, and who was clearly marked for higher command. Although Allon also clashed occasionally with Ben-Gurion on tactics and operations, he later supported Marcus as a professional who understood the situation of the Jews better than most outside observers.[37]

The history of the Zionist struggle up to that point gave its home-grown warriors a persuasive argument for their tactics. Their defense of settlements and roads with small arms created commandos and experts in small-unit actions such as patrolling, ambush, raids, and targeting and disabling communications systems. They performed well when under attack by irregulars, and this had brought them to the edge of statehood; but now the Yishuv needed combined-arms infantry-armor-artillery formations able to execute flank and enveloping attacks, encirclements, and tactical withdrawals, all while coordinating air and artillery support. That would require broad-based officer and large-unit training and exercises, a deep administrative infrastructure—with little time to spare.

The universally shared ideal that every settlement must be held, no matter how isolated or weak, had fueled the Palmach's home-grown tactics. Their casual attitude regarding rank, discipline, and organization structure was partly due to isolation, but their insistence on holding every inch of territory, coupled with this less than professional attitude, was a liability regardless of its historical underpinnings. It was at odds with the theory of maneuver warfare, which required flexibility about temporarily yielding territory during a campaign. Even a fully unified and nation-based Jewish army established and ruled by the international conventions of war would be difficult to achieve. Some thought the leaders of Palmach, Irgun, and Lehi might try to maintain independent militia, something Ben-Gurion considered abhorrent.[38]

If he had indeed looked to the British Army and its veterans for their professional attitude, Ben-Gurion was also open to the advice of a few foreign experts he deemed worthy, especially those recommended by people he trusted. At the top of both lists stood a legendary name of Israel's military history, then Captain (later Major General) Orde Wingate, an intelligence officer and exceedingly rare British Christian Zionist. A man radiating authority, passion, and charisma, he was a master of deception, a founder of modern special operations, and is easily imagined as a fiery biblical character—say, a captain of a hundred under Joshua, an idea he certainly would have appreciated.

Wingate proved to Ben-Gurion during the Arab Revolt of 1936–39 that a sympathetic outsider—bizarre idiosyncrasies and religious motivations aside; Wingate ate raw onions during his meetings—could be a forging instrument of the emerging Jewish army. Assigned to Palestine soon after the Arab Revolt broke out in 1936, Wingate overcame the resistance of the British and Jewish Agency, and by working closely with Yitzhak Sadeh, a veteran of the czar's army and Haganah leader, he created, trained, and led the combined British-Jewish Special Night Squads (SNS). A counterinsurgency force made up of Haganah volunteers and British regular cadre, its mission was to defend the completely isolated Jewish settlements. By instructing them to shift from perimeter defensive tactics, he taught the Jews to take the fight to the Arabs through night patrols and ambushes, to stop attackers before they could even get started. His ethos entailed leading from the front, doing so with speed, surprise, daring, and imagination. The SNS veterans included Moshe Dayan, Yigal Yadin, and Chaim Laskov.[39]

Even more unusual in the fractious Yishuv, Wingate had admirers across the political, cultural, and religious divides, his obvious total commitment embodied by his courage on the battlefield, the depth of his religious zeal, and the cost of his devotion to his career. His superiors and colleagues shunned him, displaying open hostility, including personal insults and anti-Semitic slurs. That made the Jews feel he was truly one of them. Transferred out of the British mandate because his views were deemed contrary to British interests in preventing the formation of an independent Jewish state, Wingate went on to fight in Sudan and then Burma, where he founded the Chindits, a long-range special forces unit that proved modestly effective in fighting against the Japanese. He was killed in an air accident in 1944.[40]

No small factor in Wingate's aura was the messianic power of his physical presence despite his slight stature. In one of history's reminders of individual agency, he foreshadowed Marcus's direct personal appeal, from the top on down, and ability to win over more than a few soldiers, bureaucrats, and politicians who otherwise agreed on nothing. Ben-Gurion, facing the destruction of the yet-to-be-born Jewish homeland, his life's work, and possibly both at the same time, now envisioned using such a man—if he could find him—to build a modern professional army with a ready-to-go general staff. That would have been hard enough during peace, but Ben-Gurion foresaw a period of civil war between Jews and Arabs in Palestine following a vote for partition, and invasion by surrounding Arab states when the legally mandated occupying power, Britain, withdrew. Ben-Gurion was not risk averse as the end of the British mandate approached, nor did he shrink from controversial personnel choices, like seeking the help of an outsider when his own high command was rent by internal political tensions that he felt directly affected military readiness.

Shamir, who as a low-ranking officer had a rare view of higher political considerations, grasped the military problems at hand as well. He had his own reservations about some of his colleagues, whom he thought had a cavalier attitude toward discipline and training. Shamir had repeatedly proven his discretion and bravery, as well as personal loyalty, and Ben-Gurion assured him that he would be called back from the United States and given a combat command when the conventional war began. Shamir's last undercover assignment, however, was as important as any of his other duties and had the highest priority. Now Ben-Gurion gave him a face-to-face order: "Find an American expert who can help us build an army."[41]

That would not be enough, however, as Shamir related later about the assignment: "Along with this senior general we needed to bring back a group of officers as his assistants. No matter how respected, one person transplanted to *Eretz Yisrael* would accomplish nothing." This group would form the core of a general-staff-level advisory group to structure a fully equipped initial combined-arms corps-sized force and train its commanders and staff. All Jewish Agency assets in America and contacts would be available for support. Within reason.[42]

Shamir could also rely on Moshe Sharett, born Shertok, longtime political affairs director of the Jewish Agency and unofficial foreign minister of the Yishuv, who planned on being in the United States before the partition vote and afterward. Shamir would be free to seek the advice of local Palestinians and American friends of the Haganah who had helped raise money to acquire weapons, equipment, and recruit personnel. As the vote neared, security would be increased. When Shamir asked if the top choice had to be Jewish, Ben-Gurion replied, "Not necessarily," but he stressed that the candidate should be more than a technician, and had to bring "combat experience, a broad national outlook and the intellect to convey his ideas to the entire army and a new state, and he also had to be sympathetic to the Zionist idea."[43] They were not interested in mercenaries or soldiers of fortune. After a difficult journey including a delay linked to cholera-ravaged Cairo, Shamir returned to Hotel Fourteen on November 5, 1947.[44]

The Barberry Room, Berkshire Hotel, Fifty-Second and Madison, November 1947

By the time Mickey Marcus left the US Army in spring 1947, the greatest demobilization in American history, more than sixteen million veterans over the course of eighteen months, was complete. New York City hardly suffered from a shortage of lawyers with impressive wartime resumes, including in many cases combat experience. Words of encouragement and advice from friends and family did not produce clients, and Mickey began to feel the pressure of starting a postwar career late. Still, he had made certain promises to Emma, and himself, that he was determined to keep. Although Mickey was never good with money, Emma certainly was, and with his savings during the war, and now financed with a low-income GI Bill home loan, they managed to land their dream house. A large two-story Victorian on Westminster Road in Brooklyn's busy Flatbush neighborhood, it was big enough for Emma's piano and collection of pets, not to mention the perfect setting for the renewal of their social life. The living room was soon filled with music and the laughter of their friends and large families on both sides.[45]

Mickey put out feelers to his Republican party contacts, and reestablished connections to former close colleagues from the Southern District of New York, including now Republican governor Thomas E. Dewey. Defeated in his presidential bid by FDR in 1944 in a landslide, Dewey would nevertheless prove to be a strong challenger to President Harry Truman in 1948. Mickey's earlier associations with Dewey also helped him reestablish contacts with prominent judges and attorneys with whom he had prewar relationships. Many of them were also active in Jewish philanthropies and had been mobilized for wartime service as civilians or reservists. Mickey arranged drinks with former mayor Fiorello La Guardia, who welcomed him back with a characteristically sarcastic observation bemoaning his decision to pursue the law rather than jumping right back into the political fray.[46]

At local Republican club meetings Mickey spoke about prison reform and human rights, the issues he had always supported but now sharpened by his civil affairs experience, especially in postwar Germany and as head of war crimes at the Pentagon. He confided to Emma and a few others, like Steve Stevenson and Lowell "Wampus" Limpus, the existential questions that descended over his spirit in the aftermath of his visit to Dachau, and what he had learned about the Holocaust. He also renewed his close relationship with Rabbi Sidney Tedesche and other leaders in the Brooklyn and Manhattan Jewish communities. The rabbi had been extremely helpful when Mickey's mother passed away, and if anyone had access to Mickey's inner self, he did. Mickey also knew some New York City rabbis who had served as chaplains in the military from his work with refugees in postwar Germany and SHAEF.[47]

By that spring, office space was in short supply, but Mickey found an office on Fifth Avenue with a prewar associate and younger Boys High athlete, Colgate University fullback Jules Yablok. Shortly after their association was announced, however, Mickey balked at a big dinner partly intended to promote his wartime achievements, preferring to build his practice on competence and relationships, not by profiting from his national service. Or at least not openly; as Thanksgiving approached, the pressure of a late start in a competitive market was starting to change his perspective.[48]

When Shamir got back to New York City in early November, he contacted Sharett, who was staying in a small apartment in the Berkshire Hotel during the UN partition debates. Sharett had emigrated to Palestine from Ukraine in 1908 and was among the very first inhabitants of Tel Aviv. A lawyer, World War I veteran of the Turkish Armed Forces, and labor-oriented politician, he played a leading role in creating the Jewish Brigade and knew Shamir well. Sharett had recently been released from the British prison at Latrun, along with the other leaders detained by a British crackdown leading up to partition. In those raids, Ben-Gurion and Golda Meir, an American-born Zionist and Jewish Agency executive who would later become prime minister of Israel, had managed to avoid arrest. Having replaced Sharett as head of the Political Department, Meir lobbied the British for the release of her colleagues. Renowned for his oratorical skills, Sharett led the effort for partition at the UN, and would go on to sign Israel's Declaration of Independence and serve as the new nation's first foreign minister and second prime minister.[49]

Sharett heard from one of his contacts, a local lawyer and former colonel in the US Army named Murray Gurfein, that one of his friends, a man known for his wide contacts in the US military and

Jewish communities, might be willing to help. That man, David Marcus, had just completed service in top-level civil affairs and occupation jobs, and Gurfein knew him well. Both men had been high-ranking World War II staff officers as well as ex-federal prosecutors and New York Republican politicians with strong links to Republican governor Dewey.

Stocky and prematurely gray with a mild manner that belied his legal, professional, and military stature, it is difficult to imagine a better intermediary. Murray Irving Gurfein owed his rise in the face of anti-Semitism to academic excellence. A Phi Beta Kappa graduate of Columbia University '28, and second in his class and editor of the *Law Review* at Harvard, he built a solid record of busting rackets on the NYC waterfront in high-profile cases during the Great Depression. When Mickey's National Guard unit shipped out to Fort McClellan in Alabama in October 1940, Gurfein was there at the train station to see him off. After Pearl Harbor, Gurfein tapped into his NYC legal contacts and joined the OSS, reporting directly to director William "Wild Bill" Donovan. Gurfein worked on Balkan operations before transferring to Eisenhower's SHAEF headquarters in early 1944 as first chief of intelligence in the Psychological Warfare Division, one of the three pillars of US Army and Joint Special Operations Command, along with Special Forces and Civil Affairs. In the months right after VE Day, the onetime office colleagues crossed paths again when Mickey was in Berlin and Washington and Gurfein was chief assistant to Judge Robert Jackson, the lead US prosecutor at the first Nuremberg trial—and Telford Taylor's boss.[50]

Both Sharett and Shamir were interested in meeting Mickey, not only because of his connections but also due to his relationship with Major General John H. Hilldring, a friend of the Jewish cause. There is evidence that Sharett discussed Ben-Gurion's search for advisers with Hilldring in December in the aftermath of the partition vote.[51] Sharett explained to his friend the need for US help in obtaining military equipment and "two or three competent American officers who would be prepared to proceed to Palestine and advise on defense arrangements." Hilldring advised Sharett to go "to the very top" but added that he knew someone, his onetime aide, who might be willing to help.[52] By that time Hilldring was well acquainted with Mickey's work with Shamir, so this encounter might have been a reference check on Mickey for Ben-Gurion and Shamir, but the recruitment link to Gurfein is confirmed by the Israel Defense Forces History Museum site.[53]

On July 31, 1946, shortly after Mickey came back to the Pentagon for his war crimes assignment, Hilldring retired from the army and assumed the position of assistant secretary of state for occupied areas, "directly responsible to the Secretary of State for the Department policy with respect to all occupation matters." He resigned from that position in September 1947 and was appointed alternate US delegate to the UN General Assembly and "the principal U.S. spokesman in the 1947 debates about Palestine," but soon afterward retired for health reasons.[54] An outspoken Christian Zionist voice, his recall to State Department, due to pressure from the White House before the vote, was not welcomed by the professional diplomats. The press described Hilldring as the Truman administration's liaison to the American Jewish community, as the president had long been distrustful of the deeply entrenched pro-Arab US State and War Departments. The authority of secretary of state George C. Marshall now buttressed both, as well as the so-called Wise Men, whose views ranged from Marshall's outright hostility to partition to a range of strong reservations about supporting a Jewish state.[55]

Three weeks before the anticipated partition vote in late November, Gurfein, Shamir, and Sharett met Mickey at the Berkshire Hotel at Sharett's suggestion. A nondescript limestone residential establishment in Midtown, the Berkshire featured the private Barberry Room, described by the *New York Daily News* as "the most exclusive restaurant in New York" and "attractive in every detail." The restaurant had been designed for the hotel in 1937 by architect Norman Bel Geddes, who arranged arrays of mirrors set in copper on the facing east and west walls, installed a two-story-high ceiling of beaten copper and bronze, and illuminated the room with light fixtures set in the ceiling, evoking stars, all of which created a "theatrical spectacle of reflected images."[56]

Originally a vanity project of Broadway writers and producers coveting the literary prominence of the Algonquin Hotel's Round Table, the venue opened as the Elbow Room and within a year had foundered as a financial wreck. At this point the founders got serious, christened the place with a new name, rejuvenated the decor, and hired a veteran speakeasy manager. The Barberry Room soon became a favorite convenient gathering spot for theater people, the media—even though reporters were banned—and influencers in business and politics.[57]

Gurfein set up the meeting and made the introductions, describing his companions as an ex–British Army major and the "official representative of the Provisional Jewish Government in Palestine." Mickey listened as Sharett outlined the diplomatic situation at the UN, where a vote on the partition of Palestine into a Jewish and an Arab state was expected around the time of Thanksgiving, just weeks away. The diplomat soon became engaged with Gurfein over refugee aid and other issues of mutual interest. Shamir engaged Mickey directly as they began to feel each other out:

> I asked him about his past and I got the impression that he was easy to talk to, that he had some field experience, and fulfilled many jobs where he had access to a wide range of acquaintances at the top echelon of the US Army. I considered this important for the search. Amongst the jobs which provided top-level access was secretary of the four superpowers in Berlin, he participated in formulating the surrender agreement in Italy, participated in the European theatre during the landing and took part in the Far East theatre. From this point of view, it was unusual to find a low-ranking officer who was able to name many of the generals who fought in such a large army.[58]

Marcus made such a good impression that after lunch the two men took a stroll along Fifth Avenue, and Shamir told him the reason for the meeting. David Ben-Gurion, he explained, the leader of the Jewish Agency in Palestine, needed at least one general officer with combat experience, along with an adjutant and several assistants, to work directly for him as military consultants, providing advice about organizing and training the Jewish forces for the war to come. The top position would be under contract, for $1,000 per month plus expenses. It isn't clear whether Sharett disclosed the extent of General Hilldring's involvement with Jewish affairs at this point.[59]

Mickey expressed immediate interest. The American demonstrated an informed grasp of recent events and of diplomatic issues regarding the Palestine debate, the British position, the vacillations of US policy, and the precarious situation of the Jews, made more apparent by the urgency of Shamir's mission. He agreed to help in the recruitment effort in any way he could. He showed no interest in any position for himself but dove right into the project with energy and no expectation of financial reward. At that stage he undoubtedly viewed the involvement as another extension of his commitment to his community and was happy to draw on his contacts discreetly for a cause he now supported.[60]

A week later the two men met at Marcus's office to begin compiling a list of potential candidates. As described, the requirements were high: a combat general with field and HQ staff experience, familiar with army-wide policies about enlistment, coordination of military branches, and quartermaster organization, all while facing the pressures of the battlefield. Shamir noted that "the job was especially demanding given that the staff needed to apply their experience and knowledge to a different people, culture, and habits. Another requirement was that the candidates must be reservists." That turned out to be an obstacle for most candidates; reservists with the required number of years on active service would usually be eligible for or receiving a pension.[61]

Haganah's intelligence arm called "Shai" had its own lists of Jewish American officers and had interviewed several during this same time. Shamir also had a list of a dozen candidates developed from input by US Army chaplain rabbis who had served in Europe. Shamir reviewed with Mickey the working list of twenty-four names, along with his handwritten observations. That list had five names cited by order of preference, including Ralph C. Smith (commander, Twenty-Seventh Infantry Division), Harry Collins (division commander who liberated Dachau), William Simpson (commander, Ninth Army), Ernest Harmon (commander, First and Second Armored Divisions), and Robert Richardson (fighter pilot and Pentagon staff). All those on Shamir's list were prestigious generals in the US military, a number of whom discussed employment with Shamir and his agents.[62]

Moshe Sharett and others had passed along suggestions, too, but from the beginning of the search, Mickey had a specific candidate in mind, his last boss in Hawaii, the division commander who led the Twenty-Seventh Infantry Division into combat and controversy, Major General Ralph C. Smith. Recently retired, Smith was then beginning a career as a foreign affairs expert at Stanford University. Mickey considered him the best man for the job. If they could land Smith, Mickey reasoned, the rest of the staff would follow. Wasting no time, Mickey made telephone contact with Smith soon after the meeting in the Barberry Room and was discussing details with him as early as November 12, 1947.[63]

During the next week Shamir met Mickey at his Fifth Avenue office, where they planned a trip to San Francisco to discuss the matter face-to-face with General Smith. A friend of Mickey, former army major Morton Strauss, accompanied them to California. A parallel objective of the trip was for Smith to meet Strauss, who was being considered as one of the assistants "if Ralph says yes."[64] It was already apparent during early phone calls that Smith was worried that employment with the Jewish Agency, which was now, in effect, an underground government, might jeopardize his general officer pension. He also wanted credible assurances that even if it were legal neither American nor British officials opposed the effort, as he feared that working against the interests of an important US ally might present diplomatic and public relations problems for him and the government. Later, as Mickey and Shamir worked through the list, these turned out to be universal concerns shared by the other candidates, among whom were some of the most esteemed generals in the US military.[65]

After the visit in late November, Shamir wrote of General Smith, "I was much impressed. Smith had a broad point of view, you could talk with him on any military subject, and he had the necessary experience. He could not, however, take on the job without the blessing of the US government. As it turned out, this was difficult to manage partly because we were ambiguous about military matters with the Americans as we were not ready to divulge some intelligence. We wanted approval without being fully under surveillance."[66]

Months of debate about what to do about Palestine at the UN ended in the General Assembly on November 29, 1947, with a vote on Resolution 181, which proposed the creation of separate Jewish and Arab states in the territory of the British mandate, with the city of Jerusalem united under international administration. The results were thirty-three votes for partition, thirteen votes against, ten abstentions, and one absent. The resolution required a two-thirds majority of the fifty-seven member states at that time for passage, or a minimum of thirty-three yes votes, a hurdle it cleared. Those in favor were an odd mix of Western allies, including the United States, Europe (except for Greece), Latin American countries, and the three Soviet republics. Those against were Arab and Muslim-majority countries, with the United Kingdom, the mandate power, Mexico, and China abstaining.

In addition to ending the mandate, the resolution called for two states with defined boundaries and suggested an economic union between these states. Given its religious significance, Jerusalem was designated with a special international status, to be managed by the United Nations. Both proposed states were called upon to draft constitutions that ensured the protection of religious and minority rights and citizenship of all residents in each of the proposed states. Britain soon announced it would withdraw its forces by mid-May 1948. There was no agreement on the forces that would be necessary to enforce the decision of the UN General Assembly or contain the violence that was now almost certain to intensify in the aftermath of the vote.[67]

Jews in the Yishuv rejoiced even as the civil violence started the day after the vote. Local Palestinian religious and militia leaders, including the Sunni grand mufti, a religious leader of Jerusalem who supported Hitler, called for the Muslim world to conduct a holy war against the Jews. Since the title of mufti signifies great learning in Islamic law and jurisprudence, and thus a mufti is able to issue legal opinions or interpretations in every situation, this gave religious sanction to a policy of extermination. The Arab League, a new organization claiming to represent all Arab countries and interests, denounced partition and swore to prevent its implementation, by regular armed forces if necessary.

Discussion in the UN began again on various proposals for delay, some kind of UN trusteeship arrangement to replace the mandate and partition, and creation of a large international police force. But as fear grew about a power vacuum in the aftermath of British withdrawal and another potential bloodbath for Jews, which no country moved to stop, these talks went nowhere. This uncertainty about the near-term security outlook in Palestine complicated Mickey's discussions with potential candidates about legal and pension problems for consultants in what increasingly looked like a potential war zone.[68]

Still, Smith reassured Marcus and Shamir that if they could address his concerns, he would seriously consider the offer. After returning from the West Coast, Mickey spent several days conferring with contacts in Washington at the Pentagon and State, visiting General Hilldring, among others. This gave him the opportunity to get a fuller picture of the current situation in Palestine and the surrounding states. Negotiations with Smith and other contacts on Shamir's list of twenty-four continued, but no one in the US government could offer any assurances that pensions would be protected in the uncertain situation.[69]

As Arab villagers started to attack Jewish neighborhoods and road traffic between Tel Aviv and Jerusalem the day after the UN vote, and intracommunal Jewish-Arab violence spread, US support for partition began to weaken. The British, who still hoped for some role in Palestine, pursued diplomatic efforts surrounding some kind of international trusteeship for Palestine if the violence led to regional instability. In the United States, bureaucratic preoccupation with the postwar National Security Act of 1947 reorganization across the entire national security and intelligence community led to caution about the diplomatic cost of full support of partition, or premature recognition of a new state of Israel.[70]

Over the course of December, as Mickey worked on the consultant search, he learned as much as he could about the military and diplomatic situation on both sides of the hill, as seen from the perspective of the Yishuv. He knew that the rules of the game meant that Shamir could not share secret information with him, but he also had his own sources of information from his West Point days, and more than seven years of active service, including contacts at State and the Pentagon. It was a certainty that if the Jews declared independence after two millennia of dispersal, persecution, despair, and Shoah ("catastrophe"; specifically, the Holocaust), they would have to fight, and do so without any real outside official support.

The UN would debate the best course of action, but that they would approve of any outside military intervention was inconceivable. On the other side, troops of varying quality from Egypt, Transjordan, Syria, Lebanon, and Iraq, along with local and foreign volunteers, were ready on multiple axes of advance, backed by dozens of airplanes and warships, and hundreds of tanks, armored vehicles, and heavy artillery, with plentiful supplies and ammunition. Less than thirty miles away to the south, the Egyptians, accompanied by Muslim Brothers volunteers, could advance on the coastal cities and ports of the Yishuv. That much was common knowledge, but Shamir was able to offer a fuller picture, within security limits.

The Arab nations, while unified in professing dedication to a Palestinian state over the whole mandate and to the destruction of the Jews, were fragmented over religion, culture, politics, and the ambitions of their respective rulers, as well as conflicting territorial objectives in the postcolonial struggle. They were unable to capitalize on the strategic, material, and operational advantages they otherwise would have enjoyed as united allies. Some among the

Fig. 14. British general John Bagot Glubb, "Glubb Pasha," Arab Legion (right), with King Abdullah of Transjordan (IWM)

adversaries—most immediately Transjordan's Arab Legion, which was loyal to the Hashemite king Abdullah I, a British-created monarch—were nevertheless already in a threatening position. The soldiers of the Arab Legion, professionally trained and led by British officers, gathered just over the border.[71] The legion's commander, General Sir John Bagot Glubb, known as Glubb Pasha, was trying his best to destroy the emerging Jewish army and maintain de facto control of the mandate, even as the British Empire's grasp of the region was quickly fragmenting. Despite the UN vote, and history, support for maintaining a strong presence in Palestine, both open and clandestine, was ubiquitous in the British government, as well as in the corresponding cabinet departments in the United States.

In the Arab-Jewish communal fighting immediately after the UN vote for partition, the Jews used stolen or smuggled small arms and homemade weapons, not unlike the ghetto fighters and partisans in the forests. Owning arms was illegal under British rule, so the Yishuv had almost no heavy weapons, although news reports openly referred to arms smuggling. The Haganah had just fifteen thousand rifles and several hundred machine guns scattered in secret arms caches around the country. Securing weapons for an operation was a commander's nightmare. Secret workshops stamped out Sten guns and grenades using smuggled machine tools, and the air service numbered a dozen single-engine sport planes from which the pilots and passengers bombed the enemy by dropping hand grenades and Molotov cocktails out the rear door. They had plans to buy heavy weapons, but the shipments could not arrive in quantity before the British withdrawal, which was not scheduled until May 15, 1948.

Marcus had been a witness to the early Cold War maneuvering, with all parties looking for the others' secret agents. Palestine was seen at State, the Pentagon, and in the media as another region under Soviet threat, and one in which Americans had little experience of the languages, religion, and culture of the inhabitants. A lack of real intelligence about what was going on, on both the Arab and Jewish sides, led the Americans to defer to their British colleagues' assessments of the Arab side, considering the British more experienced in the region's nuances and politics. Although US Army G-2 had contacts among the Jewish Agency agents immediately after the war in Italy and Vienna, they viewed them as unreliable sources of intel. The wartime Allies were suspicious of the Jews' Russian and Polish origins, despite their strong anticommunism, notes on which frequently appear in State Department and Pentagon position papers. Strains of anti-Semitism, a strong if understated tendency among the WASP patricians who had dominated American diplomacy since the founding of the republic, is evident from a reading of the records.

The Americans at that time were more interested in recruiting and utilizing former Nazi war criminals who claimed intelligence about the Soviets and the states under their domination in Eastern Europe than Jewish agents. The results of that operation, as revealed by declassification of CIA records, do not appear to be worth the moral stain left on America by the intelligence community's contempt for justice. Instead of prosecuting some of the worst serial torturers and murderers in history, American officials paid them as informants and experts about the new Cold War enemy.[72]

During the period of Mickey's recruitment by the Jewish Agency, attempts to increase the immigration of Jewish survivors from Europe into Palestine continued. There were two tracks: Aliyah Aleph, or legal immigration activities; and Aliyah Bet, illegal smuggling operations to bypass the British blockade. Each track had been supported by the British Army's Jewish Brigade until its demobilization in 1946. The main routes over which immigrants to Palestine were shepherded had before the establishment of Israel run from southern Europe, especially Italy and southern France. Mickey already knew something about that, but Shamir brought him up to date and described his own experience with the brigade.[73]

The immediate challenge for the Haganah was how to survive until help—diplomatic and material—came from the Jewish diaspora and the UN. This was the same problem George Washington's Continental Army had faced while waiting for unofficial US diplomacy to garner support for their war of independence from the French king and Dutch bankers. In the Palestine case there was no guarantee, or even a decent probability, that help would come at all, or that diplomatic efforts could prevent a slaughter of Jews in the Yishuv as the British withdrew. Britain remained implacably against partition and continued to arm its Arab clients while confiscating Jewish arms, jailing those who bore them, and incarcerating Jewish refugees in Cyprus and elsewhere. After the civil war intensified across the Yishuv following partition, the Western allies hesitated, avoiding any mention of armed teeth. The Soviet Union, which continued to fully support an independent Jewish state in Israel, blocked Britain's every move in early Cold War skirmishes. The Soviets aimed to be the first nation to recognize the new state as they cheered on the British evacuation, aggravated divisions among British allies, and stirred their own Soviet agents to action.

During the recruitment process, Shamir began to recognize Mickey's manifold talents and qualifications, but it was their failure to find anyone who fit the original requirement for a combat general that forced events. At some point, Shamir's gut feeling that "this is the man" prevailed. One of the things that impressed him was Mickey's demonstrated ability for immediate rapport with a range of people, his willingness to jump right into any given situation, and his clear talent for planning and organization. In truth, Mickey was coming to the same realization, although the same worries about the sensitivity of the job that had hung up the other candidates still nagged him. If official permission were out of the question, he still needed to be sure that the assignment would not lead to any political fallout or embarrassment, or even to criminal prosecution or risk to his reserve status or rank. He was not eligible for a pension, so that was not a consideration.[74]

Finally, word came back through Hilldring that Mickey could work for the Jewish Agency, but only under a cover identity. In addition, he could not in any way link his activities to his status as a Judge Advocate General (JAG) colonel in the Organized Reserve Corps. The US government was not looking for trouble; given that Mickey's would-be employer was an underground government, Mickey could not use official US assets or facilities to create his cover identity. In addition, US diplomats would not inform their British colleagues about the job, leaving Mickey on his own.

Someone with Mickey's talents and background could certainly secure for himself fake passports, visas, and supporting documents capable of fooling ordinary British authorities, including those he might encounter on the odd road patrol. He undoubtedly conferred with Stevenson, John Valentine "Frenchy" Grombach, or other senior contacts in the intelligence community, including Murray Gurfein. He also might have collected favors from unsavory types he knew from his prison commission tenure and dealings with bootleggers, some of whom were now legally selling liquor. Emma's correspondence with Berkman hints at many such contacts.

Mickey's first cover identity was as an American wine dealer interested in local varietals. That fits in perfectly with his underworld connections from his prison days and has exactly the right touch of Hollywood to work. Mickey was satisfied that he could operate under the Pentagon guidelines and risks, but he knew it was dangerous. There was no official arrangement for him to report back to anyone at the Pentagon, and no one had responsibility for monitoring or taking care of him. He was operating in what had already become the beginnings of the Cold War, and he would have no consular or other official recourse, even from his employers in the Jewish Agency, if he got in over his head. At that point this was still a very risky business.[75]

There was one final and decisive voice in the decision, and Shamir, who had drawn close to Mickey, understood fully whose it would be. Emma had every right to ask her husband not to go off, after all she had endured, on one more adventure. Although she had been a soldier's wife for a long time, this time their parting would be especially difficult, coming as it did on the heels of what Mickey had just declared as his final homecoming from war.

Shamir would well remember just how difficult the whole episode was on Emma:

"The drama was not so simple. I had already visited Mickey at his home and met Emma who was a teacher in Brooklyn, a genuinely nice woman. I saw the family album, learned where they had gone on their various holidays, where they lived together. Mickey told me his life story, how he got into West Point, showed me his medals, so I understood the challenge."[76]

What Shamir didn't know was that Emma had been up against this kind of situation before: first during Christmas 1934, when she started to think about Mickey leaving public service as a prosecutor and making a good living in partnership with Arthur Schwartz, and again when Mickey preempted the US Army in 1940, well before Pearl Harbor, signing up to return to active service even after having reached a career pinnacle. But no matter what promises Mickey made, by that time Emma understood that her husband would respond when he heard the echo of duty. "She was the wife of an officer," as Shamir put it, "and Mickey had gone off many times before without too much explanation. I cannot say what was in her heart, but I can only judge by their parting and the meeting we had at their home."[77]

If Emma eventually accepted Mickey's decision, his conviction that he was needed in Israel had steeled him to it, as his letters home from wartime conferences on the postwar world order, which framed his conversion to Zionism, attest. Thinking of the hundreds of thousands of Jewish soldiers in World War II, ten thousand of them fallen, compared to the treachery of the Arab nationalists who sided with the Nazis against the British, he was outraged.[78] The Arabs' argument had been that they were fighting their actual oppressor, Britain. Now some of those same Arab leaders swore openly and violently to destroy their longtime neighbors and immigrant survivors of the Holocaust in their only refuge, with British support, or at the least silence. Despite his positive experiences with the soldiers and diplomats of Great Britain, Mickey saw that nation's policy of leaving the Yishuv defenseless as a betrayal of the fight against Nazism. After his briefings by Shamir on the military situation as seen by the Haganah, and what he knew from his contacts in the American intelligence community, he had no reason to doubt that Arab leaders would make good on their oaths to crush the Jewish army at birth. Israel's only hope for survival as a state was to midwife that army before the struggle began in earnest.[79]

As the new year approached, Shamir concluded that Ralph Smith would not commit without guarantees that were impossible to provide. The choice was either returning to the Yishuv empty-handed or asking Mickey to accompany him, despite his lack of qualifications as originally outlined. Mickey had no illusions about being the first choice and probably reasoned that he could use the money and would have a chance to play a role in what he saw as an important event, the building of a Jewish army. As he also noted often, in an evocation of a boxing match long before, there was no one else. It remained to be seen if his lack of combat command experience would matter, and if he would be satisfied to be an adjutant without a boss.[80]

On December 30, 1947, Shamir and Marcus met in the late morning and then went to lunch.[81] That night David Ben-Gurion recorded in his diary the first serious discussion of Shamir's potential recruit:

> Marcus, 40 [*sic*], from Brooklyn, studied at West Point. Was in the war from the start. Saw action on the staff in Europe and East Asia. An adjutant to Hilldring. Willing to come here but not to be the first. Has promised to get the first and recommends General Ralph Smith. Shlomo and Marcus went to San Francisco to see Smith. Has agreed to come provided his government consents and the English are informed. Moshe [Sharret] has consulted Hilldring, now in private life after leaving the UN General Assembly. Served on the delegation only under pressure from David Niles, a pro-Jewish Truman aide. Hilldring speaks highly of Marcus, especially for planning. Says he is the best in the United States. Also praised Ralph Smith, but he has a drawback: he was relieved of his command though not due to his own fault. Advised that we take someone else. Marcus disagrees with Hilldring. For personnel and equipment, Hilldring thinks we should go straight to the President and recommended that Bernard Baruch make the pitch.[82]

Soon after, it was clear that Smith would not accept the offer. On January 13, 1948, Mickey contacted Shamir: "Affairs here necessitate your earliest return. Hand over (to) Teddy Kolleck. Cable when coming."[83] Two days later, Mickey signed a contract with the Jewish Agency, with a three-month term (January 15–April 15) at $750 per month plus expenses, a 25 percent premium over the pay for assistants under the original plan envisioned by Shamir, but a 25 percent discount from the market rate for the consultant services of a retired US major general.[84]

While Mickey and Shamir were making travel arrangements, Syrian volunteers crossed the border of Mandatory Palestine in the north, attacking Jewish settlements in the Safad area. On January 29, 1948, the day Mickey left the United States for Palestine the first time, Fawzi al-Qawuqji, the charismatic commander of the Arab Liberation Army, personally led a thousand-man-strong pan-Arab volunteer battalion with twenty armored vehicles across the Adam Bridge to the west bank of the Jordan River. His forces occupied the Arab cities of Nablus and Jenin, claiming to support the Palestinians in those areas, who were supposed to be part of the independent Arab part of Palestine. The civil war between the Jews and Arabs living under the mandate was two months old, and outside-sponsored groups were already intervening. As violence intensified, the British avoided involvement as they withdrew. The Jewish fighters in the separate militias were starting to inch closer in the face of common enemies, which now included foreign forces, through still not regular units of the surrounding nations.[85]

On the snowy evening of January 29, Emma's brother Alfred Chaisson drove her, Mickey, Shamir, and his wife Mina to Idlewild Airport. Mickey promised Emma that he would be back in a few months, and the couple embraced. It fell to Shamir to separate them:

> I extracted him elegantly from the embrace of Emma. I was responsible for bringing him to the country . . . to take up my offer. On the way from New York, we talked and talked. About Germany, past and future, higher echelons of command, human happiness, values, realities of life, probing into our selves, philosophizing. He loved this no less than I did. I asked him in that mood what made him agree to come and was surprised by the immediacy of his response, "*because the blood of Abraham our father runs in my veins.*" A simple clear and unambiguous reply.
>
> I have to say that dark clouds also crossed his mind during the flight. He had doubts, it was far from clear what would happen

to him. He had been lucky so far, he felt, and had come out unscathed from serious incidents in his life. I asked him, where we should bury him if he was killed, and he said, "*West Point. That's where everybody goes.*"

After spending a night in Paris, Haganah headquarters in Europe, the two men left the next day for Palestine.[86]

CHAPTER 5

Mickey Marcus and the Jewish Army

> I am pleased to appear before you and make my report. I made my inspections bearing in mind a quote from a most successful General and Chief of Staff, "Military books emphasize tactics, strategy, at the expense of administration. This is unfortunate, a blunder, as experience demonstrates that success in battle depends on the efficiency of administration."
>
> —Mickey Marcus, quoting Omar Bradley,
> March 16, 1948

Gat-Rimon Hotel, beachfront,
Tel Aviv, Thursday, February 2, 1948

Mickey and Shamir arrived at the beachfront Gat-Rimon Hotel in Tel Aviv after a long journey delayed by bad weather in Paris. Mickey checked into room 23. The hotel where they decamped was a place of quiet intrigue hosting both the American and Soviet delegations, their two banners flying next to each other on the outside masts. Journalists, businessmen, and secret agents moved in and out of the hotel, the pace quickening as the struggle intensified. An American diplomat who lived there at the same time described the rooms as "tiny, there was no lavatory and opened to friendly eyes or otherwise from three sides and no telephone in the room. . . . There was a shortage of everything . . . No one was starving, but food was of limited variety. It took weeks to get a telephone or to get utilities hooked up and a new refrigerator had to be ordered from the States."[1]

Fig. 15. Gat-Rimon Hotel, Tel Aviv

After cleaning up, Mickey and Shamir headed to the Red House, Haganah HQ, and that night Mickey wrote Emma his first letter from Palestine: "We came into the airport last night at ten but had to remain there because the road from Lydda to Tel Aviv is not secure for travel during the night. It took about 3 hours to transverse a 15-mile road stretch this morning. I had lunch with Ben-Gurion. This man is really a great person, but the problem is difficult only because of the need for support and assistance is denied to them. Oh, what a spirit and determination, yes, they will have victory."[2]

The next day Ben-Gurion wrote in his diary, "Shlomo arrived tonight (Tuesday) after leaving on Friday. Brought with him Colonel Marcus who calls himself 'Mickey Stone.' " It was the first time Ben-Gurion had heard the alias.[3] Shamir confirmed that Ben-Gurion and Mickey immediately established a personal rapport. The Jewish leader reaffirmed the mission and its importance: Michael Stone would prepare his recommendations for the command structure, unit organization, training, and doctrine for the soon-to-emerge Jewish army.

Shamir observed that from the first, Mickey's special gift of empathy took hold of the wily Zionist leader. Mickey had the ability to identify with people in the most immediate way; when he was in your presence, it was total. This sense that he was not on the outside created "a huge resonance," along with the symbolism of his coming at the critical moment, when no one could be sure what would happen. Shamir compared him to Wingate. Ben-Gurion was also impressed with the clarity of his military thoughts, and his intense focus on making sure everyone knew who was responsible for whom, and what. Unity of command with absolute clarity was his constant mantra; "He drummed this point home in the morning, the evening, and at night, to anyone who would listen."[4]

After the meeting with Ben-Gurion, whom he immediately started calling "boss," Mickey took a brief tour of the Red House, chatting briefly with anyone he encountered. The next day he met the key Haganah commanders gathered to meet Michael Stone. The most important person among the group was Yigael Yadin, chief of operations and de facto head of the Haganah because of Dori's chronic health problems. Mickey, in a play on his first name, started calling him Eagle, the same nickname he used with Palmach officer Yigal Allon, causing some confusion.

Yadin, a homegrown Haganah veteran and brilliant archaeology scholar, was thorough, thoughtful, and cautious. He viewed Stone as just another outside adviser who had captured Ben-Gurion's fancy. Escorting the visitor to the operations room in the basement of the Red House, Yadin described the enemy deployment and the general disposition of the Jewish forces into eight territorial commands. Mickey listened, scanning the map, and then offered his opinion that it was impossible to efficiently command so many secondary fronts.

Yisrael Galili, the head of the Haganah High Command, recalled that at that first meeting the discussion was about organization and training of the army, and even at the beginning Mickey argued strongly in favor of separating the headquarters responsible for combat—e.g., the front commander—from the high command to maintain independence and avoid harmful interference by those unfamiliar with the ground or the actual situation in the field. After these exchanges, everyone agreed that an extended field orientation would acclimatize Mickey to the actual problems at hand, so arrangements were made for his extended inspection of Haganah and Palmach troops in the field, to see things firsthand and up close. Ben-Gurion was most interested in Mickey's recommendations for practical steps necessary to shape the underground partisan-type Haganah militia into a citizen-soldier-based professional army, one ready to hit the ground running as soon as Israeli independence was declared and the Arab armies attacked. Even before the tour, Mickey estimated that they had only a few months to get ready.[5]

Leading by looking around: Galilee, Negev, road to Jerusalem, early February-early March 1948

Mickey's first cover identity as Michael Stone was, as mentioned, as a wine salesman, after which the story switched to make him an American foundry supervisor under contract for the construction giant Solel Boneh. His local work permit and internal travel documents, provided by the Haganah and matched to his cover identity, afforded him relative freedom of movement as an American citizen on business in the Yishuv. He set out to get a firsthand look at the fighting, and the people who would defend the country when the real war began. As suggested by Ben-Gurion, Mickey visited with many Palmach and Haganah commanders and soldiers as he visited the fighting fronts.

During one such early visit Mickey, in a car with Irene Broida, his secretary and translator, and a Haganah bodyguard who was driving, was stopped by a British patrol. Irene knew the men with her were armed, the American carrying a small pistol, the driver a Sten. As they slowed down, approaching the checkpoint, Mickey, thinking quickly, put the weapons on the back seat and told Irene to wrap herself in her coat and lie on her back on top of the guns with her legs raised while moaning, feigning pregnancy. The ruse worked. One of the British soldiers ordered the men out of the car to undergo a search, eyeing Irene suspiciously but without searching her or the car. When the soldier remarked on Mickey's muscles and asked what he did for a living, Mickey immediately answered that he was a blacksmith. Irene thought that apt "because he looked so much the part, a solidly built athlete, with a cherubic oval face, a pointed nose like a chopped-off carrot, small ears and huge boxer's hands."[6]

Fig. 16. Mickey visiting Palmach positions. Magnum

Mickey spent a lot of time with Yigal Allon, then head of the Palmach. Initially Allon, like most of his comrades, was wary about the foreigner introduced as Michael Stone: "He was an outsider from the richest and most powerful army in the world. How could he understand our inadequacies, the untrained, ill-clad boys, the lack of arms? How could a foreigner fathom the nature of the enemy, the special conditions of the country and its politics, which were an inseparable part of the fight?"[7]

As part of his initial tour of the areas where Palmach forces were stationed, Allon took Mickey to the headquarters on Mount Canaan in the Galilee just days after the successful raid on Sa'sa on February 15, 1948, by a Palmach battalion. It was the first time Mickey had a chance to see Jewish troops who had fought in a unit larger than a few platoons. By this time, the three Palmach brigades, Yiftach in the North, Harel in Jerusalem, and Negev in the south, were all fully mobilized and operating under the central Haganah command. They were still on the defense against pressure from local Arab militias, small groups of neighbors, and growing infiltration across the borders.

An important road junction, Sa'sa was an Arab village fifteen miles from the nearest Palmach troops. It had been occupied by elements of the Arab Liberation Army, a volunteer militia under the famed Arab soldier Fawzi al-Qawuqji, deployed nearby. As part of a series of offensive operations to take the fight directly to the enemy and lift morale after several severe setbacks, the raid on Sa'sa was consistent with the active defense that Wingate had instilled in his disciples, including Allon. The raiders achieved surprise, and in less than ten minutes after beginning the operation had penetrated the village, placed explosives, withdrew, and blown up their intended targets. Withdrawal from the areas proved more difficult, taking all night, rain and the ensuing mud hampering the platoon carrying the wounded.[8]

When Mickey arrived at Mount Canaan, the men of the Yiftach Brigade had not yet been relieved and were short on supplies, battle-weary, sick, disheartened, many of them in rags. The raid had been successful, but it had exhausted the battalion. The weather was still miserable, and the men were sheltering in their mess hall, having been told to assemble to listen to a visiting guest speaker. A soldier named Gabby recounted the event to the journalist gathering accounts of Mickey a year after his death:

> We couldn't pick out which of them was the American. Yigal spoke to us first, and Mickey listened quietly, sitting among us. Yigal reported about the situation in the rest of the country and then he called on Mickey to speak. A sign on the wall attracted his attention and he asked one of the boys to translate it for him. It was a quote attributed to the revered Italian military hero Giuseppe Garibaldi: "I have neither pay, nor beds, nor food. I promise you starvation, thirst, exhausting marches, and death.

But he who loves his country with more than lip service, will rise and follow me."

Now Mickey stood and began to speak,

"Soldiers of the Palmach. I see what you're up against, I see how you're dressed. I hear you coughing, I heard of your raid on Sa'sa. I've just been told what the motto on the wall says, listened to your questions, and the answers you received. And from all this, I conclude this is one of the best armies I have ever seen. I haven't seen infantry better than this anywhere. And I am sure that with such men victory is in the bag."[9]

Gabby conveyed the anecdote with the immediacy of an intense relived experience, feeling again the terrific impact of Mickey's remarks on this exhausted, shabby, ill-shod band of partisan fighters:

He spoke of plans, and told us we needed only time to organize, and then we'd go on the offensive. That was the kind of talk we liked to hear. Like mercury, it raised our morale immediately. It went straight to the hearts of the men.[10]

During this period Mickey and Allon spent many hours discussing the military situation. The Palmach leader was impressed by the scope of the adviser's knowledge but agreed with others that he didn't appreciate the situation in the field and the tensions between the political objectives and the tactics suitable to the facts on the ground. He told interviewer Porath,

We could not always go along with Mickey's ideas. Basic to our strategy had to be a program of tactics aimed at achieving boundaries for the newly emerging state. Sometimes we had to sacrifice good military strategy for a more immediate goal. It was impossible to conduct some of the activities he had in mind.

> When he would suggest a drill, or to organize a large unit and move it from one part of the country to another, we would have to tell him if he moves more than two vehicles at a time it would alert the British and that would result in searches, confiscation of arms and curfews.[11]

Oval Office, the White House, Washington, DC, February 1948

As Mickey set out on his inspection tour, the rhythm of political maneuvering and unexpected shifts of policy abroad intensified. Early in the month, just as Dr. Chaim Weizmann, head of the World Zionist Congress, came to New York to lobby for US support for Jewish independence, a countermove played out across the Atlantic. The UK started to shift strategy, favoring annexation of Arab Palestine by Transjordan, a dramatic maneuver threatening to realign the Middle Eastern balance of power and challenge the intent of the partition plan. In the United States, the national security and intelligence restructuring mandated by the National Security Act of 1947 continued, as did the normal rotation and promotion of senior officers.

On February 12 General Omar Bradley, wartime commander of the US Twelfth Army Group, postwar leader of the US Veterans Administration, and onetime math teacher of the West Point class of 1924, was appointed chief of staff of the US Army. Mickey undoubtedly took note. Clarity on US policy toward the situation in Palestine, however, remained elusive. Defense Secretary Forrestal voiced concerns at a National Security Council meeting about potential US military mobilization if partition led to instability in the region. Secretary of State Marshall did not give a firm opinion, indicating that the Palestine issue remained under continuing reevaluation as the security situation worsened.[12]

President Truman's stance added another layer of complexity to the policy formulation. Publicly, he emphasized the theoretical nature of trusteeship, one of the proposed UN alternatives to the previous November vote, and reiterated support for partition. Yet he also instructed Marshall to stand ready to proceed with Ambassador Warren Austin's latest draft speech to the UN Security Council, which hinted at a shift in US policy away from partition.

The political dynamics took a dark turn in Jerusalem on February 22, 1948. A synchronized car bombing struck the office of the *Palestine Post* on Ben Yehuda Street and the Jewish Agency offices in Jerusalem simultaneously. The strike was orchestrated by popular and competent Palestinian Arab militia leader Abd as-Qadir al-Husayni, scion of a prominent family that included the anti-Semitic, pro-Nazi mufti of Jerusalem. The devastation was extensive, claiming eighty-eight lives and injuring many hundreds. This act of terror shook American resolve, further eroding the initial staunch support for partition. On the ground, tensions soared. The Arab Liberation Army maneuvered around Arab Galilee and Samaria, and al-Husayni's Army of the Holy War bolstered its presence around Jerusalem, with the added strength of Muslim Bosnian Waffen SS veterans.[13]

During these political tremors, personal interventions at the highest level of US policy continued. Eddie Jacobson, President Truman's World War I army buddy from Battery D, close friend, and onetime St. Louis business partner, was a longtime Zionist and knew many of the movement's leaders personally, including Chaim Weizmann, a leader of the Jewish Agency and the World Zionist Organization. A man whose unrelenting goal for decades had been a Jewish homeland in the British mandate of Palestine, Weizmann would later become Israel's first president. Jacobson dispatched a poignant telegram imploring Truman to confer with Weizmann, but his friend's response was noncommittal, indicating that he had no plans to meet with the Zionist leader.[14]

Haganah HQ, The Red House, Hayarkon Street, Tel Aviv, March 16, 1948

After returning from a month-long orientation tour of all fronts, during which he had free rein and many encounters, Mickey gave the "boss" a brief oral report on March 3, 1948. "I found less than I expected and more than I hoped for," he said, citing the basic shortcomings in organization, transport, and equipment and then waxing eloquent about the emerging Jewish army, especially its young leadership.: "The Haganah has educated a type of commander who could easily be converted into a first-rate officer." Mickey saw the ordinary people as "a new breed of Jew." He viewed their intelligence and street smarts, spirit of improvisation, and devotion to duty as the substance of a top rank army. One of his favorite expressions when addressing a soldier was, "come here young hero" said with total sincerity.[15]

The bottom line, in Napoleonic terms, was simple: the moral outweighed the material by just enough, and the Haganah could be forged into an effective fighting force in time. If they could be reinforced quickly with heavy arms, diplomatic and economic support, and increased mobilization of all national assets, Israel could hold the ground through the British withdrawal in mid-May and the immediate aftermath. As his confidence grew during his tour, Mickey communicated his optimism to soldiers of every rank, and his spirit became infectious in soldiers ranging from his assigned Palmach driver up to Yaacov Dori, Haganah chief of staff.

Now Ben-Gurion came under the fabled Marcus spell. The next day he sent a message to Teddy Kolleck, who took over from Shamir and now ran Haganah North American operations: "The expert who came with Shamir (Marcus) has been a great blessing to us. It would be good if you could send at least ten more like him—all at once." Kolleck was talking to others, including two who were on Shamir's lists of generals, but no one came close, and some were a distraction.[16]

Mickey took several weeks to gather his thoughts, notes, and impressions and to confer with commanders and staff officers, including Ben-Gurion, Dori, and Yadin, developing his recommendations for a formal presentation to the Haganah high command. He spent a lot of time at the Red House, often waiting for meetings to end, where he displayed his usual behavior: turning to a secretary, he would say, "Loveliness, please bring me a file," or spontaneously he would speak authoritatively about opera, art, or history, quoting the Bible, Keats, or his favorite, Shakespeare. He would start to tap-dance, or sing a favorite aria, daven aloud, or engage in conversation on religion or science. Everyone agreed that despite that behavior, on military matters, he was "strictly business."[17]

Parallel to those few weeks after his return from his tour, global political events shook the pathway to actual partition and the previous approach to the Palestine issue. In America, on March 8, President Truman received a memo from domestic adviser Clark Clifford titled "US Policy with Regard to Palestine," emphasizing that the partition of Palestine was the policy of the United States and was viewed favorably by influential parts of the US administration. The next day, March 9, Marshall signaled his view that if the UN Special Assembly convened, the United States should back trusteeship, a theoretical concept and deviation from the partition sentiment that Clifford had expressed the day before. By March 12, the US Committee on Palestine (USCOP) voiced their assessment that when the British mandate ended, the region would plunge into chaos, civil strife, and bloodshed.[18]

Amid this whirlwind of official discussions and policy reports, a poignant personal moment fraught with global significance unfolded on March 13, when Truman's old friend Eddie Jacobson made an unscheduled visit to the White House. Without an appointment, he entered the Oval Office and strongly urged his friend to meet with Chaim Weizmann, the president of the World Zionist Organization and a longtime leader of the Zionist movement. Truman, whose motives are still debated, responded with a mix of humor and resignation, "You win, you baldheaded son-of-a-bitch. I will see him."[19] Once again, Truman's stance had shifted.

Back in the Red House, as early as March 12, Ben-Gurion had been discussing an official position for Mickey, identified in the diary as "Mickey Stone (Col. David Marcus)," first considering the title of deputy chief of general staff, after positive reception from Israel Galili, the chief. Nothing came of that, but a notation just six weeks after Mickey's arrival points to the speed with which he had gained the confidence of Ben-Gurion, who was already thinking of how he could use the American to increase the professionalism of the Jewish army. By March 16, 1948, Mickey was ready to present his blueprint for organizing that force, including its doctrinal and operational principles.[20]

Because of his conversations with Shamir, and his own sources, Mickey knew the history of Jewish self-defense efforts in the early decades of the twentieth century, especially during the mandate. Mickey was also aware that Ben-Gurion was not the only one who had been pursuing the goal of forming a Jewish army under its own flag. As early as 1942, various American groups had sponsored and lobbied for a "Jewish Legion," to be drawn from the Allied countries but fighting Nazism under their own flag. At the time, one lobbying target was then Democrat Missouri senator, and later vice president, Harry Truman, who was outspoken about the plight of European Jewry when reports of their slaughter emerged. Truman did not support the creation of a separate military force but, sympathetic to the cause, maintained contacts with some of the proponents thereof right up until his sudden ascension to the presidency.

In the immediate aftermath of World War II, the focus of American Zionists shifted to the plight of the survivors of the Shoah still languishing in Europe, and the necessity to immediately create both a homeland and an army to secure any hope for a Jewish future in Palestine. One of the loudest, most persistent and influential voices pressing this case directly to Truman was Eddie Jacobsen, the old artilleryman. [21]

Mickey had an instinctive understanding that the roots and traditions of the emerging Jewish army would reflect the history of both the Yishuv and the diaspora. He also had his own strong views, reinforced by his extensive exposure to general staffs of a half dozen nations during the war, that the American army tables of organization, general and special staff structure, and maneuver formations and principles provided a flexible model for the organization of the Jewish army. He also believed that the American experience, especially during the Revolution and World War II, had fundamental lessons for the Jewish army as it went through its struggle to help its people gain freedom and independence. [22]

Indeed, Mickey's outline, both material and inspirational, drew heavily from his understanding of both the American and Israeli revolutions. He well understood that the struggle for independence from foreign occupation and foreign invasion required the development of a unified—and unifying—national army out of a multitude of militias before the onset of the main engagements. Well before the United States was a self-declared independent nation, its provisional government established the Continental Army under a broadly respected and politically unopposed leader, George Washington. Like the Jewish army forming in mid-May 1948, the Continental Army had its roots in a massive occupation of the national homeland by, as it turns out, the same colonial master, and its commander had welcomed the advice of foreign military experts whose skills were broad and motivations complex. For Ben-Gurion, Mickey had emerged as the most important such figure since Orde Wingate. Because Ben-Gurion was not a soldier, this was more than a luxury.

As Mickey saw it, Ben-Gurion faced the same problem as George Washington had. Ben-Gurion, too, had to organize and lead a national army that would establish its people's independence in the presence of an occupying army with strong lines of supply and maritime supremacy as well as depth and reinforcement. In Ben-Gurion's case, his nascent army also would have to fight off a coalition of neighbors. The very roles of commander-in-chief and a military high command were still in flux and buffeted by local politics on a near daily basis. In local historical terms, the most striking and depressing analogy was that of the First Jewish Revolt against Rome, culminating in the siege and destruction of Jerusalem and its second temple in 70 AD. In that national liberation struggle, despite early Judean successes in repelling the initial Roman operations, including early siege efforts against Jerusalem, the various political and religious factions continued their endemic internal squabbling without a central leadership ever emerging.

From the point of view of an American in a position to shape a foreign army, the parallels to the early republic after independence were also striking. The fighting spirit of the Continental Army had been the key to American independence, but only because it survived long enough for diplomatic efforts to secure outside military and financial intervention by France and Holland. Decisive victories at Saratoga and Yorktown made independence possible, but only because diplomatic efforts by Benjamin Franklin and John Adams had prepared the ground in anticipation of—or desperately hoping for—an American victory and change in momentum.

The Jewish army would need victories in the field early to sway outside powers to give support. Patience and long-term commitment were not oft-practiced virtues in the Western democracies. Neither America, a weakened Europe, nor Stalin were willing to send forces to the area to enforce diplomatic dictates. The Jewish army, if it survived, would be the key to the reestablishment of sovereignty over Zion, first by consolidating its hold on their ground against neighbors who claimed nationhood or territorial rights on the same land. The political and diplomatic elements of the struggle were not, however, part of Mickey's assignment or the focus of his contract. His political opinions, even if solicited by those he met in Palestine, were irrelevant. He did not advise on politics or propose any sort of theory or doctrine of counterinsurgency in his written materials, which—had he done so—might have touched on the challenges and claims of Arab and Palestinian nationalism.

But if Mickey believed strongly in the efficacy of the American command model, he also recognized that history had provided the founders an equally powerful practical model for the structure and ethos of their new army. Much like the Continental Army during the American revolution, the Jewish army looked to its most recent adversary for its basic organization, administrative system, and general approach to warfare. Practically, in the Yishuv, the most dominant common influence on security matters, dating from Edmund Allenby's conquest of Palestine in 1917, was the British Army. From the beginning of World War II, and years before the organization of an officially organized and sanctioned Jewish unit was established in the British Army in 1944, the Yishuv had sent its people into service under the Union Jack. Even before the arrival of foreign volunteers—mostly World War II combat veterans—in Palestine in 1948, many soldiers of Israel had British military experience. A few had achieved field grade rank up to colonel, but there was not a single officer in the Yishuv who had commanded a formation larger than a battalion.

Mickey advised the nascent government of Israel to establish a general headquarters (GHQ) to immediately bring all the various militia components of the Jewish army, with no exceptions, under a central command. Unity of command was Mickey's core unifying principle of defense. The GHQ would not command directly but through the front commanders, replacing the regional brigade organization of the prewar Haganah with a geographic Northern, Central, and Southern Front organization, which would deploy multi-brigade maneuver forces against an enemy, capitalizing on internal lines of communication to concentrate forces for the offensive. The organization of training and administration would be general staff functions, led by officers who would command reserve units during wartime.[23]

These steps recognized the complex political dynamics at play but provided a common context for military organization. The brigades in the field at that point, though varying, were based on territorial roots and responsibilities. Nine were deployed: six under direct Haganah command and three Palmach brigades, the Harel, Alexandroni, and Yiftach. None had ever deployed at full strength, nor had any ever engaged in brigade training or actual combat operations.

At every opportunity Mickey hammered home a few key points to the Haganah leadership: the need for more mobile army units; the necessity to use the initiative and intelligence of soldiers as the army's primary resource; and an aggressive approach that would attack the enemy sharply rather than adopt a defensive strategy. Special units would be employed, based on terrain requirements, availability of weapons, and the nature of the mission. Mickey knew the traditions and history of the American general staff system as well as the British command structure, having experienced both at the highest level, but quickly understood the initiative, quality, and potential of the Jewish soldiers. Especially impressed by the company and potential battalion and brigade commanders, he made his recommendations suited to their unique characteristics, experiences, and actual conditions. He advised that the Haganah high command immediately focus on staff organization and training at battalion and brigade level, especially coordination of logistics, planning, and intelligence.[24]

If there is a close American analogy to Mickey's situation, Friedrich von Steuben, the drillmaster of Valley Forge, fits best. Recruited by Silas Dean for his training abilities, Steuben made his greatest contribution by codifying and publishing a standard drill system for the Continental Army. He adapted contemporary European military drill and its traditions and organizational foundation to meet the needs of the new nation's citizen-soldiers. In so doing he established the tenets of military professionalism in a democratic army. Like Mickey, distinction as a battlefield commander eluded Steuben, although after America established its independence he reaped the tangible rewards of being hailed a hero of the Revolution. For Mickey, the reward was his legacy and the endurance of his name.[25]

Zipporah Porath, the young American journalist caught up in the 1948 war with the Haganah and then looking into Mickey's time in Israel, saw his broad influence clearly: "Everyone I spoke with was in awe of his magnetic personality, quick grasp of situations, phenomenal memory, and enormous capacity for work. They praised his courage and his humanity, his integrity and valued his unwavering optimism and ability to inspire confidence."[26]

Training Manuals, Eli Kirschner's apartment, Tel Aviv, March 1948

As the pace of events on the path to conflict gradually accelerated, Haganah intelligence decided that protecting the secret of Mickey Stone was impossible at the Gat-Rimon Hotel, now a known object of intense surveillance. During the period he was working on training manuals and consulting at the Red House, Mickey operated out of a Tel Aviv safe house apartment owned by Eli Alan Kirschner, a thirty-seven-year-old Oxford-educated lawyer and Haganah officer. Scion of a prominent South African Zionist family and longtime associate of Ben-Gurion, Eli was knowledgeable about every aspect of the military situation and had personal contacts with many of the principals. His wife Eva (née Zerinsky) was a sergeant in the Third Battalion of the Palmach Yiftach Brigade.

Mickey spent many evenings with the Kirschners discussing their war experiences, recent history, and mutual observations of the British, religion, and philosophy. Mickey argued hard with Eli about the need for the Haganah leadership to immediately bend all efforts to the rapid formation and supply of a large Jewish army based on the brigade as the basic maneuver unit, and eventually division-size formations. As Mickey saw it, if Israel had any hope of survival, let alone winning the pending war for its independence, the divided politicians, and their patchwork of underground militias, would have to put aside their parochial perspectives, radicalize their thinking, and ally against common enemies. They would have to cooperate and pool their resources, in soldiers and material, to form a combat army while under the greatest pressure of all, actual battle. And—what might prove most difficult for them to comprehend in such a situation—they had to shift most of their planning efforts to administration, logistics, and training. Mickey stressed that these were equal in importance to, indeed would shape the outcome of the actual fighting.[27]

Mickey also spent a good deal of time visiting the cadets enrolled in the Haganah platoon commander's course, focused on tactics and run by ex-major Chaim Laskov, veteran of the Jewish Brigade. The course had three main goals: to build the character of each officer cadet; to train each cadet to command an infantry platoon, both independently and as part of a company; and to inculcate good order, discipline, and esprit de corps among their soldiers. While Mickey was impressed with Laskov's course, he immediately recognized that any new Israeli force also needed a course for higher-level commanders up to battalion and brigade level. Tactics were important, but the new Israeli military could not win on the battlefield unless it had officers who understood and were conversant with maneuver and the operational level of war.

Consequently, when Mickey submitted his official report to Ben-Gurion on March 16, among his recommendations was the immediate creation of a four-week-long course for battalion-level commanders. Since no such course had ever existed in the Haganah or other Jewish paramilitary groups, Mickey suggested that he command the proposed school for battalion commanders along with four other men, all of whom had served as officers in the British Army, Shamir, Laskov, and Herzog. Ben-Gurion agreed, and Mickey wasted no time in starting to develop doctrine and other literature for the course and sketching out a four-week lesson plan. He was the only person in Palestine at that time who had experience at all three levels of war—tactical, operational, and strategic—since he had served as a staff officer at the division and higher levels of the American army. That was his perspective as he began.[28]

Over the course of the weeks after his presentation to the Haganah high command, Mickey prepared manuals and booklets that lay at the core of the enduring image of Michael "Mickey" Stone as one of the major influencers of the Israel Defense Forces (IDF). Many sources claim that Mickey wrote the documents totally from memory, that he or the Haganah could not bring his US doctrine manuals with him because of British security, or variations of that story. The archives of the IDF, however, house copies of US doctrine and operational manuals of that period bearing Mickey's initials and other identifying marks. Shamir's memoirs reference that the manuals were in Mickey's possession while he was in Israel, and that his work adopted the American style and presentation for his Jewish army training and doctrine. While the manuals may have been sent to Mickey after he arrived in Palestine, clearly he didn't write his manuals from memory.[29] His experiences training troops in the Twenty-Seventh Division in Hawaii and as a War Department planner in the Pentagon also shaped the documents. Mickey wrote two manuals, one on the duties of the battalion staff, suited for a brief training course, and the other a tactical field manual. The first book opened with these words: "The commander himself is responsible for the actions and inactions of his unit. He must not blame his staff officers or secondary commanders." The brochures were written in English, translated into Hebrew, typed up, and then distributed. A theme in both books was that doctrine, combined with improvisation, a trait especially prized by those having served in Palmach, were the keys to combat success at the tactical and operational levels of war.[30]

Working at so furious a pace of dictation that he outran the translators, Mickey's focus remained on the brigade as the primary maneuver formation. In his manuals, Mickey harkened back to the Ranger-type training course he ran in Hawaii for the Twenty-Seventh Infantry Division, stressing the offensive, taking the fight to enemy territory quickly, upsetting their plans, deep penetrations, hit-and-run raids, and cavalry type supply-severing operations that hearkened back to Wingate and the Civil War generals (and West Point grads) Philip Sheridan, George Custer, and J. E. B. Stuart. Mickey urged the use of complex ambushes and other harassing tactics, imperative for an army having to mobilize quickly, build up strength, and eventually hit back hard in one of the enemy's weakest places. The final aim: to deliver the best possible results on the battlefield, thus gaining an advantage in the political negotiating phase.[31]

The immediate purpose of the manuals was to serve as course materials for the four-week program to quickly train fighting battalion commanders selected from the ranks of the best company-grade Haganah, Palmach, and Etzel officers. In Mickey's organizational plan, the enrollees would be trained to lead elements of large, mechanized infantry units with attached armor and artillery, along with trained staff members who would also be graduates of the training school. His texts became the basis for training officers when the IDF established a professional military education infrastructure. The titles of his Tactical Field Manual chapters, 230 pages altogether and grouped under the title "For Company Commanders and Above," outline the basic course:

1. Staff Officer Training
2. Tactical Usage of Infantry Units at Battalion and Company level
3. Tactical Usage of Infantry Units at Platoon and Squad level
4. Troop Movement
5. Attack and Defense
6. Fortified Positions and Urban Warfare
7. Tanks and Their Usage[32]

Oval Office, the White House, Washington, DC, March 1948

During the period when Mickey was writing the manuals, official US policymakers began to discuss delaying the actual partition of Palestine in the hopes that doing so would allow time to figure out how to limit the violence that was certain to follow it. On March 18 Truman met with Weizmann. He strongly endorsed a solution that would lead to "justice without bloodshed," but added that if the Jewish state were declared, the US would recognize it. That would be the extent of his support. The next day Ambassador Austin told the Security Council that partition of Palestine was no longer viable, and Secretary Marshall reiterated that US diplomacy was focused on some kind of temporary solution. An American arms embargo had been placed on all arms to Palestine on December 5, 1947, obviously hurting the Yishuv more, as it rendered the once tolerated arms activities of the Haganah fully illegal. That was not likely to change.[33]

In Palestine, Ben-Gurion faced growing pressure about whether to declare independence at, before, or after the end of the British mandate still scheduled for May 15, 1948. He knew the declaration would mean war with at least four Arab armies and outside volunteers. Even as the UN continued to debate delays, other powerful voices, including some prominent American and British Zionists, joined in, arguing that diplomatic efforts needed time to gain political and economic support and end the boycotts preventing large-scale arms imports to the Yishuv.[34]

President Truman was watching events with growing frustration. On March 21 he wrote to his sister Mary Jane Truman that the "striped pants conspirators" in the State Department had "completely balled up the Palestine situation. But it may work out anyway in spite of them." The next day he wrote his brother, Vivian Truman, regarding the backing of partition, "I think the proper thing to do, and the thing I have been doing, is to do what I think is right and let them all go to hell."[35]

History had come full circle. After initially supporting the 1917 Balfour Declaration to gain Jewish support in the Great War, the United States gradually changed its policy. By 1945 President Franklin D. Roosevelt had assured Arab nations, increasingly worried about Jewish immigration to Palestine, that US involvement in the Middle East would be conducted with extensive consultations with the parties—that is, a Jewish state would never happen. The strong suggestion was neutrality in support of the status quo. The British opposed Jewish or Arab states in the mandate, as well as unrestricted immigration of Jewish refugees even after the war. Their interests lay in positive relations with Arab nations to protect their political and economic interests in Palestine as part of a wider regional strategy. Even after the UN vote and the end of the formal mandate, they still hoped to wield influence.[36]

Truman was more sympathetic to the Zionist cause than his predecessor, and in May 1946 he supported immediate admission into Palestine of one hundred thousand Jews still languishing in Western European displaced persons (DP) camps. Soon after, he empowered a cabinet-level committee led by Dr. Henry F. Grady, an assistant secretary of state, to negotiate with the British about Palestine. In October 1946 Truman publicly declared his support for the establishment of a Jewish state. During 1947 the United Nations Special Commission on Palestine (UNSCOP) made its own inquiry and proposed a partition plan to divide the League of Nations mandate for Palestine into separate Jewish and Arab states, with some type of separate international protectorate arrangement for the holy city of Jerusalem. The passage of UN General Assembly Resolution #181 then set events toward independence in motion. Civil violence and maneuvering for tactical advantage between the Jewish and Arab forces began the day after the vote. As the date of the end of the British mandate and final departure of British troops on May 15 neared, the pressure on Ben-Gurion for declaration of statehood intensified. So did the pressure on Truman from his State Department to stand down from any kind of formal recognition of Israel to wait to see what would happen post declaration.[37]

As in the case of the Balfour Declaration back in 1917, at first the United States had supported the partition of Palestine into separate Jewish and Arab states, but after the initial spout of Arab-Jewish violence, the State Department backed away. They put forward the idea of a trusteeship under the UN, an alternative that would limit Jewish immigration and rule a collection of Jewish and Arab provinces rather that two independent states. The concept of a trusteeship was as theoretical as any forces for enforcement or quelling the violence that already engulfed Palestine. Behind State's thinking was concern about potential Soviet influence in the Middle East and the risk that Arab oil producers would cut US supplies. The armed forces chiefs pointed out that the necessary forces were not available. Anti-Semitism also played a factor. [38]

On March 22, Truman said at a press conference that some kind of trusteeship, or rule by the UN, for the territory being given up by Britain might be a temporary measure, but not a substitute for partition. By early April, the United States was calling for a reconsideration of the Palestine problem in the UN. On the ground, irregular Arab forces were crossing the Mandatory borders, and Haganah was getting ready to launch Operation Nachson by the Palmach Harel Brigade, their largest operation to date, to break though the roadblocks along the road to Jerusalem just outside the city to allow the Jews to bring in food, ammunition, and other humanitarian supplies.[39] With everything moving in a whirl, just as he had promised Emma, as well as for other reasons, Mickey returned to America the first week of April.

Back to the US: Prospect Avenue, Brooklyn, April 8, 1948

Before he returned to America, Mickey went to see Ben-Gurion. "I'll be back even if I have to swim," he reassured him, personally repeating the promise to Shamir, the disheartened commanders, and secretaries at the Red House. When the British withdrew, he told them, he would be with them. The realization that no one, not even Ben-Gurion or Shamir, believed him troubled him a great deal, as he related to a friend during his return to America, asking more than once, "Why don't they trust me?"[40]

On April 8, 1948, Mickey arrived in Washington, DC, via Switzerland after stopping for an overnight visit with Emma's cousin Regina Gabel in Bratislava, Czechoslovakia. He spent the night captivating the family, with Regina writing to Emma soon after, "I don't know how to give you the highlights because the entire visit was a highlight for us. The minute he walked out from the plane and walked over to us, we felt that we knew him a long time, so friendly was his approach." Anticipating that he might be back via the same route, Mickey left some clothes and money with Regina before he headed home. On arrival in America, Mickey took the train from Union Station to Penn Station, a ride he knew well, and was reunited with Emma.[41]

Mickey had come back for several reasons. First, as mentioned, he wanted to honor the promise he had made to Emma, who had in letters been complaining about ill health, but he also returned to help in the procurement of men, weapons, and equipment for Israel's defenses, despite having to skirt the legal edge now that an embargo was in place. Parallel to that effort, he hoped to influence the attitude in Washington toward Israeli independence, and the new nation's chances for survival. That meant persuading his diplomatic and military contacts that the Jewish army he was helping to build could stand against the power and fury about to descend on it, forces that, according to the best intelligence as well as common sense, were in a good position to crush it.[42]

Emma's desk calendar from April 8 to May 2 documents Mickey's heavy work schedule at his law office and Hotel Fourteen, mixed with numerous visits with his family members, social gatherings with friends, and several dinners relating to Mickey's work. He was consumed with work during the day while Emma went to her job or meetings of community groups. Except for social events, the couple spent little time together and had just one date, dinner and a movie, the entire time. To complicate the situation, during one meeting at Hotel Fourteen their Oldsmobile was stolen off the street. A generous friend lent them a spare car until theirs was recovered.[43]

Benny Edelman, a Haganah operative who worked on supply, described Mickey dropping in right after he got back to check out what was going on. "He told us about the situation he had just left. How brave our boys were and what stamina they had under bad conditions. He said B-G had given him a shopping list of important supplies to buy."[44] Mickey helped select items that matched the most important priorities with scarce funds. He enjoyed modeling the clothing. "A pair of fatigues he was checking out had pockets all over the place. Delighted, he grabbed anything in sight, the secretary's purse, the desk stamp, the paper weight, stuffed them into the various pockets and did a fast tap dance around the room. When told we didn't have the funds for new supplies, Mickey urged we buy vintage army surplus even as old as the First World War, he urged, 'buy what you can, but where shoes are concerned, only buy new shoes!' "[45]

That attitude strongly echoed the experience of an infantry soldier and recalls an earlier episode after Mickey's visit with the Palmach in Galilee. On his way back, passing through Tel Aviv, he expressed outrage to Allon that the stores had shoes while the men were barefoot. "I would break in and raid them, confiscate them. First you must make up your mind that we are at war, then you'll be able to mobilize the country. If you continue to look at this war as a series of episodes, then you'll never have the power to enforce your requirements."[46]

This was the civil war phase, right after the partition vote but before the British withdrawal, and Allon believed Marcus didn't truly understand the Haganah's situation. Whatever Mickey's plans, Allon's men were still underground partisans, freedom fighters; no matter the circumstances, they could not take what they wanted and thereby surrender their legitimacy. Nonetheless, Mickey pushed his position right up to the Arab invasion, including in his discussions with the Haganah high command. He had other clashes with Haganah commanders, whom he called "Olympus," complaining to his friends during his visit to America, "They treat me like a stray dog who landed in their lot. They can't make up their minds whether to befriend me or to defend themselves."[47]

On April 11 Eddie Jacobson made another visit to the White House to meet with Truman. "He reaffirmed, very strongly, the promises he had made to Dr. Weizmann and to me; and he gave me permission to tell Dr. Weizmann so, which I did. It was at this meeting that I also discussed with the President the vital matter of recognizing the new state, and to this he agreed with a whole heart." Mickey's American Zionist contacts kept him appraised of political developments in Washington, where he would soon be going for the ceremony to honor his award of the Order of the British Empire (OBE). As he planned for his trip to the capital, he took the opportunity to set up appointments with friends and contacts to further his lobbying efforts. After the first week of work and socializing he finally got a chance to have his own party in his new Brooklyn home.[48]

On Saturday, April 17, Emma and Mickey hosted eighteen mostly long-standing friends for dinner, aided by their longtime maid Dorothy Chappelle and her husband Theodore. It was not a joyous scene of homecoming. Emma describes arguments at the gathering about whether Mickey should return to Palestine, replete with shouting and the airing of sharp differences of opinion. Naturally, all this dampened the mood, so much that this time not even Mickey, the consummate party lover, could reverse the damage. Thinking he might defuse the situation by splitting, he ducked into the kitchen and found Ted Chappelle in the room alone. The two men had an easygoing familiar relationship, with no hint of racial tension. At one point in their conversation in the kitchen, according to Chappelle, Mickey pulled up his pants leg and showed Ted a scar on his calf.

Ted: "How did you get that?"

Mickey: "Have you heard of a little group of people called Jews? Well, I got this scar helping them in Palestine."

Ted: "Are you going back?"

Mickey: "Yes, I'm going back, but I don't know if I'm coming back."

Dorothy Chapelle, who knew Mickey's moods well, had a similar recollection that during the party the host was wistful and expressed the desire to return to a quiet and normal life, but added that what he was doing to help the Jews in Palestine was a moral responsibility he couldn't put down. Others report that Mickey had a similarly fatalistic attitude about returning to Palestine. No other account claims that Mickey was wounded in Palestine, though, as the anecdote relayed by Ted Chappelle suggests.

By this point Emma had grown exhausted in her fruitless pleas that Mickey not return to Palestine, and the tension between the two was growing. The next Tuesday he went to Washington to collect his medal.[49]

Medal presentation, British Embassy, Washington DC, April 20, 1948

While Mickey was still in Palestine, Emma received a telephone call from the British embassy, inviting her and her husband to a formal presentation of the OBE he had earned in 1945. As it turned out, Mickey attended the ceremony in his US Army uniform in his rank as colonel, but alone. He never suggested that Emma should accompany him, or asked what she thought about the affair. This was consistent with his behavior as reported by Maginnis and others, making light of all such decorations, but Emma didn't see it that way. Writing to Berkman about the ceremony, she confided, "I can still get frustrated and angry that I was never asked to attend the ceremony. Mickey didn't feel it was important enough for me to take time off from teaching, therefore I had to rely on his account of the ceremony. To a sentimentalist it was devastating."[50]

During the ceremony, the military attaché read the citation:

> To Colonel David Marcus, US Army, Honorary Commander of the Military Division of the Most Excellent Order of the British Empire. In 1943, Colonel Marcus became the first chief of Planning Branch of Civil Affairs Division, US War Department. His able work in the fields of combined planning for military government, from the time the problem first arose, was characterized by a cooperative and liberal outlook which paved the road for Anglo-American agreement on many complex problems.

Mickey recounted the details of the ceremony which began promptly at 4:15 on April 20 at the British Embassy on Massachusetts Avenue. When Ambassador Lord Iverchapell draped the pretty blue ribbon around the American colonel's neck, he admired the recipient's "fine coat of tan." Mickey said nothing but remarked afterwards, "Gosh, it was a temptation to explain that I got it dodging British patrols in Palestine." The two men did not speak any further, the ambassador did not ask where the colonel got his tan, and if he had any knowledge of Mickey's prior two months' activity, there was no mention of it in Emma's accounts.[51]

Mickey told Limpus and Stevenson that when he was in Washington for the ceremony, he met with General Omar Bradley, their old math teacher, recently appointed the seventeenth chief of staff of the United States Army. After a brief non classified discussion of the Pentagon's assessment of the situation in Palestine, accompanied by Stevenson, Bradley asked, "How long can the Jewish army hold out?" Mickey answered, "Since we're not an army, but a nation at arms, we'll only be defeated when we are destroyed." In that response, one can hear the cadet still going the extra round with an injured arm.[52]

Dinner at Emmanuel Neuman's apartment, New York, April 30, 1948

A few days before Mickey went to Washington, April 18, Emma took a rare sick day from work and visited her doctor, from whom she received a diagnosis of nervous exhaustion. Unfortunately, things didn't get better. Mickey persisted in constant work and socializing with family, friends, and even strangers, spending time with Emma only in rare moments between. At this point she was finding it increasingly difficult to feign interest in her husband's singular topic of conversation, or even remain civil. Looking back at that time and thinking of the affection and warmth Mickey had expressed toward her in his letters, Emma was struck by the contrast between their relationship on paper and during the time of his brief return to America, one "full of indecision, dismay and the knowledge that we were hurting each other." Obviously, Emma didn't want him to go back to Palestine, but he argued that what he would be doing would be no different than what the foreigners fighting for America had done during our fight for independence. Mickey had written in February, "I doubt if I have ever done anything—anywhere—any time, which is more worthwhile." In other letters, and since his return, he had confided that the situation was desperate and despaired over how little help was coming from the outside, as well as expressing his frustration with the level of responsibility he had been given without authority to change things.[53]

After the OBE ceremony in Washington, and just before returning to Palestine, Emma and Mickey attended a farewell dinner in his honor at Dr. Emanuel Neumann's house in New York City on April 30. Neumann was a prominent American Zionist leader who had aided Haganah efforts for years and was a friend of Sharett. Also attending were Bartley Crum, publisher of a leftist newsweekly called *PM* and an adviser to the White House pushing for recognition, and Melvin Krulewitz. Mel was also a boxing champion and a Marine war hero of World War I, and had just returned from a tour of Palestine, accompanied by former army staff officer and Bulova heir Harry Henschel. The trip was arranged by Kolleck with the Pentagon's approval but was not related to recruitment, and Krulewitz made an unofficial report to his friends at Marine headquarters when he returned. Neither man had made it to Shamir's final lists for possible staff officers, and by this time the search for an American general was over. The Haganah was focused on specific military skills, pilots and ground crew, most of all, not command officers.[54]

After dinner, the discussion turned to prospects for victory, delay, or compromise on independence, and concern for the helpless who might be left without a defense. Mickey expressed optimism and dismissed delay or surrender. Emma wrote in a letter describing the exchange that he said, "After two thousand years of suffering and waiting history is knocking at our door. If we don't open the door, we may never get another chance. We must try. We must put up a good fight."[55]

The next day, May 2, Mickey packed his army canvas bag and put on his rubber-soled field shoes, comfortable in any terrain. This time Emma's brother Alfred Chaisson drove them to the recently renamed Fiorella La Guardia Airport in honor of The Hat, who had given Mickey his first important job. No one talked, and the atmosphere was strained. At the departure gate, Mickey turned to Emma, promised her he'd be back in June, and kissed her in a final embrace. Then he slowly walked on the tarmac to the DC-3 airplane, climbed the portable steps, turned back, and waved goodbye.[56]

CHAPTER 6

"Aluf Michael Stone" and the Siege of Jerusalem

> He was like a shot in the arm for the army, injecting confidence, and optimism. He strengthened in each man he met faith in our special abilities and his stamp of approval meant a great deal to us. He taught us to learn the weaknesses of the enemy and to use this knowledge to our advantage. He pressed us to consider the practical side of military organization. We were in awe of his quick grasp of situations, his courage and humanity. He was a most unconventional regular soldier.
>
> —Yaacov Dori, Israel Defense Forces chief of staff, 1949

Haganah HQ, Red House, Tel Aviv, May 10, 1948

Mickey got back to Tel Aviv at the end of the first week in May via Czechoslovakia, flying on a C-47 piloted by a South African volunteer, with Teddy Kolleck, some Haganah members, and other volunteers on board. They landed at a small strip outside Tel Aviv because the main airport at the town of Lydda was no longer secure with the final British withdrawal only a week away. After decamping at a safe house, Mickey checked in at the Red House to catch up with developments since his departure.[1] Soon thereafter, on May 6, Yigal Allon, in command of Yiftach Brigade, took Mickey to the outskirts of Malkiya, an Arab village that the Yiftach Brigade was about to attack. Mickey was not pleased to find the soldiers lounging about, lying on the ground, spread out over a large strip of open, level ground while awaiting the order to form ranks and assemble. Looking nervously at his watch with a half hour to go, Mickey turned to Allon.

"Look, Eagle, those men must get on the trucks now. They're not going to make it."

"Give them a quarter of an hour more," Allon said.

It was the first time Mickey had observed a brigade-size formation of the Jewish army, and he was anxious. Allon later admitted he wasn't sure he could pull off the mission at hand. Suddenly a whistle rang out, followed by shouts. Minutes later the brigade's trucks were loaded with troops, their morale high, singing robustly. Mickey, smiling broadly and heartened by the smooth assembly, quoted Patton. "An army that knows how to sing before a battle," he encouraged Eagle, "knows how to win it too." Allon remembered that moment as the one in which he had come to believe that Mickey Stone truly understood the soldiers of Israel.[2]

On May 10 David Ben-Gurion recorded in his diary that he had lunch with Mickey, for the first time since his return, during which they discussed Mickey's contacts in Washington, especially with Hilldring, who had advised his protégé, "You should hold on to the borders as of May 15 and be prepared for any eventuality. If there is no outside threat or attack across these borders, then you should be prepared to cross them ourselves; otherwise, we should stay put.' "[3]

Two days later, on May 12, Truman met in the Oval Office with Secretary of State George Marshall; his assistant secretary, Robert Lovett; and White House domestic adviser Clark Clifford. In one of the most examined episodes in US diplomatic history of the second half of the twentieth century, Marshall openly accused Clifford of pandering to American Jews for domestic political reasons. He threatened Truman with a breach, specifically pledging not to vote for him in that year's election and making that stance public, in essence accusing the commander-in-chief of putting domestic political considerations above the national security interests of the country. As reported, Truman betrayed no outward emotion, and did not commit one way or another to recognition of the state of Israel in the meeting. Over

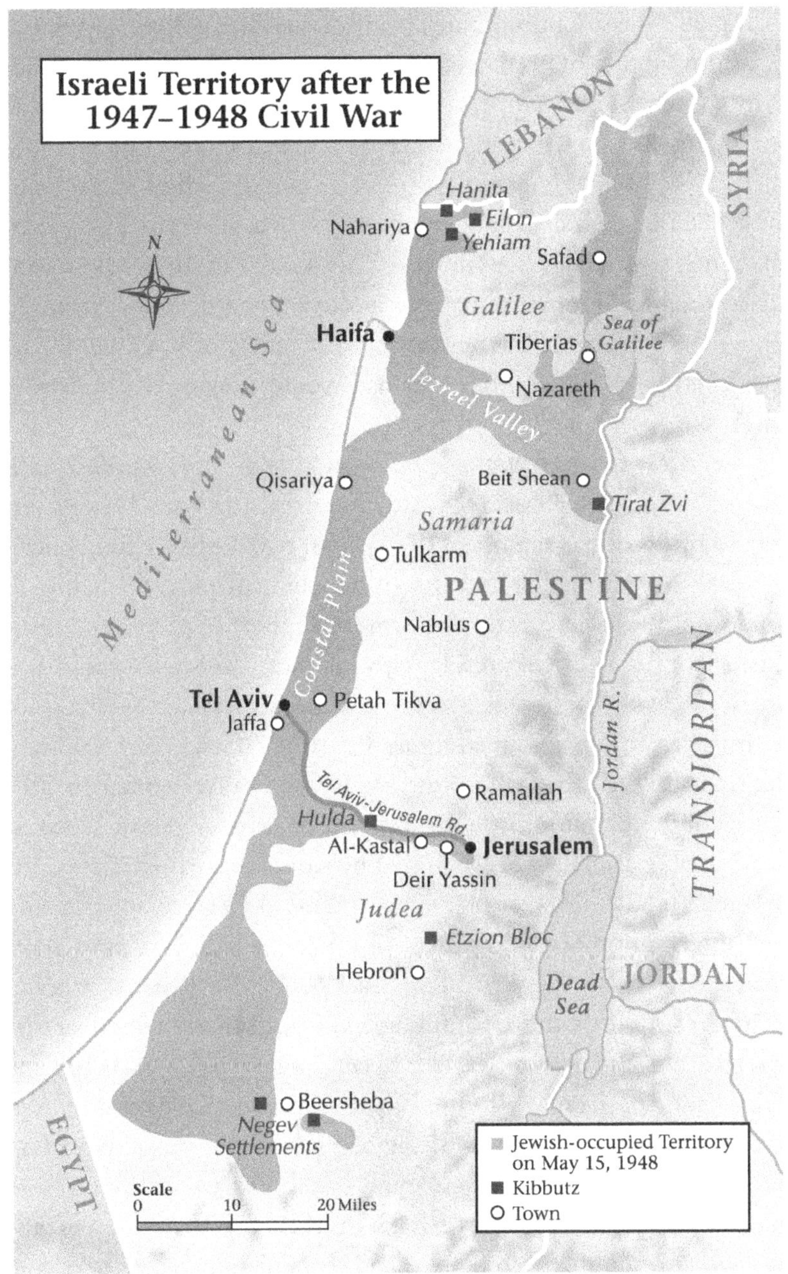

Fig. 17. Civil war in Palestine from partition to independence, November 1947–May 14, 1948. HistoryNet

the next few days, Clifford and Lovett discussed conflicting views in the White House, State, Defense, and intelligence community with the intent of calming tempers. The day of the meeting Zionist leader Weitzman wrote to Truman, "I deeply hope that the United States, which under your leadership has done so much to find a just solution to the Palestine situation, will promptly recognize the Provisional Government of the new Jewish state. The world, I think, would regard it as especially appropriate that the greatest living democracy should be the first to welcome the newest into the family of nations." In the end, Lovett told Clifford that Marshall would "stay out of the entire matter."[4]

It was no secret that winning Governor Tom Dewey's New York was crucial for the Democrats in a tight presidential race. Dewey, undeterred by his defeat against FDR in 1944, was the likely Republican candidate that November and already attacking Truman for failing to support his own Democratic platform for support of partition. When Marshall threatened the president to his face, the stakes could not have been greater for Truman in the upcoming election. Every diplomat involved in the administration's Palestine effort, except for John Hilldring, backed Marshall's position. It was unprecedented for this tightly controlled faithful public servant, revered by many, to be so disturbed about a policy decision that he would make such threats. At the Pentagon, the newly created Department of Defense opposed any direct intervention or commitment of US forces and warned of other strategic risks of an aggressive pro-Israel policy. No one was arguing for an expansion of the US military's mission in the region or the deployment of the necessary forces to support it.[5]

The leaders of the newly formed Central Intelligence Agency (CIA), most vocally the Office of Strategic Services (OSS) veterans among them, endorsed Marshall's view, some—such as Kermit Roosevelt—doing so publicly in the press, relying on their British colleagues' advice. The surrounding Arab nations and their allies in the Arab League openly threatened to intervene militarily and destroy the Jewish state as soon as the partition resolution had passed. Since then, they had been getting ready. By the time Ben-Gurion was readying his independence speech, hours before the end of the British mandate, the Egyptian air force was preparing to bomb Tel Aviv.[6]

Fig. 18. David Ben-Gurion reads Israel's Declaration of Independence, May 14, 1948. *Newsweek*

On Friday, May 14, 1948, at 4:00 p.m. local time, the leaders of the Yishuv, journalists, foreign observers, and a few invited guests gathered downtown in Tel Aviv for an important announcement. Days later, *Newsweek Magazine* described the proceedings:

> A small man with shaggy white hair stood in the main gallery of the modern, two-story Tel Aviv Museum of Art on Rothschild Boulevard. He spoke slowly: "We hereby proclaim the establishment of the Jewish State in Palestine, to be called Israel." Thus David Ben-Gurion, chairman of the Palestine National Council and now Premier of Israel, brought to a climax the half-century struggle of the Jews to recreate their ancient homeland. Dr. Chaim Weizmann became president of the Council of Government of the new State. . . . That night Tel Aviv was blacked out, but behind

> the cafe doors the celebrations went on. Just before midnight, when Israel became officially established, doors were flung open and rejoicing crowds again poured into the streets. The news of the United States recognition had just reached Tel Aviv.[7]

The Israel Declaration of Independence is based on the indigenous and unbroken physical, historical, and cultural connection of the Jewish people to the land of Israel, and the vision of a modern democratic state deriving legitimacy by the will of its people. While the Jewish roots were established in archaeology and the Bible, the horrors of the Holocaust proved the need for a homeland as a refuge for Jews and guarantor of Jewish life by force of arms in a hostile world. The document declared a Jewish state in the land of Israel, to be known as the State of Israel, in accordance with UN Resolution 181 of November 29, 1947, which recommended the establishment of separate Jewish and Arab states in the former British mandate of Palestine.

The declaration outlined the principles on which the State of Israel would be based: equality of social and political rights regardless of religion, race, or gender; freedom of religion, conscience, language, education, and culture. It called for peace with its neighbors and appealed to the Jewish people in the diaspora to rally around the new state, support it, and contribute to its development. Nowhere in the document does the word *God* appear; instead, the signers, thirty-seven in all and representing the full array of political affiliations and communities within the Jewish population, relied on the "the Rock of Israel" (Tzur Yisrael) to protect the new state. As full-scale conventional war loomed literally the next morning, the declaration laid the foundation for Israel as a modern, liberal, democratic Western state.[8]

That night Ben-Gurion wrote in his diary, "The whole world was sure that within ten days, two weeks at the most, not a soul would be alive in Israel."[9] That is not how Mickey, who attended the ceremony, saw it as he wrote to Emma two days later, describing the exhilarating moment of independence in the last letter she would receive from him:

As you can imagine, I have been busier than ever before in my life and the results are most gratifying. I was in the north during the victories there and returned just in time to hear Ben-Gurion declare the State of Israel. My eyes filled and I embraced you a thousand times, as I know the two weeks ahead will be most difficult. All here wept with joy at President Truman's recognition of the state.

The Egyptian army has invaded, Syrian army is on the move, Iraqi army is concentrated. King Abdullah's forces are across the Jordan River. If our new army arrives on time, be assured of victory. Everyone is brave, courageous, and determined to stop the onslaught. Sweetheart, my dear, it was the correct and proper thing that I came. We will lose much in matters such as money,

Fig. 19. US president Harry Truman, the most important Christian in two thousand years of Jewish history. White House

etc., but I know that I shall come home safe to you, with both of us knowing that the sacrifices made were justified.[10]

Amazingly, despite the State Department's outright opposition, the skepticism of US military leaders, the best advice from his intelligence community, and pressure from Great Britain and his onetime Senate colleagues, Harry Truman granted almost immediate de facto recognition of the State of Israel. As biographers tell it, this was not least because of commitment to and warm feelings toward Eddie Jacobson, his Jewish friend and persistent visitor at the White House during that period, whose friendship with him had begun during World War I in Battery D, 129th Field Artillery, of the Missouri National Guard.

At 6:11 p.m. EST, the US sent a telegram: "This Government has been informed that a Jewish state has been proclaimed in Palestine, and recognition been requested by the provisional government thereof. The United States recognizes the provisional government as the de facto authority of the State of Israel."

At exactly that same time, the State Department negotiator at the UN, Warren Austin, was in the middle of yet another debate on the Palestine crisis when he received word of Truman's recognition. He angrily walked out, and Marshall had to send a staffer to prevent the entire US delegation from resigning in protest and sympathy with him. US policy did not change dramatically, and the arms embargo would continue until the end of the fighting in early 1949, but this single decision gave instant diplomatic legitimacy to the State of Israel and added weight to the Balfour Declaration and the UN partition vote. Harry S. Truman of Missouri established a special relationship with Israel literally at its birth—becoming a godfather of sorts—and remains the most important president since Israel's founding, and the most important Christian in two thousand years of Jewish history.[11]

After Egyptian aircraft attacked Tel Aviv that night, on the first morning of independence, the regular armies of Egypt, Transjordan, Syria, Lebanon, and Iraq—some thirty-five thousand soldiers of varying quality and readiness—attacked Israel from multiple directions. With no common objective, or war plan, and a divided and uncoordinated command, the disparate forces occupied the areas set aside for the Arab part of the partitioned state. In unsynchronized attacks, these forces attacked frontally, and when checked attempted to isolate, besiege, and destroy the Jewish settlements. Their initial efforts to occupy Jewish territory were slowed by Haganah, Palmach, and Irgun detachments and civilian volunteers defending Jewish villages all over Palestine. The governments of the invading states and their mostly Sunni religious leaders openly declared their intentions in explicit and bloody detail to strangle the infant nation at birth and torture, rape, and murder its inhabitants. Even in those first hours of Israeli history, the Jews believed their enemies' threats, their issuance prompting many of their neighbors, some of whom now hired unemployed Nazi officers, openly to cheer.[12]

The most immediate threat was that posed by the Egyptian army poised along the Mediterranean coast in Gaza. The day after the declaration, May 15, 1948, a large Egyptian mechanized regiment of six thousand soldiers and fifty armored vehicles crossed the border and began moving north along the coastal road. Another column of Muslim Brotherhood militia moved to take the large town of Beersheva and flank the Jews.[13] On an earlier visit to the Negev with Shamir to inspect Haganah forces and assess the defensive preparations and fortifications, Mickey met with Negev Brigade commander Nahum Sarig at his HQ. They were not impressed:

> We sat with him for two or three hours, heard his positions, the arrangements Sarig made to familiarize himself with the terrain and what he planned. Sarig bombarded Mickey about how well-prepared he was with "I have this" and "I have that" and Mickey said nothing out of politeness. When we left, Mickey said to me, what I believe was the most critical statement he made about a commander, "he does not know how weak they really are."[14] But understanding how desperate their situation was, he promised Sarig, "When the showdown comes to free the South, I'll be there with you."[15]

Now the defending Negev Brigade, consisting of two small battalions comprising some nine hundred men, was exhausted from months of fighting with local Muslim Brotherhood gangs and other Sunni militias prior to independence. So far, they had managed to hold on to the more than two dozen kibbutzim in the Negev with tolerable losses.[16] Chastened and now unsure how best to defend against the coming Egyptian attack, Sarig requested that Haganah HQ send a liaison officer to assess the situation and advise him. The Egyptians had already attacked two Jewish settlements—one of them Kibbutz Yad Mordechai ("hand of Mordechai"), founded by survivors of the Warsaw Ghetto and named for one of the uprising's fallen commanders, Mordechai Anielewicz—on the road to Tel Aviv using artillery and armored vehicles.[17]

While these assaults were beaten off by the civilian defenders of the villages and units of the Negev Brigade, the Israeli general staff took special note of Sarig's request. They were alarmed that the Egyptians, having bypassed the besieged villages, had continued moving north toward Jewish settlements in central Israel. After the past skirmishes and redeployments that took some of their defenders away for the next stage of the war, the communities in the Negev were not well defended. They had no heavy weapons and were ill prepared to face the mechanized forces maneuvering toward them.[18]

In response, on May 17, Ben-Gurion dispatched Mickey by small plane south. Still under cover and introducing himself to soldiers in the field as Mickey Stone, he got an update from Sarig and his officers, reviewed the maps, and decided to attach himself to an infantry company under the command of Captain Aharon Spector, already deployed in the field along the likely route of the Egyptian advance. After spending the night at Sarig's headquarters, Mickey and his assigned aide, Haganah lieutenant Alex Broida, the husband of Irene, Mickey's secretary and driver, arrived at Spector's HQ near Kibbutz Negba. Alex was working in New York during Mickey' visit to the city in April and came back with him as an aide when Mickey returned in early May.

As their jeep pulled up, the Egyptians, having spotted Spector's trucks grouped together, bombed the vehicles, causing major damage. The troops were frozen with fear in the face of strafing Egyptian Spitfires and light tanks and armored cars advancing under a rolling artillery barrage. Fortunately, a newly arrived shipment of armored cars equipped with machine guns that Mickey had directed to the Negev Brigade before his departure were not damaged.[19]

Mickey urged Spector and his platoon leaders to take the initiative: "Act with what you've got. Shoot the planes down with rifles, attack the columns with small mobile units, hit-and-run attacks in surprise night-time raids. Jeeps will do the job until we get tanks. David did it with a slingshot, didn't he?" Famed photojournalist Robert Capa, on the scene of the skirmish on assignment for *Illustrated* weekly, described how a Palmach woman shot down an Egyptian plane with a burst from her Sten gun. Mickey wrote Emma about the same episode, and she wrote that "if he hadn't seen it with his own eyes, he wouldn't have believed it."[20]

Later, when they were alone, Mickey chewed out Spector in old infantry fashion for having parked the vehicles together and told him to get them scattered and hidden. Returning to the soldiers, he then gave an impromptu field demonstration with a stick, drawing diagrams in the sand to illustrate how to properly employ the automatic weapons mounted on the newly arrived armored vehicles. This type of vignette appears in several accounts, along with Mickey getting right down in the dirt with the soldiers, and those who had this firsthand instruction never forgot the impact of these battlefield talks about tactics and weapons. As Shamir noted in explaining the appeal that Mickey had for professionals and soldier in the field, he knew the basics about the military, and years of top-level staff-experience "did not detract from, or damage his ability to hold a rifle, lift it, roll it and aim it well, to demonstrate, feel and check. These are basic things in army life. He could do it himself, and he could put the theory into action, and this gave him a common language with all professionals and could speak to everyone at their level."[21]

A week after he arrived for his tour of the Negev front, on May 23, Mickey sent a telegram to IDF headquarters, saying, "The situation is critical but there is no reason to panic." He reported that the kibbutz at Yad Mordechai was being attacked by an Egyptian battalion. Defended by its eighty inhabitants and a platoon of the Negev Brigade, it had suffered twenty killed and thirty wounded. An Egyptian motorized brigade had renewed attacks on two other kibbutzim in the Negev. Ben-Gurion recorded in his diary Stone's report on the active defense tactics employed around the besieged communities on the road to Tel Aviv: "Our men went on the offensive and inflicted heavy losses on the Egyptians, who sustained about one hundred casualties, several tanks. They retreated. Stone demands three hundred rifles, 150 Stens, machine guns, mortars, Piats, flamethrowers and grenades. Two hundred fifty Palmach have gone to the Negev, 70% armed with little training."[22]

Heartened by the results of a recent IAF air strike and the rising morale of the men, Mickey also suggested that the best course of action was to cut the Egyptian supply lines by attacking the rail line as well as the fortifications and artillery emplaced at Gaza. The rail line ran along the coast from Lebanon to Alexandria, and the Egyptians were using the southern portion to resupply their forward units. Mickey advised sending all available armored vehicles and artillery south. Now the Negev Brigade staff, with Mickey's advice, started to plan Operation Pharaoh, aimed at shifting the brigade to an offensive posture and changing the momentum. Having approved the operation, the Haganah general staff notified the Negev Brigade command staff on May 23 that it was planning an air strike the next day to strengthen the defensive capabilities of Yad Mordechai and the company defending it, but the air strike had to be postponed.[23]

Operation Pharaoh finally kicked off on May 25, the day after the fall of Yad Mordechai, with three objectives: to capture or destroy Egyptian artillery emplacements near Beit-Hanun, to neutralize Egyptian forces at Gaza's airport, and to immobilize artillery northeast of Gaza at Gaza-Ritz. This time the Negev Brigade requested an air strike by the Israeli air force, which was conducted later that night, destroying the enemy artillery at Beit-Hanun and the Gaza airfield. An attack on the Gaza-Ritz battery was canceled after a truck carrying explosives needed by the engineers overturned. A mixed tactical picture, Operation Pharaoh was nevertheless an operational success for the IDF, having exposed the eastern flank of the enemy attacking force, threatened the Egyptian lines of communication, and slowed the momentum of their advance. Instead of moving forward on May 27, the Egyptian high command ordered the spearhead infantry battalion to secure the city of Gaza and dig in. The forward momentum of the main southern thrust was checked two days later at Ashdod, just twenty miles from Tel Aviv, which also had a significant positive impact on the morale of the Jewish soldiers.[24]

The fictionalized account of this episode in the movie *Cast a Giant Shadow*, with Mickey organizing a mobile jeep and armored half-track ambush of Egyptians besieging a kibbutz, captures the essence of the actual battle. In fact, as described earlier, Mickey's arrival coincided with the delivery and deployment of a shipment of thirty radio- and machine-gun-equipped jeeps. These, combined with locally fashioned armored vehicles, provided mobility, firepower, and coordination. Heartened by the arrival of the jeeps and inspired by their adviser, who offered them encouragement and guidance, the remaining troops of the Negev Brigade did indeed change the course of the battle.[25]

Mickey returned to Tel-Aviv on May 28 after having inspired the Negev Brigade in the spirit of attack it would maintain throughout the rest of the war. As soon as he arrived at the Red House, he walked into Ben-Gurion's office unannounced and, holding up a hat and pair of trousers perforated by shrapnel and bullets, asked, "Boss, what do you think?" The older man was shocked until Mickey explained that the clothes had been hanging on the laundry line outside the assembly area when the attack happened.[26]

Mickey felt so optimistic about the posture of the Negev forces and the outcome of the offensive raids in Operation Pharoah that he told Ben-Gurion he thought they could even have captured Gaza with just 1,500 men, and that the Israeli forces need only to mount another raid and to take the necessary weapons from the Egyptians to accomplish just that.[27]

Aluf Michael Stone, commander, Jewish Forces, Jerusalem Front, May 28, 1948

While Mickey had been busy in the south, Jewish operations near Jerusalem had not been going well. Under the UN plan for Palestine, the city of Jerusalem and its suburbs was supposed to be part of a special international zone administered by an international body, not part of either the planned Arab or the Jewish states. After the outbreak of conventional war on May 15, however, the importance of taking control of Jerusalem with its hundred thousand Jews was increasingly clear. Both the Jewish quarter of the Old City in the eastern sector and the newer Jewish neighborhoods in the west came under sniper, artillery, and infantry attack.

Heavy house-to-house and room-to-room fighting between Jewish and Arab forces had raged in the city even before the formal declaration of independence. When it seemed likely that the Jewish forces would gain the upper hand, King Abdullah of Jordan ordered the Arab Legion, Transjordan's army, to enter Jerusalem on May 17, 1948. The unit was led by British officers under the command of John Bagot Glubb, a British lieutenant general whose résumé Mickey knew well. The Legion was a formidable foe, with the Jordanian forces eventually seizing the Jewish Quarter of the Old City and today's mostly Arab East Jerusalem. Some fifteen hundred Jewish civilians living there were expelled, the soldiers and military age men taken as prisoners. While most of the Jewish population in Palestine lived in areas along the Mediterranean coast, the Jewish residents in greater Jerusalem now found themselves in territory under Arab control or under constant threat of being taken by a foreign army.

On May 16, Mickey responded to a request by Ben-Gurion to advise on what it would take to secure the supply route to Jerusalem from the east. After consulting with Yitzhak Rabin, commander of the Harel Brigade, which had fought over the road for months and held the eastern part of the main road, Mickey presented a plan to the Haganah general staff, offering specific organizational recommendations for the immediate creation of a mechanized infantry brigade that could act as an offensive force. This suggestion reflected his original thinking in his earlier memo to the Haganah general staff in mid-March. On May 16, Ben-Gurion recorded Stone's plan in his diary:

> Two battalions should entrench themselves along the ridges to prevent the enemy from reaching the road. The enemy has four 75-mm. field guns, and we need similar weapons for operations. Each company should be supplied with four mortars and four Piats. The road must be kept in good condition so an engineering platoon and four armored cars should be ready to deal with problems arising out of attacks, roadblocks, or enemy ground action. There should be a strong, motorized striking force at *Sha-ar Hagai* gorge to defend convoys should they be attacked. The convoys should travel only at night. The General Staff accepted the Stone plan.[28]

The plan didn't mention the looming threat on the western part of the road, but it was too late anyway. The next day, May 17, an Arab Legion infantry regiment occupied the highway crossroads village of Latrun, west of Jerusalem past the gorge, effectively cutting off Tel Aviv. Legion troops took over the high ground, dominated by a British-built fortified police station called a Tegart fort that sat at the Latrun crossroads and put the main road in Palestine, linking the coast with Jerusalem, under direct fire. During the fighting before independence, Latrun had been occupied by Palmach forces, which had mistakenly withdrawn before May 15 without any forces to relieve them.

As pressure built to do something about the intensifying siege of Jerusalem and morale began to flag, Ben-Gurion heeded Mickey's advice to organize an offensive formation able to intervene in the battle at the decisive point by establishing the Seventh Armored Brigade on May 14, 1948. Honoring his previous assurance that Shamir would be given a combat assignment, Ben-Gurion selected him to command the new unit, effectively a strategic reserve, and named fellow Jewish Brigade veteran Chaim Laskov to muster and command its main striking force, the Seventy-Third Armored Battalion, the latter unit to be built around a shipment of infantry fighting vehicles due to land at Haifa imminently. The NCOs and junior officers would come from Laskov's training program. Since the mobilized manpower was already distributed in other units, Shamir had to scrounge for men and equipment, including a muster from a contingent of recently arrived immigrants speaking a babel of languages, but rarely Hebrew, a minority of whom had some military training.[29]

The new brigade would never train together at any level of command, was deficient in every category of equipment, lacked basic supplies, actual armor (tanks), or any heavy weapons such as mortars, howitzers, or anti-tank weapons, and had only a few machine guns—and no intelligence on the enemy. Its staff, bolstered by thirty-year-old former British Thirtieth Corps intelligence officer Vivian (Chaim) Herzog, came together in a matter of days. Like their men, the officers had never worked together or trained at any level as a staff or command group, and they were in no way ready for the combat they would soon face.[30]

Latrun, Ayalon Valley, Mid-May 1948

The village of Latrun lies in the southern Ayalon Valley, where the Judean Hills and coastal plain meet, two kilometers southwest of the New Testament town of Emmaus. The name Latrun is a distortion of the French *le toron des chevaliers* (the tower of the knights), recalling a crusader fortress atop the hill east of the fort. The name is also associated with Saint Dimas, the repentant thief crucified alongside Jesus, because of a mistaken similarity between *le toron* and *latro*, Latin for "thief."

Latrun was fought over by Joshua, the Hasmoneans, and Roman legions in two Jewish revolts; the Byzantines and Arabs battled near it or used it as a base in their conquest of the land the Romans renamed Palestina. At the base of the heights around the village, the main road between Jerusalem and Tel Aviv runs through the ascent of Beth-Horon to the northern Judean Hills. It has always dominated access to

Jerusalem. Taken in June–July 1099 by Duke Godfrey de Bouillon of Lorraine from Fatimid forces, the village of Latrun fell to Saladin less than a century later, in October 1187. Eventually Palestine became a province of the Ottoman Empire, which ruled it for more than four hundred years. Ascetic French Trappist monks built a monastery there in 1890 that is still known for its fine wines.

During the conquest of Palestine in 1917, Lord Allenby launched a two-pronged attack against Jerusalem from Latrun, one via the gorge of Bab el-Wad and the other near Beth-Horon, which resulted in the capture of the city. Allenby entered on foot, as a pilgrim, not a conqueror. To the northwest of Latrun, the British Mandatory police built one of their cookie-cutter Tegart forts, a heavily fortified police installation with thick walls that dominated the crossroads near Latrun as well as the adjacent pumping station of the Jerusalem water pipeline.

In World War II the British established a prisoner-of-war camp next to the pumping station, and later they set up a detention camp for Jews along the Gaza road, where Haganah, Palmach, and political leaders of the Yishuv, including Jewish Agency and other civil society groups, were interned. In May, after the declaration of independence and the British evacuation, several days passed before the Arab Legion occupied all the key terrain features. The Haganah did nothing after clearing the bottleneck at Bab el-Wad.[31]

By May 20, the Arab Legion Fourth Regiment under Colonel Habis al-Majali took control of the five-kilometer section of the road between Latrun and Bab el-Wad. To the east, units of the Second Legion Regiment blocked the road farther east at Biddu. Although Jerusalem had been cut off from Tel Aviv several times during the civil war phase of the war, that was sporadic, the result of uncoordinated attacks and retreats by irregular militia forces. Now the road between Tel Aviv and Jerusalem was controlled by a professional army rather than local militia and tribal gangs, and the supply convoys were effectively stopped.[32]

Frustrated by mounting Jewish losses, the immanent fall of the Old City, followed by the capture of the Etzion block of villages and massacre of its residents, Ben-Gurion decided to take Latrun by frontal assault. There was bitter opposition on operational grounds from Yadin and Shamir, who pleaded for more time to get ready. Ben-Gurion would not yield to military advice or facts and ordered his brand-new brigade to take the fort and open the road to Jerusalem.

The first attack, called Bin Nun Alef after Joshua bin-Nun, the conqueror of Jericho, was a coordinated effort from west and east by elements of two brigades. The main thrust, from the west, would be carried out by the newly organized Seventh Armored Brigade, commanded by Colonel Shlomo Shamir. The Seventh Brigade's assault on Latrun and the nearby crest would be executed by two battalions—an Alexandroni Brigade battalion attached to the Seventh Armored and led by Major Zvi Germann, and the newly raised Seventy-Third Armored Battalion, commanded by Major Chaim Laskov. Some of the immigrant soldiers were World War II veterans who had served in the armies of their countries of origin, but they had only a brief training period together and with their Haganah leaders before this operation.[33]

In the secondary attack from the east, elements of the Harel Brigade would pin down as many as possible of Latrun commander Majali's troops to keep them away from the main effort. Once Shamir's brigade had achieved its initial objective of occupying the Latrun crest, the Harel troops would occupy the Latrun–Bab el-Wad section of the Jerusalem to Tel Aviv Road, then move north to secure the rugged hills between there and on to Ramallah, a large Arab city north of Jerusalem.

The assault was planned for shortly after midnight, in the first hours of May 25, but it was delayed by the late arrival of the Alexandroni battalion, which did not manage to begin its movement until 4:00 a.m. By this time, a previously scheduled but premature bombardment from the handful of Israel's very few 65mm howitzers had alerted the legion, so Majali's troops, far from being surprised, were ready to fight. As the offensive proceeded, both Israeli battalions suffered very heavy casualties, particularly the men of the Alexandroni. Bin Nun Alef ended in defeat for the Israelis, and an Arab Legion company took Radar Hill overlooking the road between Abu Ghosh and Biddu. Taken by surprise, the Harel men on the hill were driven off, and the legion consolidated their blocking position to the east at Latrun.[34]

That same day, May 26, 1948, less than two weeks after independence, the Israel Defense Forces was founded by ordnance and officially established in an Order of the Day on May 31, 1948. Signed by Prime Minister and Defense Minister David Ben-Gurion, it stated that the IDF would represent the exclusive military force of the State of Israel, that all other military forces would be dissolved, and that Israel's army would be made up of air, naval, and ground forces, not separate services but a single integrated armed force. All IDF soldiers would pledge allegiance to the protection of the State of Israel, its laws, and its authorities upon recruitment.[35]

Despite the official establishment of the Jewish army, the mood at the Red House had now reached a new low. The Jewish population of Jerusalem was starving, the first attempt to lift the blockade having failed with heavy loss of life.[36] Two days later, on May 28, Mickey came back from Gaza after Operation Pharoah. Faced with an increasingly dire situation in Jerusalem, Ben-Gurion made a dramatic decision. He knew he needed a commander to take charge, rally the troops, and inspire them to try again to take Latrun. This he decided to do despite the resistance of Yadin and the field commanders, who insisted that they needed more time to regroup, and that a weak and hurried effort would be suicidal. Ben-Gurion remained adamant: "I sent Stone to Latrun to speed up the capture of the town and the liberation of Jerusalem. With Yigal's approval, I have appointed Stone as commander of the Jerusalem Front. He will oversee the Harel Brigade plus troops serving under David Shaltiel and Shlomo Shamir."[37]

Ben-Gurion had ordered the formation of the IDF's first division-sized force, and the Jerusalem Front would become the forerunner and model for the IDF Central Command, responsible for the security of Jerusalem and the territories taken some twenty years later in war in 1967.

Both Yisrael Galili, now chief of staff, and Yigael Yadin, operations chief, agreed with Ben-Gurion that Mickey was the best (and only) choice to command the forces trying to open the supply route to Jerusalem's desperate Jewish inhabitants. None of the other prospective choices, the other brigade commanders, commanded persuasive support after the initial setback at Latrun. Mickey would oversee operations, and when the Seventh Armored broke through and linked up with the other units, Mickey would have operational control over the division from his own headquarters. In appreciation for what Mickey had already done for him, and no doubt to signal his own place in future military operations, Ben-Gurion declared that Michael Stone, already an important unifying figure, would henceforth hold the rank of *aluf*. The word itself has been variously translated as head of tribe, supreme commander, or champion, equivalent to what we call a general in other languages. No actual rank structure existed in the IDF at that point, and none was mentioned in Ben-Gurion's diary until after the first truce.[38]

The question of whether the rank of *aluf* even existed in the Jewish army at that time, or whether Mickey—or, more accurately, Michael Stone—technically held that rank before the formal commissioning process of the State of Israel, persisted after his death. None of it dented the image nor diminished the reference. On the scale between technical detail and tolerable exaggeration, the claim of generalship tilts to the latter. The evidence overwhelmingly argues that David Marcus officially held the rank of *aluf* in his own name only a full year after his death.[39] In this regard, he was exactly like his associates in the Haganah, all of whom had lived underground with code names. Had he lived longer, it would be impossible to imagine Mickey Marcus taking an oath of service to a foreign government, or honoring Ben-Gurion's demand to take the legal name Michael Stone, as the other *alufs* did. It is nevertheless possible that Mickey and Ben-Gurion could have found a way to work together.[40]

The passion and sincerity with which Mickey held his opinions and his position of moral authority within the Jewish army was palpable.

The other commanders knew he had not been a combat general, but whether they recognized the symbolic nature of Ben-Gurion's creation of the new rank or not, they accepted Mickey's authority as a rally point, which he knew how to wield, doing so quietly, carefully, and professionally. As a reserve army officer employed as a consultant, Mickey observed certain boundaries he would not cross, including revealing secret US information or trying to discover the secrets of his employers. He exchanged and received intelligence information from his friends and contacts in Washington, but there is no evidence that he was a spy for Washington, despite some uninformed family gossip or other hearsay that gained credence by persistence.

David Ben-Gurion, a student of history, knew that the last soldier in sacred texts called *aluf* was Judah the Hasmonean, leader of the revolutionary Maccabees (hammers) in the second century BC. Along with the others in his family, Judah led the still-observant Jews against their foreign Greek overlords in the land that had been called Judea since Alexander the Great. The local Jewish Hellenistic, and assimilationist, collaborators did not oppose the desecration of the Second Temple in Jerusalem in the interests of order. Some two millennia later, charged with overseeing a conflict that was part fight for freedom from colonial British rule, part civil war with hostile Arab neighbors, and part the long struggle for Jewish religious and political freedom, Ben-Gurion chose the honorific title of *aluf* for Michael Stone. If anyone needed a miracle and a new Hanukkah to give Jewish sovereignty a chance, it was Ben-Gurion. And like the hero of the menorah, Aluf Michael Stone would not live to see a Jewish army parade through David's capital, but he became an enduring mythic hero of two peoples, in a sense, one-upping Judah.

On May 28, the day of his appointment as *aluf* and front commander, Mickey arrived with his aide Lieutenant Alex Broida at Seventh Armored headquarters at Kibbutz Hulda, just a few kilometers west of Latrun, where he planned to stay during the next stage of the fighting. He did not form a headquarters staff at that time, although planning began and candidates for staff positions were being considered. On

May 30, forces spearheaded by Shamir's Seventh Armored, now under Mickey's command, attacked Latrun again in Operation Bin Nun Bet. The plan for this action, already formed before Mickey arrived, was a refinement of the earlier effort, with Laskov's battalion again spearheading the attack but with Major Yaakov Peri's Fifty-Second Battalion from the Givati Brigade replacing the Alexandroni battalion to provide infantry support. Mickey attended the final orders group before the battle but offered no suggestions.[41]

The Givati battalion took Deir Ayub, a village north of the main road east of the fortifications at Latrun, without resistance, but as they moved toward Latrun they came under heavy Arab Legion fire and retreated without coordinating with Seventh Brigade HQ. Laskov's Seventy-Third, reinforced with newly arrived armored vehicles but uninformed about the Givati withdrawal from the area, attacked the Latrun police station. The assault penetrated the outer fortifications and was initially successful but faltered due to the Arab Legion's intense firepower from the high ground and lack of infantry support. Facing significant casualties, Laskov's battalion, the IDF's first armored unit, retreated again in the face of heavy losses, including the death of one company commander. Mickey was with Laskov at his command post, just fifteen hundred meters from the front lines, supporting him in the decision to withdraw, and later in a telegram to Haganah general staff Mickey wrote, "Was present on the battlefield from 11:00 to 05:00. Plan, Co-ordination, Artillery, OK—Performance by Armor excellent. Infantry disgraceful. 2 fighting companies will take Latrun." Shamir wasn't sure which infantry Mickey was talking about, but it was soon clear to everyone that taking Latrun was beyond their capabilities. Mickey's division had failed to capture Latrun—but what proved to be more important is that for the next ten days the main elements of the Arab Legion remained pinned down at Latrun in a defensive posture. Although the road to Jerusalem was still in enemy hands, the Arab Legion's momentum and the threat it posed to the coastal plain had, for the time being, been checked.

At first the situation remained grim; Ben-Gurion concluded that the Arab Legion would not only capture all of Jerusalem but use the momentum from its success at Latrun to capture more land and/or advance farther west toward the coast. On Mickey's recommendation, the Yiftach Brigade was attached to the Jerusalem Front to relieve the badly mauled Seventh Brigade. Military operations now began focusing on two efforts to lift the siege of Jerusalem: bypassing the main highway through an emerging engineering solution; and Operation Yoram, a third attack on Latrun.[42]

Road 7 and the Siege of Jerusalem, June 1948

During late May, several soldiers discovered a path in the hills south of the main road shielded by defilade from Latrun, linking several villages. Those accounts conflict, but soldiers in Palmach and the Haganah were familiar with potential alternate passages to Jerusalem before the Latrun battles, but none of them could support heavy traffic. The main road lay in a valley, but the footpaths in the hills along an alternate southern route might offer a way to establish a new continuous road link to Jerusalem, thereby bypassing the Arab Legion forces holding Latrun.[43]

There were serious engineering hurdles in the grade differences between the two most promising stretches of the bypass, including a steep drop from one to the other, but Seventh Armored engineers agreed that the gap could be made into a usable road. Stone wanted to see for himself, and after Bin Nun Bet he conducted a personal reconnaissance, along with Chaim Herzog and Amos Chorev. Upon returning from his reading of the ground to the Red House, with preliminary construction underway, he backed the Seventh Armored effort wholeheartedly, working to secure construction equipment and labor (mostly from civilians in the city) to construct the new road. Meanwhile foot traffic and hauling supplies would continue on a barely passable temporary track through the hills.[44]

The new route would run south of the main road connecting Beit Susin to the stretch of road at Bab el-Wad and straight to Jerusalem.

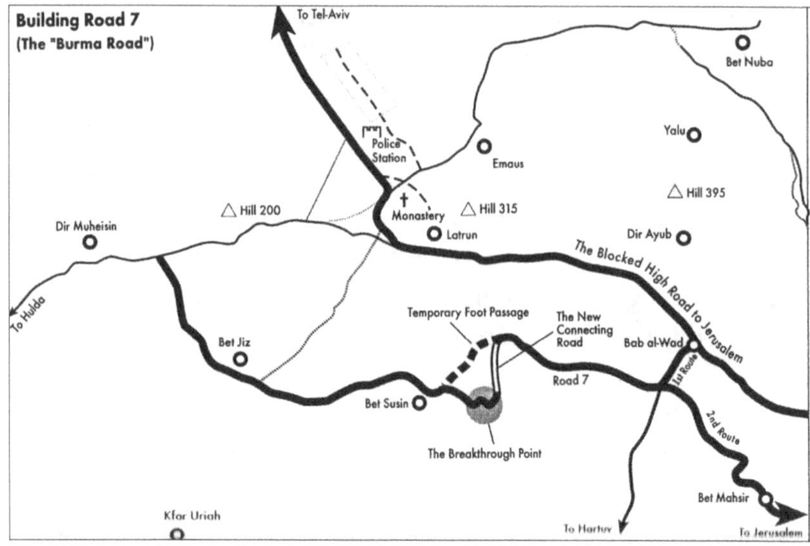

Fig. 20. Latrun area and Road 7, the Burma Road, 1948. Shamir, *The Battle for Jerusalem*

After the first few site-preparation visits along the proposed route and confirmation that access points could support equipment, construction began directed by Shamir's engineers on what was soon christened "the Burma Road," after the famous supply road built to link Burma and China in World War II. The irony was not lost on the British journalists and veterans of the East Asia theater, some of whom claim Mickey came up with the name. In negotiations with the Israeli civilian authorities, his experience on civil/military building projects, especially during his service at Fort McClellan and later in Hawaii, proved useful in expediting support.[45]

To provide security for the effort, forces from Seventh Armored went on the defensive and kept the legion pinned down, their attention directed away from the construction sites. This ambitious engineering feat, conducted at night by the engineers, soldiers, and scarecrow citizens of besieged Jerusalem, proceeded simultaneously with the planning for Operation Yoram, a third effort to capture Latrun and, hopefully, remove the Jordanian threat from the main road to Jerusalem once more by maneuver. The operation, planned by Mickey and the top officers from the brigades involved, began on

June 8–9 and resulted from Ben-Gurion's decision, based on a recommendation from Mickey, to withdraw Allon's Yiftach Brigade from the Galilee and attach it to Mickey's front. He now commanded the equivalent of a reinforced division-sized field unit.

The main objective was Hill 346, located between the two Arab Legion regiments defending the Latrun area. The plan reflected Mickey's battlefield experience, but the attacking unit took a wrong turn, mistakenly attacked Hill 315, and then lost momentum. After this failure, Stone's forces on the Jerusalem Front no longer had the capacity to mount an attack on Latrun, but he still argued hard to renew Operation Yoram. The Arab Legion renewed the fight in Jerusalem and moved aggressively west, but they had lost the initiative after the IDF's three operations at Latrun—Bin Nun Alef, Bin Nun Bet, and Yoram. The local legion commander reported to Glubb that they had annihilated the superior enemy force, killing hundreds of Jews. For the time being, Glubb figured he had won a major victory. For his part, Ben-Gurion remained focused on the completion of the Burma Road.[46]

On other fronts, Israeli forces managed to slow down the Egyptian invaders by a daring combination of hit-and-run attacks and night raids against the enemy's flanks and long supply lines, their advance slowing to a crawl and eventually halted. In the north of the new nation, Palmach units under Moshe Dayan checked the Syrian advance toward the Jordan Valley, and the Iraqis and the various Muslim militias stalled after uncoordinated and unsuccessful attacks on border settlements. By the beginning of June, the Haganah command was fixed on Jerusalem. The Arab Legion already held the ancient Holy City and were trying to cut off the remainder of the new city before any possible UN-brokered ceasefire took effect. The IDF held its ground, and the legion made no further advances.[47]

At this point, the second week in June, photojournalist Robert Capa arrived at the Seventh Armored headquarters at Hulda. He had met Mickey before in the Negev and knew Stone's real identity. Capa immediately sensed the spirit he had experienced in Spain with the International Brigades now made manifest again in Mickey

Stone, with whom he bonded as battlefield friend. As Capa learned, all Mickey's efforts were directed toward finishing the Burma Road as an alternative way of getting supplies into Jerusalem against the pressure of the imminent ceasefire that had been negotiated through the United Nations and scheduled for the morning of June 11. Failure to establish a secure supply route to the city before the ceasefire took effect would leave West Jerusalem outside Israeli control, according to the UN's rules. By this time nearby Arab villages had been forcibly evacuated to further protect the road, and the government sent out hundreds of laborers and as much heavy equipment as could be found each night to assist the Seventh Armored engineers responsible for the project.

Under desultory Arab artillery and sniper fire, Capa took pictures of the laborers and heavy equipment. As David Eldans, head of the government press office photo department, recalled,

> Whenever Marcus told Capa not to go to a certain area, you could take it for granted that he would go. So then began a game, Marcus claiming that one place was dangerous to keep Capa away from the real danger elsewhere. But in the end, Capa always found him out, so Marcus had to turn to other methods. There were strict security regulations, and the commandos and patrols had orders to turn the photographer back from places that were too hot. But Marcus failed to take Capa's cleverness and personal charm into account. He simply made friends with all the soldiers with fascinating stories and with the brandy flask he always carried in his hip pocket and so he went everywhere. So much for military discipline. But Marcus wasn't angry for he had come to like and admire Capa.[48]

The two men were clearly cut from the same cloth, building a strong attachment to one another in just two weeks.

Stone's driver Rivka, while taking him to Hulda during a legion artillery barrage, commented to his passenger, "You know you could get killed in a war like this. What made you come here?" Thrusting out his arm and pulling up his sleeve, Mickey replied, "See these veins? The blood of Abraham flows in them. That's what brought me here." According to Zipporah Porath, the journalist gathering stories after his death, at least four of the people she interviewed remembered Mickey saying the same thing. Others said a favorite response was, "You gotta help your brother out in a fight."[49]

A Palmach soldier nicknamed Ra'anana was in one of the early supply runs to transverse the jeep and foot path road from the Jerusalem side. He described arriving at Seventh Armored HQ on May 31 to ask for reinforcements and a bigger jeep-based operation for the temporary footpath while the main construction effort proceeded with Road 7, which was not yet able to bear fully loaded trucks. Until then, cargo had to be moved by small vehicles and Ra'anana found himself taking to the Front commander: "Mickey supported us, and with his help we rounded up ten jeeps. These we filled with 2 mortars, four new 'Besa' machine guns, and one hundred shells for each of the mortars. Where the hills were too steep for any jeep to pass, we loaded the supplies on our shoulders and carried them to vehicles waiting on the other side for transport to Jerusalem. The following night one hundred men each with one shell strapped to his back, scrambled over the hills by foot, about eight miles, to make it to the beleaguered Jerusalem area."[50]

Friendly fire: Abu Ghosh Monastery, outside Jerusalem, late the night of June 10–11, 1948

On the evening of June 8, only a week after construction had begun, Mickey and Capa drove together over Road 7, bypassing Latrun and connecting to the road to Jerusalem, which was passable but still dangerous. Capa slept most of the way, even though the road was so pitted he was nearly jolted out of the jeep, and in the morning he photographed Haganah troops near the Arab-held Old City. The next two days Mickey and Broida inspected the front and stayed at Allon's headquarters at Abu Ghosh, which Mickey intended to use as his headquarters for the next few days until the announced truce took effect. After that, he would set up a new headquarters for his fourth attempt to capture Latrun.

On June 10 the first convoy of military supplies, food, and other humanitarian assistance and provisions traveled Road 7, now openly called the Burma Road, from Tel Aviv to Jerusalem without unloading at any point along the route for manual transfer. That same day Capa came out to Abu Ghosh, where he told Mickey that the Eden Hotel in Jerusalem "was preparing its highest honor for an American commander: a hot bath, an experience, Capa assured him that would be 'a delirious experience.' "[51]

On the night of June 10, after visiting the construction site during the day and celebrating with the Palmach troops, Mickey went to his room on the second floor of the building housing the HQ on the monastery grounds. There had been heavy drinking at the celebration, and at about 3:30 a.m., Mickey got up and went relieve himself outside the compound's perimeter. The night was chilly, so before going outside he wrapped a white wool blanket over his shoulders. A short time later the sentry on duty, Eliezer Levinsky, heard a noise and looked up to see a white-covered figure advancing toward him. Levinsky called out, in Hebrew, the challenge for the password, but the figure continued to advance toward the compound. Mickey, who did not understand spoken Hebrew, either had not understood the sentry or had forgotten the password, which that night was *haderech shelanu*, "the road is ours." In reply, Mickey uttered something that sounded to the sentry like English, but not hearing the password, he did his job and fired a warning shot. The figure still advanced, and Levinsky, believing the unidentified intruder might be an English-speaking officer from the Arab Legion or an Arab belligerent trying to enter the base, fired several rounds from his Sten gun at Mickey, killing him.[52]

Yigal Allon, commanding Yiftach Brigade, who was sharing the second floor in the headquarters with Mickey, was awakened and told a tragedy had occurred. His first panicky thought was that all of Jerusalem had been taken by the legion, but the truth nevertheless hit him hard. Stunned, he asked Haganah HQ for instructions on what to do with the body and was told to coordinate with Dr. Meron Issachari, Harel Brigade surgeon, who performed a rare battlefield autopsy. Issachari combined Palmach, Haganah, and British training and service, embodying a unique blend of skills and experiences. Born in Germany, his path to Palestine took him through Beirut and Iraq as a refugee before he set up a private practice and became actively involved in the Haganah. In 1942 he enlisted in the British Army, serving as a combat surgeon in North Africa and Italy, and later in the Royal Marines.[53]

On the morning of June 11 Dr. Issachari examined the body of Michael Stone and drafted his report, concluding that a Sten bullet had entered the body on the left side of the chest between the fifth and sixth ribs, exiting between ribs six and seven, causing wounds sufficient to cause immediate death. There were also two superficial wounds on the right arm consistent with the chest wounds and weapon. The body was transported to Jerusalem that night and put in preservative the next morning before being moved to Bezalel Museum, where it was covered with the national flag. Candles were lit at its base, and an honor guard of Palmach and Haganah flanked the casket on both sides.[54]

Ben-Gurion was shocked by Mickey's death, and on June 11 he sent the following telegram to the new Israeli embassy in Washington for transmission to Emma:

> Please inform Mrs. David Marcus that her husband fell last night at his post in the hills of Jerusalem. The government of Israel, the Jewish Army, and the entire Jewish people of Palestine send her expressions of deepest sympathy in her grief. During the short time of his being with us—too short alas—he succeeded in making an outstanding contribution to the building and perfecting of our war machine which has secured for him a place of honor in the momentous phase of our history during which the state of Israel came into being. As a man and a commander, he endeared himself to all those who came into personal contact with him, and his fame spread through all the ranks of our armed forces. They

> all admired his superb courage, his remarkable military intuition, his quick grasp of new situations, his unlimited devotion, and his natural spontaneous human fellowship. He was recently appointed as supreme commander of our forces at the Jerusalem front and immediately became the moving spirit of that campaign, the most difficult and farreachingly important of all those which we have had to fight so far. His name will live forever in the annals of the Jewish people, and we feel confident that American Jewry will be proud of its great and gallant son who has given his life for the liberation of Israel. David Ben-Gurion.[55]

That same day, Ben-Gurion called on Yaakov Shimshon Shapira, newly appointed legal adviser for the government and later Israel's attorney general and minister of justice, to look into what had happened. Ben-Gurion was suspicious that the Palmach had somehow participated in an assassination. By striking the symbol of professional efforts to unify the militias, he thought, they sought to preserve an independent militia separate from the army. A week later Shapira filed his brief four-page report. It described the number and type of shots reported, the wounds Mickey suffered, how he died, where he was and why, and the sentry's testimony. It was a terrible accident, Shapira concluded, the truth more embarrassing than sinister. The official finding substantiated the sentry's claim that he fired his weapon in the line of duty. Levinsky, a promising cadet in Laskov's training camp for squad commanders, became a horse breeder and receded into obscurity until his identity was revealed in 1983.[56]

Mickey was killed in one of the most famous friendly fire incidents in history. Think Stonewall Jackson. Some people couldn't accept that. It was not a sniper, an assassin, or stray bullet, as various rumors had it that were passed along by various friends, family, and classmates of Mickey. The stray bullet theory was repeated for decades after the event by credible sources. It had begun with Steve Stevenson and gained credence with Emma herself.[57] But the text of the report does not contain any evidence, or even hint, of conspiracy or foul play, or implicate any other person. Ironically, the Palmach, despite its well-known early suspicions of Stone, embraced Mickey fiercely in death, especially its top commanders, Yigal Allon and Yitzhak Rabin. On the personal or institutional level, the view by that time was that Stone was a symbol of the struggle for Jewish independence, and a unifying figure. Even in the absence of any evidence, it's hard to see how any Jewish group gained by his death.[58]

West Point Cemetery, July 1, 1948

Troops of the Seventh Armored Brigade prepared the body according to Jewish law and escorted it to Tel Aviv in a plain coffin strapped to the hood of Robert Capa's jeep. He photographed the soldiers and statesmen carrying the coffin. After some brief communication with Emma about burying Mickey in Israel, Stevenson took charge of the arrangements to transport his friend's body back to the United States for burial at West Point. Ben-Gurion, Sharett, and other leaders of Israel accompanied the body to the Tel Aviv airport. A specially chartered flight was arranged by Stevenson and paid for by an ad hoc committee of Mickey's friends and associates, organized by judge Arthur Schwartz, an old friend from Mickey's prosecutor days.

The Israeli escort in America included Colonel Moshe Dayan, accompanied by his wife Ruth, and Harel Brigade captain Yosef Hamburger, the American Haganah commander of the blockade-running ship *Exodus*. Neither man had been particularly close with Mickey; they were there mostly for political and other reasons. Alex and Irene Broida, who had been working for the Haganah in New York before Alex was assigned as Mickey's aide, came back with the body to return to their assignment in America. They became close to Emma. The airplane was welcomed at La Guardia Airport in New York by an official delegation of police, NYC prison officials, and local and state politicians, also facilitated by the ad hoc Marcus memorial committee.

After a funeral service at Union Temple, David Daniel Marcus was buried at West Point on July 1, 1948, exactly twenty-eight years to the day that he had first reported there as a plebe. Governor Thomas E. Dewey of New York and Major General Maxwell D. Taylor, commander in Normandy during Mickey's time in the European Theater of Operations and superintendent of West Point, attended. The Marcus family rabbi, Sidney S. Tedesche, presided over the ceremony, its events unfolding according to an old protocol: prayers, eulogies, bugler, a gun salute according to an official order of the US Army. The mostly silent mourners, family, friends, and associates gathered around an American flag-draped coffin, attended by twelve members of the Thundering Herd.[59]

While more than a few West Point graduates have died fighting under foreign flags, David Daniel Marcus, class of 1924, the Thundering Herd, Cullum Number 7556, is the only graduate buried in the West Point cemetery who died fighting in the army of another nation. But that is an accident of history; any graduate can be buried there. Emma is buried with him, and next to them lie Steve and Mair Stevenson, as all four had planned when they were young. Marcus's epitaph reads: "A Soldier for All Humanity."[60]

Emma Marcus outlived most of those who shaped the public perception of Mickey Marcus. She appeared at memorial events and traveled to Israel a half dozen times, during one visit getting press coverage that corresponded with the shooting of *Cast a Giant Shadow*. If the movie would turn out be the principal embodiment of her legacy preservation efforts, the organizational foundation already had been laid immediately after Mickey's death by the ad hoc efforts of his friends. Soon after he was buried, a dozen men set up the Colonel David Marcus Memorial Foundation, Inc., in New York under leadership of Judge Arthur H. Schwartz. Joined by Stevenson, Limpus, and other family members and friends, Emma served as the foundation's secretary and screener. Its purpose was to maintain the integrity and quality of official efforts to honor Mickey's memory.

During the closing days of the 1948 war and after, the foundation arranged donation of ambulances and dual use material to Israel in his honor. Over its lifetime, the foundation also sponsored athletic awards at Boys High and West Point for sportsmanship and boxing. It had a hand in all official and semiofficial NYC Mickey-related functions, among them annual Mickey Marcus Days, programs at museums, and NYC prison-system-related events like the Jewish American Gibborim Society, a Jewish prison employee retiree group. Best friend Steve Stevenson often served as organizer and speaker at these presentations, in which he reminisced about his closest friends, as well as their wives, often with them present. A highlight of all these efforts came on the tenth anniversary of Mickey's death, when the foundation held a gala at the Jewish Museum that attracted national attention.[61]

Mickey died a few hours before the first month-long UN ceasefire, which turned out to be a temporary truce, took effect. It formalized what had been a campaign-winning battlefield engineering miracle. That day marked the conclusion of the most important two hundred days in Jewish history since Titus of Rome destroyed the Second Temple in 70 AD and ended any degree of Jewish sovereignty in the land of Israel for two centuries. Mickey's official West Point service record lists his last assignment as "Supreme Commander, Jewish Forces Jerusalem Front," where the restoration of that sovereignty met its greatest physical challenge during the second phase of the war for independence. The first phase lasted from the vote for partition until the Declaration of Independence, November 30, 1947, to May 14, 1948; the second phase, from the Arab invasion until the first truce, May 15 to June 11, 1948. More phases followed two more truces, with war-ending armistices signed in 1949 between Israel and Egypt (February 24), Lebanon (March 23), Jordan (April 3), and Syria (July 20). Since then, Egypt and Jordan have signed peace treaties; the others remain in a de facto state of war with Israel.[62]

On December 7, 1948, Prime Minister Ben-Gurion, IDF chief of staff Yaacov Dori, and many others who fought at Latrun and built the Burma Road, formally inaugurated K'vish Hagvura, the Road to Jerusalem. The original Road 7 was broadened and paved even before the end of the war. At the dedication Ben-Gurion stressed Jerusalem as the pivotal theater in Israel's War of Independence:

> This road, which we inaugurate today, embodies the summit of our war for a homeland and independence, and the most heroic and tragic campaign since we were forced to stand up against our many enemies—the campaign over Jerusalem. This campaign is the essence of Israel's war of independence, waged for over a year now all over the country. It has been conducted not only over Jerusalem and its immediate surroundings but mostly over the road to Jerusalem. Our fate has depended on this road since the beginning of the war when our enemies within the country and without rose to destroy us. Jerusalem was exposed to mortal danger, and from the heavy blows suffered by our settlements during the war, Jerusalem took lessons. The enemy knew that the most fatal blow, and the easiest one, it can impose on us, is the subjugating of Jewish Jerusalem and its destruction. This road is a monument to our heroism in war and Jewish labor—which have and will win."[63]

The multinational UN peacekeeper force dispatched by the Security Council, its first ever mission, ruled that completion of the Burma Road lifted the siege of Jerusalem, with the city at the edge of starvation. Under the armistice agreement with Jordan, the entire Latrun area, including the monastery and the police fortress, remained in the hands of the Arab Legion, an enclave linked by a single road with the Arab rear. A strip of no-man's-land interposing between the Jordan and Israel positions, it was surrounded by mines. The water pumping station there was blown up to deprive Jewish Jerusalem of its water supply, in violation of the agreement reached under UN auspices. A new water line was laid along the Burma Road.

The main crossroads near Latrun that sparked the battle remained in no-man's-land, but the plan to have supply convoys pass through it under UN protection failed after a trial convoy drew fire that killed several Israelis. In the end, the fields in no-man's-land were cultivated based on local arrangements, and the Jordanians stood down. On June 6, 1967, the fort, monastery, and hills at Latrun and the crossroads were taken by the IDF without fighting, and subsequently the main and shorter road from the coastal plain to Jerusalem was reopened.[64]

One might well ask, was the Latrun campaign decisive? Or, less delicately, were the blood spilled—139 Jewish soldiers killed and many hundreds wounded—in the first two Bin Nun operations, the bitterness left by Ben-Gurion's decisions, and the mistakes and tragic turns in the field worth the outcome? What are the elements of a decisive campaign?

First, was the strategic objective underlying all operations and tactical maneuvering achieved. The effort to secure a supply route to Jewish West Jerusalem was Ben-Gurion's main goal, from the declaration of independence to the first truce. From the early struggles to get convoys past the Bab el-Wad gorge to the sweeps of the hills of snipers and irregulars, the supply line was the paramount concern. During his first visit, Mickey traveled the route in the terrible month of March, when convoys to Jerusalem were wrecked, to observe the early plans to secure the route. He applauded the first large brigade-size Haganah offensive, Operation Nachson, in April, which briefly lifted the siege on the city while the British were still in-country but staying on the sidelines.

While the frontal and flank assaults on Latrun failed in late May, reconnaissance and intermittent cross-country trips behind the front-line fortifications unlocked the key to the real objective: supplying Jerusalem. And why was the Jewish enclave of the city so important, given that it was the most exposed position in the proposed partition plan, under which it soon would be internationalized? The city was not just the chosen capital of a new nation, but—as Ben-Gurion stressed in his dedication of the road—the symbol of national and religious identity for Jews, and holy as well to Arab Christians and Muslims. Losing the western Jewish part of the city after the surrender of the Old City might well have been an unrecoverable psychological and political blow to suffer, just before the UN-mandated truce. A more dire and desperate situation for the newly declared state is hard to imagine. Instead, the ability to supply Jerusalem boosted morale despite the death of Marcus, or even because of it, as his modest contributions to the construction of the road magnified his image and were trumpeted even by parties that fought over everything. The road Marcus became identified with was a material and spiritual demonstration of resilience and improvisation in war which helped stiffen the resolve of the IDF during the remainder of the struggle. The press in both Israel and the United States embraced the story and increasingly linked the road and the man.

The casualties at Latrun were indeed high, and the politicization of battle, including wild exaggerations about the casualties, as well as personal differences, have stained the truth of the Latrun campaign. But if it is judged in its entirety, from May 25 to June 10, the Seventh Armored Brigade and its Road 7 saved the capital city.

The building of Road 7 neutralized the Jordanian possession of Latrun and rendered it strategically useless. Worse for the Arab Legion, it shifted their posture from offense to static defense in just two weeks. Despite their tactical victory and the heavy losses inflicted on their enemy, the Arabs had been outmaneuvered, their siege lifted, and their war-winning strategy wrecked. It was a stunning tactical shift with major strategic results, even if the Arabs had not noticed. In any event, the saving of Jewish Jerusalem ensured the survival of the State of Israel. The Jordanians were the first to sign an armistice with Israel, and later Egypt followed, with a peace treaty in 1994 that has survived every crisis since. Speculation about what would have happened had Jewish Jerusalem been lost in 1948 produces no good outcomes for Israel.

Today Latrun is a museum and memorial dedicated to the Armored Corps of the IDF and houses the Jewish Warrior in World War II Museum. The first IDF Armored Corps unit, Shamir's Seventh Armored Brigade, has been deployed in every war and major confrontation since the IDF was founded in May 1948, including the Israel-Hamas War begun on October 7, 2023. The troops and citizens who labored at night at Latrun were under the command of Aluf Michael Stone; he too helped save Jerusalem. Their road made possible the continuing Jewish quest for sovereignty over the land, in defiance of man, other ideologies and religions, and history.

CHAPTER 7

Assessment and Legacy of Mickey Marcus

> For me, he was the first general of the IDF in every sense of the word. He had a sense of purpose and mission, in the establishment of the Israel Defense Forces, he taught us how to act as an army in our early days and was one of Ben-Gurion's greatest military advisors. There is no one who better illustrates the strong bond between Israel and the United States.
>
> —President Reuven Rivlin, 1948
> Haganah veteran, West Point, 2015

1948 and 2023,
Wars of Independence and Wars of Survival

This biography is not a history of Israel's 1948 war for independence. Or of the Battle of Latrun. Or of Zionism versus Palestinian nationalism/Islamism. Its subject died well before the conclusion of the war, which was punctuated by two more UN ceasefires and halted by four separate armistices between Israel and four invading Arab countries. Some of those agreements led to peace treaties; some fronts remain ablaze.[1] The subject of this biography picked a side, and the author is on the same side, so any consideration of the continuing relevance of the subject, and the image of the subject, must reckon with things as they are now between America and Israel—without a full explanation or defense of how they got there, or even where the relationship might be headed.

Fig. 21. IDF chief of staff Chaim Laskov, Abu Ghosh Memorial, June 11, 1958. Israel Government Press Office

The basic claim that Mickey Marcus has become not just a US Army or American Zionist hero but a symbol of the mutual national security interests of Israel and America has a particular relevance during a period of regional and global tension and actual war in Israel. Those mutual interests have evolved over time, shaped by domestic politics and the often colliding economic and diplomatic imperatives of large powers like America, and small but powerful regional states like Israel. As restated over the last decades, those interests at the foundation now include:

1. Supporting a western-style democracy, the only one in the Middle East, within the post–World War II global rules-based order. That, as always, is based on diplomatic, economic, and military support, and deeply dependent on domestic politics and relations with other states in the region, most of which are monarchies, authoritarian regimes, or theocracies. The dominance of the information warfare space and the interplay of journalism, technology, and instant global information networks has a dramatic impact on the actual level of support at specific moments of conflict.
2. Opposing hostile foreign powers in the region like Iran, state puppets under their control to some degree, like Syria, and various nonstate Islamist militias, like Hamas in Gaza, Hezbollah in Lebanon, and the Houthis in Yemen. This policy has relied on deterrence of varying levels of effectiveness but reached a crisis during late 2023 and into 2024 and appears to have failed.
3. Protecting economic interests, most importantly by securing the eastern Mediterranean and Red Sea transport routes from the Persian Gulf through Hormuz and west to Europe through Suez, and east from the oil fields in the Gulf through the Strait of Malacca to China and other Asian markets. The rise of Iranian influence in Yemen, and the continuing threats to the Gulf states, Red Sea and Suez Canal maritime trade by its proxy Houthi government, has weakened the interests of all western powers, including the United States, western Europe, and Israel.

The actual relationship between Israel and the United States since Marcus's death, however, has not changed because of him; it has gyrated from initial Cold War wariness after Truman's dramatic recognition of Israel to outright hostility toward it during some periods. Eisenhower was hostile during the Suez crisis in 1956, compared to Nixon's actions in the 1973 war and the strong diplomatic efforts during Trump's administration. Periods of active threat in the recent past from open enemies like Iran and its proxies tend to fortify support initially. But bloody conflict, ideological and conflicting geopolitical interests, and election year politics often lead to sharp divisions between governments and personalities, most evident during the years-long right-wing Netanyahu premiership in Israel, resulting in open and hostile arguments, especially during the Obama and Biden administrations.

But while the rhythm of the United States' relationship with Israel always has been and still is heavily shaped by the personalities and politics of successive governments in both nations, the prevailing sentiment in the United States still supports continued military and political support of the Jewish state. More recently, a hostile attitude toward Israel among the college-educated young, driven by outright Marxist ideology, blinkered progressive postcolonialist critique with a heavy tinge of Jew hatred, and intersectional ideology has been misapplied to the Israel-Palestine struggle. The progressive wing of the Democratic Party thinks the problems in Gaza are the same as those of East St. Louis or downtown Detroit. That Franco-American ideological hodgepodge has created the fiction of Jewish communities in Israel as "Zionist white settler colonists," enforcing "apartheid" and other ideologically programmed marching chant fodder, creating a new, made-for-social media blood libel on the left. The right relies on its old hatreds, tropes, and Nazi images and instincts.

The ancient Jew hatred in both the Christian and Muslim communities, whipped up by incitement by clerics and increasingly extreme rhetoric on the political right and left, now has large numbers of citizens in every major capital justifying, defending, supporting, or accepting murder, torture, and rape as "legitimate" liberation tactics, obscuring legitimate resistance to Zionism and rendering it irrelevant.[2] Effectively, anti-Zionism is anti-Semitism, but since that is an academic construction, applying Occam's razor, anti-Zionism is Jew hatred. This has previously been mostly unspoken in the West, but the same sentiments, indeed the same arguments, made by virulent opponents of Israel today are exactly those first made in the 1948 war. The enemies of Israel now demand a historical reversal of their disaster, or Nakba, their failed attempt at genocide against the Jews in 1948. A new jihad to erase an old defeat. They reject now, as they did then, any Jewish state in any part of what they still call Palestine, and call for the death, expulsion, or subjugation of its Jewish inhabitants. Openly. Many greater and actually viable countries that don't rely on handouts have historically accepted defeat and recovered.

For the Jewish children of the Greatest Generation, the generation that defeated Nazism, the current reality means their own children, millennials and Gen Z, no longer share a visceral connection to Israel as a matter of personal life insurance. Even when violent Jew-hating mobs walk the streets in their cities, claiming political grievance outside synagogues, the educated young are more likely to champion Palestinians as one of the oppressed peoples, and vilify Jews as oppressors. They are ignorant of the ethnic roots of most Israelis in North Africa and the Arab world, or that they were driven out of Muslim lands in mass ethnic-cleansing expulsions, before and after 1948. That puts Israel squarely among the nations filled with people of color, and the most welcoming to immigrants of any modern nation.

Neither has the marching mob any interest in the Jewish resistance to Ottoman and British colonialism in Palestine in the twentieth century that led to the formation of their nation. Gone is the gnawing realization that the only refuge for Jews facing actual violent threats where they live is Israel, whatever the politics or government of the moment. For liberal Jews, even in times of active war against Israel and open anti-Semitism, the reality of their children assaulted at their alma maters does not shake their progressive ideological hostility to Zionism, a hostility that evokes Soviet doctrine and practice.

The fear that permeated the first generations of Jewish immigrants in America, especially in the early years of the twentieth century, when Mickey grew up, disappeared in America with the World War II generation. The Holocaust has been reduced to popular entertainment; books about it are prime targets for right-wing censorship here and official government control in the lands where murders happened, like Poland, Hungary, and Lithuania. The fear of terrible and violent death made so real for Jews by Nazi Germany and its collaborators in World War II is gone.

The basic issue, however, facing the leaders of Israel remains the same now as in 1948. Can the state protect its land and citizens within its borders, and deter or destroy their enemies when they gather to press for Israel's destruction? What is different now than it was at the beginning of the modern state is that Israel has a technologically advanced professional Jewish army, due in small but still relevant ways to an American Army and Zionist hero, Mickey Marcus, and his final two hundred days.

After the barbaric premeditated pogrom unleashed on southern Israel on October 7, 2023, by Hamas, a Muslim Brotherhood–linked terrorist organization, only the ignorant, naive, or outright anti-Semite could argue the stakes have changed since then. If the Arabs won in 1948, or now, the suffering of the Jews would not be limited by the world's thoughts and prayers. If the Hamas massacre wasn't conclusive enough, recent history offers a lengthy list of the shattered remnants of other ancient communities, mostly Muslim sects, destroyed by religious Sunni and Shia fanatics in Syria, Iraq, Yemen, and Lebanon, all played out on social media.

The war with Hamas in 2023 brought the reality of genocidal barbarism and hatred of Jews by an invasion of the land of Israel. That was accompanied by images of tens of millions screaming for Jewish blood all over the world, including the capitals and cities of the democratic Western alliance. But it differed only in scale and atavistic barbarism from similar pogroms and massacres against Jews in the Yishuv in

1947–48, and in the years leading to the ending of British rule and the independence of the Jews in Palestine. Or after.

Although an assimilated Jew and latecomer to Zionism, Mickey Marcus became an instant hero of Israel for as long as the founders exerted influence, political and moral. Now that legacy has a diplomatic and historical foundation, and visits to West Point have become the ritual ground for marking and remembering his impact on the American army and IDF. The stretch of ground that once held the Burma Road is today a nature walk, the shattered rusted relics of war now a part of the scenery, the heights marked by a memorial to Machal near the spot where Mickey fell.

In 1993 then prime minister Yitzhak Rabin, standing on the ground he fought over forty-five years earlier, paid tribute to Mickey Marcus and the other 119 overseas volunteers who lost their lives in the struggle for Israel's independence and survival. At the dedication ceremony near Sha'ar Hagai, Rabin evoked the desperate mood of those days: "They came to us when we needed them most during those hard and uncertain days of our War of Independence."[3] Every year around the anniversary of Independence Day, there are articles or brief video spots that remember the siege of Jerusalem, spotlight the burned-out vehicles, and occasionally mention the American Mickey Marcus, code name Michael Stone. Otherwise, the state and people of Israel have no consciousness of the man. The squares, plaques, neighborhoods, and schools named after him get the same attention to their namesake as those named for anyone else from what young people consider the deep and dead past. We walk past them without stopping.

In America, Mickey became an almost instant Jewish American and Zionist military hero with a strong West Point, New York, Jewish community, and more recently a US Army civil affairs base of institutional interest. The strength of that legacy was boosted dramatically by both iterations of *Cast a Giant Shadow*, but apart from the drama swirling around his life at the end of it and the political uses of his untimely death by the new state of Israel and by the early Zionist leaders in America, what Marcus said ironically about himself might be said of any of those who came to fight, half from North America: "I am not the best one that could have come, but I am the one who did come."[4]

Certainly, no one understood the irony of that self-description better than the man who had tried hardest to recruit someone for the very job Marcus ended up doing. In the end, Shamir decided that Marcus was exactly the right man for the job, and the best man that could have come. And he told Marcus's story for his whole life. But even rarer than the strange set of circumstances that thrust Marcus to his unique place in legend is that his image remains as it began, unblemished, and when recalled it is as a selfless hero of two democracies. The much broader claim carved in the stone marker over his grave, "Soldier for All Humanity," would be hard to find chiseled anywhere in our polarized hate and conspiracy-addled environment, where history is defined as a compelling narrative opinion in short bursts of bytes.

The truth remains that David Daniel "Mickey" Marcus, US Military Academy class of 1924, the "Thundering Herd," and 1923 US intercollegiate welterweight boxing champion, is the only person buried in the West Point cemetery whose presence requires a footnote. But the epitaph conveys a status, an exceptionalism that remains striking because the footnote is about Israel. It is cited as often in descriptions of Mickey's life as any of the boldest fictions, tall tales, or true stories. But it links the universal in Mickey to the particularity and details of an American Jewish citizen-soldier in the first half of the past century. The plaque honoring him and placed by the government of Israel at the grave makes the bilateral connection manifest.

Mickey was in 1948 and remains, more than seventy years after his senseless death, a potent symbol of American Zionism rallying for Israel and Western values and notions of freedom, and he has a serious claim to inclusion as a foundational figure of the modern Jewish army. A force bound to the homeland and defense, described by Mickey to Omar Bradley, then the chief of staff of the US Army, as a people in arms, it was born from a history of persecution and helplessness endured in many places. Denial of the right to bear arms had been a common theme no matter the land. But when creating a Jewish army, the founders held firm to a code they call the purity of arms and is consciously Jewish: "An IDF soldier will only exercise their power or use their weapons to fulfill their mission and only when necessary. They will maintain their humanity during combat and routine times. The IDF soldier will not use their weapon or power to harm uninvolved civilians and prisoners and will do everything in their power to prevent harm to their lives, bodies, dignity and property."[5]

Suffusing the soldiers' spirit as powerfully as the training to kill is the realization that the taking of life in war, and wielding of powerful weapons, is such a breach of normal behavior for the ordinary Jew that it can only take place under the strictest of rules and proportionality. From its very creation, the IDF has operated strictly under the humanitarian rules of war, while its enemies frequently have not. It contains in its table of organization exactly the kinds of legal checks at the staff level that all democratic governments maintain. That innocents suffer despite the rules is in the nature of war and does not negate the code, or the compulsions under which soldiers operate.

Mickey was instrumental during the postwar occupation as well as during his time at the War Crimes Branch in providing the intellectual framework for defining genocide, war crimes, crimes against humanity, and crimes against peace. Such terms are not meant to be the accelerant in rhetorical tirades, or the charge made as lightly as on a poster. But Nuremberg provided the first real-world example that if the international laws governing such matters are breached, they will be enforced. Combat missions must be planned and executed with the greatest possible avoidance of civilian casualties and critical collateral infrastructure damage consistent with the importance of the target and rules of proportionality. There are also violations that justify active self-defense that by nature cause civilian casualties: hospitals and schools may not be used for military purposes and may be attacked if they are. And there is the chaos of warfare. War is a disaster, and at its most extreme must only be waged for self-defense and survival. There are also unwritten conventions of personal behavior. No one is abandoned on the battlefield, even the dead.

The founders of the IDF melded their experience in the Allied and Soviet militaries, Partisan forests, and the history of the Yishuv into an instrument of self-defense, consciously calling it a Defense Force. It was shaped in many places but does not bear the historical ethos, legacy, or psychological results of any of its lands of origin—at least, not anymore. It is neither militarist nor pacifist by nature and does not intervene in politics. More remarkable still, and an incredibly rare phenomenon in either Israel or America, Marcus as a symbol of what is best in both militaries has remained a constant in the two democracies for three quarters of a century. Few question his claims to official remembrance in either country except as a part of other arguments, not as a critique of one person's biography and his influence in death.

Mickey has so far escaped the political fallout of the Israel-Palestine struggle that followed his death, largely because his job was not politics. He worked for the side he wanted to win, and if that side remains an American ally, his place is secure in Israel, even if it only serves a diplomatic or cultural purpose now. Mickey's legacy is part of the history of the US Army in the first half of the twentieth century and is secure, if only at a footnote level. His end is what makes his story a tale of destiny. If the alliance fails, Mickey might be studied as a symbol of how it came apart.

Battling in a brief but bloody campaign to take an ancient crossroads, Aluf Michael Stone's division had lifted the siege of Jerusalem, the last in a three-thousand-year-long list of conquerors whose great and terrible captains include David of Bethlehem, Nebuchadnezzar of Babylon, Titus of Rome, Saladin of Tikrit, and Lord Allenby of Great Britain. Joining that list, David Mickey Marcus from Brooklyn left his mark on history. He helped save the ancient capital and has ever since been hailed as the Israeli Lafayette. He achieved everything he set out to do, and was self-aware, as revealed in a telling moment: his confiding to John Maginnis, on the ship headed for Utah Beach, that he knew he was a witness and small shaper of world events. Now he had added to his list of achievements that of serving as a field general, the dream of the most ambitious West Point cadets.

As the story goes, Mickey was ready to go home for good, an acclaimed war hero with powerful New York political connections, and to do so on his own terms. Then, in an instant, he was dead, killed by the last bullet fired before a truce—the first of dozens of UN-sponsored truces in that region since—and by his own soldier. The shock of his death reverberated for months in America and Israel. Conspiracy theories about his death surfaced in the early days, reaching a peak with the work of Israel's "new historians" in the 1990s, and have since faded. Leaks of the now public but longtime secret investigation of his death produced no real evidence of foul play. Many Yishuv officers were suspicious about foreign advisers, but as a martyr and a person, Mickey was easy to embrace, especially since he touched many of Israel's founding fathers, just like Wingate. Soon after meeting him, they found actual differences on policy, or discomfort with a foreigner, no longer as relevant.

Lingering legal issues about Americans fighting for other governments, or foreign organizations, without registering as an agent never touched Mickey. In Britain, Whitehall was unhappy with the unequal press treatment of American and Commonwealth veterans in the Palestine fighting and stung by charges that the British were commanding the Arab Legion. They reacted in the press by citing the example of Colonel Marcus. If they hadn't kept track of Mickey before then, at least a question given the timing of the Order of the British Empire ceremony in Washington, the British knew about him afterward. But they reacted through a news report and not an official protest. Coverage in the press about foreign fighters quickly faded, but others who had fought for Israel before and after independence did not escape legal consequences. Some ended up in jail, or lost basic rights, including citizenship.[6]

Except for annual remembrances at West Point and his grave, which serves as a pilgrimage ground for visiting Israeli soldiers, diplomats, or during a film retrospective about war movies that included *Cast a Giant Shadow*, Mickey disappeared from public consciousness. But the popular information sphere is only one measure of actual legacy. As recently as 2017, Marcus was honored by the US Army as a Distinguished Member of the Civil Affairs Regiment at Fort Liberty, home of Army Special Operations Command, consistent with their interest in the origins and practice of operations other than war, and in institutional memory.[7]

David Marcus saw himself as an American freedom fighter in a Jewish war of independence, a cause he totally embraced, but that was just one dimension of his career. [8] Mickey Marcus, alias Michael Stone, had a profound impact on the organizational and strategic foundation of the IDF, even though his time in Israel was brief.

But what makes someone a founder of an army; of the Jewish army, in particular? The factors below are essential activities of a founder:

- *Formation.* Marcus was not involved in the mustering of the Haganah and successor IDF forces fighting for independence but was a key agent of transforming those forces into a more structured, cohesive, and professional fighting army.
- *Organization and command.* He played a key role in creating the tables of organization of military units, shaping early command structures and doctrine, lines of authority, and defining staff functions and key staff responsibilities of logistics and administration. Further, his rudimentary front headquarters, coming together near his death, was a precursor of the IDF front command structure—Northern, Southern, Homefront, and Central—the forerunner of which was the Jerusalem Front under Aluf Stone. The concept of creating large but flexible operational level units at the division and corps level, later called *ugda* in the IDF, was born at Latrun.
- *Doctrine.* Marcus supported, urged, and helped shape the IDF's spirit of the offensive and focus on taking the fight quickly to enemy territory. He pushed for the early use of the maneuverable

mechanized task force, matched to terrain and mission, and the mixed arms brigade as the foundational maneuver unit in the IDF order of battle. His support of active and preemptive defense against the enemy's mass and logistics base was in keeping with the legacy of Orde Wingate, another charismatic and foundational character in the early history of the Jewish army.

- *Training.* Mickey's original ideas about training battalion and brigade-level commanders and staff in close collaboration with later chief of staff and PME professional Chaim Laskov, and his constant emphasis on physical training and ranger-type/special operations thinking, are still hallmarks of IDF training—even during wartime.
- *Culture.* While the core ethos of the modern Jewish army was shaped by Israeli leaders and the history of self-defense in the British mandate, Mickey's position in the diaspora and America, especially after his death, symbolized the broader global Jewish support for the establishment and nurturing of the State of Israel. The ideas surrounding the IDF concept of purity of arms were influenced, if not in fact, certainly in spirit by Marcus in his strict embrace of professionalism at all levels.
- *Political legitimacy.* No one would claim that Marcus shaped the civil-military relations between the state and the Jewish army, or the legitimacy of the latter's purpose: self-defense. His very presence, however, and his discreet discussions with his friends in America about the viability of the Jewish army he was shaping helped maintain support as enthusiasm for partition in the United States cooled. The survival of the Jewish army, and the fact that it managed to hold on to most of the assigned territory and did so against the unanimous prediction of the US intelligence community, helped justify Truman's early recognition of Israeli independence. That support has held firm for three quarters of a century.
- *Leadership.* Ben-Gurion continually called Jerusalem the critical theater of the war for independence, and at the worst

> moments right after independence, when international pressure was building for a ceasefire after a string of Jewish defeats, he turned to Mickey Marcus to unify the nation's forces fighting near the city. What Marcus did or didn't do, his decisions or lack of them, or what he might have done had he lived are not the issue. He was in command, and unity of command was his core concept for building a postindependence, defactionalized, apolitical, unified Jewish army operating according to the humanitarian laws of war despite its enemies' blood libels.

Though his time in high operational command in the IDF was remarkably brief, less than two weeks, Aluf Michael Stone commanded the first mechanized infantry division, attached to the first organized front headquarters, in the modern Jewish army of Israel. That army is the fulfilment of the long struggle for the national liberation of the people of Israel against foreign rule and restoration of sovereignty in the land of Israel. Jews have continuously dwelled in that place, or returned to it from exile willingly or driven, across an unbroken history of more than three thousand years, dating the Exodus in the Nineteenth Dynasty, or fourteenth-century BC, Egypt. Mickey's impact as a leader was felt across the spectrum from prime minister to Palmach driver and is borne out in the testimony of those he touched.[9]

While David Daniel Marcus, aka Michael Mickey Stone, might not be a founder of the IDF in the most rigorous definition thereof, someone who was there from the very beginning and played a key role over an extended period, what he did in mere weeks marks him as a foundational figure in the force's early development. Marcus was shaped by the citizen-soldier American military experience of the first half of the twentieth century, tested by the challenges of the Depression, seasoned in the exciting La Guardia years in NYC politics, and reached a peak of personal excellence and service during World War II and the US occupation of Germany. In his last assignment in the US Army, he helped lay the legal foundation and establish the first apparatus for trial and punishment of war crimes, crimes against peace, and crimes against humanity. If he had gone home for good then, it is very likely history would never have heard from him again, whatever his fate, high or low. But when *fortuna* touched him through Shlomo Shamir's hand and set him on the path to his last two hundred days, days of destiny, it cemented his esteemed place in the history of the Jewish army and the people of Israel—exactly what Ben-Gurion, the boss, had promised Emma when Mickey fell in the hills of a free Jerusalem.

APPENDIX A

Mickey's Report to the Haganah March 16, 1948 (Shamir Archive)

I am pleased to appear before you and make my report. I made my inspections bearing in mind a quote from a most successful General and Chief of Staff -

> "Military books emphasise tactics - strategy - at the expense of administration. This is unfortunate, a blunder, as experience demonstrates that success in battle depends on the efficiency of ADMINISTRATION".

The failure to understand its importance is where the High Command usually goes WRONG.

2. Tactics teaches you how to "Guard", how to strike, how to move. You need much more, discipline and faith - that is the moral side of the cause, supply the material side; leadership and organisation is the intellectual side; all are necessary. You can't neglect any one of these essentials.

3. For purposes of this discussion I assume that the Arabs are more numerous and are equally poorly equipped as we are. Our potential strength and advantages must stem from the belief that we must be better prepared to furnish superior services, administration and organisation to our forces.

4. To organise an army, you select a Commander-in-Chief, a Boss. It is his job to combine, mould the efforts and energies of thousands into a strong steel fist, and avoid the creation of thousands of weak fingers.

5. The Boss has a difficult job, as he must be in 24 places, talk to 24 people at the same time. He solves this problem by the establishment of a STAFF. Every person of the staff must know not only his job,

/but his

-2-

but his functions must be clearly stated; he must know from whom to take instructions and who are his subordinates to whom he issues orders. Then he must supervise the execution of the orders and make certain that there is strict compliance with ORDERS. The duties, functions, responsibilities have not as yet been defined. No precise written terms of reference. Under the direction of the High Command an intensive course for the training of the Brigade-Battalion Commanders and Staffs is under way. In the Army thereis never enough of anything, including time. However we are going to train the STAFF.

6. Armies win wars by fire and movement. Many believe that movement is the more important ingredient of success. "Get there first with most men" is an old military axiom. Today, you can't move a battalion for lack of control, training, of the staff,but primarily no one battalion has the transport available to move quickly and efficiently, not HAPHAZARD and by chance. This is strange, because you have the manpower here who have the vision to foresee what is required - men who have the wisdom to plan and order the execution. And many men in the field who have the courage to act to gain the ends sought.

7. There are 3 operations of WAR - 1. Offensive, the attack - 2. Defensive, so that you can secure a place to counter attack - 3. Withdrawals.

8. The Attack mustbe bold, aggressive, ruthless, determined. The Offensive wins wars. I believe that too much emphasis has been placed here on "National Defence", as it can (and I have found it so) become part of the military policy and philosophy of your army. Such a doctrine provides the road to calamity and defeat. Wars are won by victories in the field, such as Normandy, not by the disasters at DUNKIRK. The will to win requires the determination to strike overpowering blows to destroy the enemy; rather than to

-3-

await calmly, placidly the blows of the enemy. The taking of a village, blowing up of a house, an outpost, then returning to your base to eat, sleep and talk about retaliation is not WAR. In war, you take the outpost and keep going until you paralise the enemy by hitting him in his weak, vital points. That requires that you make available to your High Command a striking force that can take the offensive and if need be serve as your Reserve when you must temporarily assume the defensive.

9. Of course, I understand thatyou can't now attack. But is there any reason why plans should not be under way - blue prints created, men trained, so that if the march of events makes it necessary for survival, we make bold moves - we are in a position to do so? Things don't happen, they are caused - actions can't be left to change. It must not be HAPHAZARD.

10. Planning is essential NOW, for a proper, efficient way to stop the killing of Jews in the defile of the road from Tel Aviv - Jerusalem. Thereis no one way to plan a military operation. There are many approved solutions. Personally to safeguard the defile, I would move boldly, with vigour seize the exit and entrance of the defile: deploy my forces along the ridges, on the flanks of the road, and either kill the enemy, capture him, but certainly eject him. Then sit on the high ground. You can't do it without planning.

11. Initially, we mustbe prepared to defend. Penetration by the enemy must be accepted as NORMAL. The Nazis penetrated into one third of Russia. The Japs seized a half of a Continent. Experience in combat proved that any attempt at defence in line by the establishment of a steel ring will not stand up against modern attack. The errors of the Maginot Line are still fresh and vivid. If you accept the principle that the enemy will break through and thrust his forces like a dagger at your heart, you must agree that we must be prepared to meet the thrust of the dagger by a tough strong hammer that will halt the dagger and then take

-4-

on the attitude of the attack. That force to which I made reference as the striking force earliest - would be the same force to halt an attack. This leads me to the use of a military term - "Reservë". Every Section, Platoon, Company, Battalion, Brigade, Army, Commander is taught to fight with a RESERVE. Today, if the enemy would start from Tulkarm, it would move to the sea and Natanya. Becauseyou have not provided the High Command with a Reserve. A reserve that would stop a thrust at us - or a force that would successfully exploit a breakthrough of our forces.

12. Now to a matter of Prime Importance - the SOLDIER. I am amazed that the soldier is not physically fit. The men of the Palmach appear to have the best physical condition of all of the forces I have seen.But they can't march 35 miles in 24 hours - and be prepared to engage the enemy in combat. I know what it means to be tough, hard physically fit for combat as I have trained rangers in the Pacific. You can't subject men to difficult physical exertion - gruelling marches - obstacles courses, unless they are properly fed,clothed, equipped. Then, you can test them to go without FOOD, WATER, SHELTER, SLEEP, after you get them up to a high standard of physical fitness.

13. Morale - I shall not attempt to define it. Statehood carries with it obligations - I saw in several places men who stated to me that they did not have a reserve of food - just two meals ahead of the last one. I saw men without blankets - many men who picked up their feet to show me that their shoes were without soles. Yes, these men won't desert. They are the only military asset I have seen in Palestine. They have an eagerness, a determination that must be preserved. Failure to supply them is undermining this asset. I refuse to believe that there are not enough shoes,blankets,clothing, to give to them. I refuse to believe,and don't be mislead - these men refuse to believe it - as a walk through Tel Aviv convinces them that there is food in abundance, there are shoes and clothing.

-5-

14. The explanation that there is no funds can't be accepted. The lack of money does not excuse the failure to provide. You must seek the money and find it - here in Palestine. One can't depend on the future actions of the United Nations. You must mobilise your resources. Initiative,inventiveness,resourcefullness are needed In this day there are shortages of food - money - clothes - but make certain that the soldiers are adequately taken careof. The best quartermaster is of no value if you don't give him supplies. Do you know how to make the most of what you have here in Palestine? Do you know how to use whatyou have - you mustxxxx organise better your civilian resources.

15. The mental attitude has not reached the point where you areprepared to mobilise your manpower and resources for an all out fight to the finish. If I knew that I could return here in a few days from America with several technical army experts and staff officers, I would fly there tomorrow to seek them out and bring them here. Perhaps it may be necessary to do that - but for purposes of planning, the path of reason dictates that you must proceed on the basis that there will be no or little outside aid.

16. Wars are not won signle-handed. It requires the combined and collective strength of the community. Accordingly select your able men from the community of Palestine, delegate power to them and put them to useful work. You must secure all the competence within Palestine to win.

17. As the executive for military government,when I was stationed early in 1942, I saw the efforts of the People of the large island of HAWAII, in establishing an organisation to mobilise the strength of a community. It was admirable.

18. I speak not of arms - equipment, as I know of the desperate attempts made to secure the needed sinews of war.

-6-

19. Let me go [illegible] tell you something of your military command, the finest thing I have seen in the Hagana - section, platoon, company, battalion commanders serving as leaders depending on their own ability,personality, bearing in mind always the welfare of their men, yet possessing the ability to make the "toe the mark" - play the game - to do that, gentlemen, without RANK, authority, is a great tribute to your men in the field. Don't let them down.

20. To sum up, letme urge thatyou provide your military command with the authority to build up an efficient staff - measures and steps are being taken to train men for staff duties. Your General Headquarters must be provided with a Reserve. Your Quartermaster must be furnished with SUPPLIES - money to enable him to get FOOD, ClOTHES - TRANSPORT - EQUIPMENT. Improve also the recreational facilities for your men by providing them with the means to engage in sports which, incidentally will further their physical development.

<u>16th March,1948.</u>

APPENDIX B

Draft, Jewish Agency Contract for General Ralph C. Smith December 3, 1947 (Shamir Archive)*

December 3, 1947

SECRET AND CONFIDENTIAL

My dear General Smith,

I am pleased to announce that General Hildring has given his blessing for an American to serve as Chief of Mission "Medina". On behalf of the Jewish Agency I hereby offer you the position as Chief of Mission "Medina". In this capacity you will be the Expert Consultant and Technical Advisor on all military matters relating to all problems connected with the Armed Forces.

It is understood that there will be made available a staff to assist you.

You shall be paid at the rate of $1,000 per month. Your assistants will be paid at the rate of $600 per month. In addition all expenses will be paid.

It is further understood that the period of employment will be not less than three months and not more than six months.

Very truly yours,

Approved: __________

Accepted: __________

*Transcribed from the original in the Shamir Archive

ACKNOWLEDGMENTS

A friend wisely observed that sometimes a story takes hold of your soul and never lets go. No story seized me as early as that of Mickey Marcus. First, I thank my cousin Debby Gettinger. When I was eight, she showed me a picture book about a fallen Jewish American hero self-published in 1949 by Bronx high school students, *The Story of Mickey Marcus*. It was a gift Debby got from a teacher who knew Emma and Mickey Marcus. Years passed. I read the only biography of Marcus, *Cast a Giant Shadow*, in high school and saw the film version of it in college, and even after that, when the occasional article came, I read it with interest and remembered my feeling of strong attachment to his story. Decades passed. Then, twenty years ago, having written my first book on military history, a biography of Major General Maurice Rose, I started thinking of revisiting the life of Micky Marcus. Both were the result of youthful encounters.

Many respected historians, biographers, journalists, lawyers, boxers, serving and retired soldiers, professors, teachers, friends, relatives, and strangers have read all or parts of the manuscript, listened to my endless rap, made suggestions, corrections, and criticisms, and offered me valuable advice. Not all of them know how much or precisely how they influenced my work. Some of them are gone. Thanks to Buford Alexander, Laure Aubuchon, Gideon Avidor, Martin Blumenson, Wilson Blythe Jr., Fred Borch, Steve Bourque, Alex Bruner, Steve Bye, Mark Calhoun, Ed Castorina, Shlomi Chetrit, Roger Cirillo, Rob Citino, Bruce Cohen, Charlie Conner, Peter Crean, John Curatola, Carlo D'este, Barry Driver, Stan Falk, Greg Fontenot, Jonathan

Freeman, Laurence Golding, Victor Gourevitch, Mike Haskew, Rick Herrera, Chaim Herzog, David Hogan, Kevin Hymel, Cole Kingseed, Chris Kolakowski, Terry Kungel, Don Marsh Ben May, Jim McGee, Dwight Mears, Benny Michelsohn, Ed Miller, David Mitchell, Dave Musick, Derek Penslar, Gary Petersmeyer, Zipporah Porath, Dan Rosenheim, Troy Sacquety, Matthew Seelinger, Eitan Shamir, Stuart Shapiro, Miles Siegel, David Silbey, Richard Sommers, Jacob Stoil, Luke Truxal, Gerald White, Clair Wilcox, Bob Wintermute, and Dave Zabecki.

There are very few sources for Mickey's story, but those in America hold the raw material for unraveling the image from the man. The US Army Heritage and Education Center (USAHEC) in Carlisle, Pennsylvania, has supported my work for a quarter century. From my first visit the staff has been open and welcoming, and guided my research with great professionalism, knowledge, and sharp instincts. Special mention to Louise Arnold-French, who called me a military history rock star. Thanks, girl. You're groupie quality. Because of all their confidence, recommendations, and support, I was honored with a General and Mrs. Matthew Ridgway Research Award in 2014 from the US Army War College to support my Bradley research.

It is impossible to glimpse the man David Marcus '24, his best friend Charles "Steve" Stevenson '24, and their wives without visiting West Point Special Collections. I spent many pleasant days there and on campus and was lucky early in my writing career to make a wonderful friend, Alan Aimone, who worked in Special Collections for many years. He taught me about the academy when Macarthur was Supe and Brad taught math to the Thundering Herd, and pointed to sources, not least Red Reeder '26, Mickey's lifelong friend and corner man in the ring. Alan introduced me to the Marcus collection, donated by Emma Marcus, and told me that every new rabbi assigned to West Point began his ministry by looking at the Mickey collection and a visit to his grave. I treasure Alan's counsel and miss our lunches at the Thayer Hotel and dinners in San Francisco.

The third repository of Mickey material is the Cornell University Special Collections, which holds the papers of Edward "Ted" Berkman, the only book-length biographer of Marcus. For his biography, he contacted many of the principals. Advanced graduate student Megan Jeffreys waded through Berkman's material, unraveling and curating his peculiar method of cutting up and pasting sources in his manuscript, the archival boxes following his nonchronological, flashback-rich style. Although modern history is not her field, Megan "felt" the story and uncovered the hand of Emma, wholeheartedly supporting the heroic, universal—yet also Jewish—image of her husband, whether he was called Mickey Marcus or Mickey Stone. Here, despite the personal pain and resentments that Emma felt, she tellingly reveals her fierce loyalty to her life's great love.

Other institutions and archives helped me fill out the story, including the Lucius Clay Papers at the Library of Congress; the John H. Hilldring Papers at the Gilder Lehman Library; the Ted Berkman Papers at Columbia University; the Machal Archives at the Center for Jewish History; and the New York Public Library. The list also includes various archives in Israel, and I used those available in English and online.

Thanks to the US Army Center of Military History in Washington, DC. When I first started my second career as biographer and military historian, this was my first stop for World War II general officer files. It's been my good fortune to write for a related publication, the US Army's *Professional Bulletin of Army History*. The editor, my friend Bryan Hockensmith, in the winter of 2016 published my cover article about Mickey's contributions as a founder of modern civil affairs operations in World War II, now a part of US Special Operations. Soon after, Marcus was posthumously recognized as a Distinguished Member of the Civil Affairs Regiment at Fort Liberty, North Carolina, on October 26, 2017, my birthday. What a terrific present! It's incredible to see one's work become part of the legacy of the US Army. To Bryan, Fred, Dave, driver Ed, and others involved in that effort, a heartfelt thank you. It was one of the proudest moments of my life.

Very special thanks to Yael Shamir Driver, daughter of IDF Aluf Shlomo Shamir, whose incredible life story is a binding thread in the last two hundred days of the life of Mickey Marcus. Yael's Shlomo Shamir Archive, containing many original items, offers a completely unique, consistent, original, and fresh perspective on the story of Mickey Marcus and the man behind the public image. It is a writer's dream to uncover such original material and consistent second-hand witness. That also was *fortuna*. One of the first things I saw in the archive was the title page of *The Mickey Marcus Story*, sent by Emma and inscribed to Shlomo. Yael, your father was a hero of the Jewish people, the Jewish army, and the Seventh Armored Brigade.

I am lucky to have a publisher who believes in my work and commits the resources of the University of Missouri Press to make sure my voice is heard. Thank you David, Robin, Drew, and especially copyeditor Miranda Ottewell, a sharp, discerning writer and wonderful interlocutor. My editor, Andrew Davidson, and his team have carved out a niche of excellence in military history. I consider Andrew as my friend and trust his advice even when we're negotiating. If there is a better working relationship and partner in the academic publishing business, I'd be hard pressed to imagine it. Andrew, I set out to achieve a personal legacy in a demanding field, and you were essential for a long-shot success. In your shoes, I'm not sure I would have done it. Hey man, thank you doesn't go far enough.

My series editor, John McManus, is a much-decorated and world-recognized military historian. One of my first articles is in the same magazine as one of his. It was more than a decade ago that John and I first discussed a two-book deal for his series at Missouri: Brad, then Mickey. Life intervened and all looked dead for a time, but thanks to you, John, it happened. You're a master of the craft, with even greater recognition ahead, and I'm proud to brag that you're a colleague.

My dear friend in London, Francis Bennett, respected novelist and still active publisher, is my closest adviser on all things writing—and anything else that touches on the human condition. Visits with him and Tessa are part of *my* London. He always brings far-ranging wit and worldly wisdom to our times together, especially when I hit a block or take counsel from my fears. During one such time, not long after Covid, I went to London to see Francis, hoping that once again he could help. The advice he gave me, from his own experience I later thought, was both admonishment and encouragement. He said that it was my moral responsibility to finish what I had started as a boy and tell Mickey's story. With the events swirling around us as I write this in July 2024, and the newly realized relevance of the story I tell in these pages, his voice now seems prophetic. If I didn't do it, he said, no one else would; or even worse, someone would, and fail the subject. Thanks, my dear friend Frances. I know you're right. The Special Relationship is more than just my own blood.

Every day I remember my parents, Alex and Laya Ossad, and honor them always. I am who I am because of them in every way that matters, and this book is partial payment for what they gave me—freedom, the sweetness of living, a great childhood, a Jewish background, and a life in America, the Golden Land of equal justice under law at its best. Their memories are a blessing every day.

My children, Jordana, Tova, and Matt, have always offered encouragement, forbearance, and support. Tova knows her obligation is to nurture at least one historian, and what could be better than a salon of freewheeling discussion at the Champagne Brunch at the Harvard Club with Jordana? They both endure Daddy's endless chatter about deadlines, the cosmos, Middle Eastern history, and the crisis of western culture, but I've learned as much from them as they have from me. Especially about politics. What is virtue?

Sandra, top corporate communications exec, partner, companion, and first to hear my ideas and share my highs and lows, deserves a decoration for "unflinching tolerance with Special Mention in dispatches for deadline times." No one could be a worse client than I am. Thanks for the second time, San, I hope it's worth it. You are the essence of fashion and totally dominate your demographic.

Finally, I acknowledge with great respect my teachers, colleagues, the profession, its society, journal, and traditions, and those from that world who helped and encouraged me from the start. From leadership to the ranks, they welcomed and helped me despite my being outside their profession and eased the isolation in ways large and small. My philosophy teacher Victor taught me that in such a venture as this, you have to passionately pursue the passionless truth while preserving the essence of your own core. Sometimes I get it wrong, or even inverted, but in all cases the mistakes, faulty arguments, and other limitations of this biography are entirely my responsibility, as is what evokes your image of Mickey.

Chronology of the Life of David "Mickey" Marcus

1900
April 18: Marcus family arrives on SS *Amsterdam*, Ellis Island, New York

1901
February 22: Born at 103 Hester Street, Manhattan, New York[1]

1905
July 19: Emma (Chaison) Marcus born

1910
September 21: Father, Mordechai "Max" Marcus, dies

1915
June: Graduates from PS 109, Brooklyn

1919
June: Graduates from Boys High School, Brooklyn

1920
July 1: Enters US Military Academy, West Point, New York

1923
Wins US intercollegiate welterweight boxing championship

1924
June 12: Commissioned second lieutenant, Infantry, Regular Army
Enrolls at Brooklyn Law School

1926
November 29: Resigns Regular Army commission

December 23: Commissioned second lieutenant, field artillery, Organized Reserve Corps

1927

July 3: Marries Emma
Awarded LLB, Brooklyn Law

1928

Awarded JD, Brooklyn Law

1929

Appointed assistant US attorney, Treasury Department, Southern District of New York

1930

September 5: Promoted to first lieutenant, Field Artillery, Organized Reserve Corps

1930–1934

Assistant US attorney, Southern District of New York

1933

March 15: Mother, Lina Leah (Goldstein) Marcus, dies

1934

January 1: Appointed Deputy Commissioner of Corrections, NYC

1936

Summer: Appointed New York City temporary magistrate

1939

March 15: Film *Blackwell's Island* released
November 30: Promoted to captain, JAG Division, New York National Guard

1940

April: Promoted to commissioner of corrections
August 17: Promoted to major, JAG Division, New York National Guard
September 6: Appointed JAG, 27th Infantry Division (ID); promoted to lieutenant colonel, JAG Division, New York National Guard
October 15: 27th ID nationalized; leaves New York for Fort McClellan, Alabama

1942
April: 27th ID Deploys to Oahu, Hawaii from California
Fall: 27th ID Ranger School established

1943
March 1: Civil Affairs Division (CAD) established in War Department
April: Transferred to CAD
July 26: Promoted to colonel, JAGD, Army of the United States

1944
May 12: Arrives in England, attached to 101st Airborne Division
June 8: Lands via LCI (Landing Craft, Infantry) on Utah Beach with Major John Maginnis
June 25: Departs Normandy for Washington
August: Dumbarton Oaks Conference
September: Quebec Conference

1945
February: Yalta Conference
Late May: Assigned HQ, US Forces, European Theater, Germany, Secretary, US Control Council, Berlin
July–August: Potsdam Conference
August 27: Named assistant to Major General Oliver P. Nichols, Berlin
September 9: Attends Allied victory celebration in Berlin

1946
February 4: Appointed head of War Crimes Branch, CAD
July: Commissioned major, JAGD, Regular Army

1947
April: Resigns Regular Army commission
Commissioned colonel, JAGD, Organized Reserve Corps
Returns to Brooklyn
November 6: Approached by Shamir at Berkshire Hotel
November 29: UN votes on partition of Palestine
November 30: Jewish-Arab Civil War begins

1948
Jan 15: Signs contract with Jewish Agency
Jan 29: Leaves for Palestine with Shamir
February 4: Meets Ben-Gurion at the Red House, Haganah HQ

March 2: Completes tour
March 16: Authors report for Haganah High Command
April 8: Returns to United States
April 20: Presented with Order of the British Empire at British Embassy, Washington
May 2: Returns to Palestine
May 14: Attends declaration of Israel's independence, Tel Aviv
May 15: Egypt, Syria, Transjordan, Lebanon, and Iraq attack Israel
May 17: Dispatched to Egypt
May 25: Operation Bin Nun Alef, Latrun
May 28: Appointed "Aluf Stone," commander, Jewish Front
May 30: Operation Bin Nun Bet, Latrun
June 2–10: Construction of the "Burma Road"
June 10–11: Killed by Palmach sentry at Abu Ghosh
June 11: First UN truce declared; it will last until July 11
July 1: Buried at West Point

1949
June 28: Posthumously appointed *aluf* in the Israel Defense Forces

1951
May 10: Prime Minister David Ben-Gurion visits West Point grave

1962
August: *Cast a Giant Shadow*, biography by Ted Berkman, published

1966
March 30: Film version of *Cast a Giant Shadow* released

1982
April 16: Emma Marcus dies

1995
June 10: Machal memorial dedicated along the Burma Road

2017
October 26: Named distinguished member of the Civil Affairs Regiment, US Army Special Operations Command

2024
June: Fifty-eighth annual Marcus celebration at West Point

Principal Awards and Decorations Earned by David "Mickey" Marcus

Army Distinguished Service Medal

Bronze Star Medal[1]

Legion of Merit[2]

Army Commendation Medal

Presidential Unit Citation

World War II Victory Medal

US Army Occupation Medal with Bar (Germany)

American Defense Medal

American Theater Campaign Medal

Asiatic-Pacific Theater Medal

European-African-Middle Easter Theater Medal, with one campaign star (Normandy)

New York State Conspicuous Service Cross (Military)

Foreign Awards

Commander, Most Excellent Order of the British Empire

Israel Order of Independence Ribbon

BIBLIOGRAPHY

Archives and Manuscript Collections

Ben-Gurion Archive, Sde Boker, Israel. https://bengurionarchive.bgu.ac.il/en.

Berkman, Ted. Papers, 1942–2001. Columbia University, New York

Bradley, Omar. Papers. US Army Center for Army Education & Heritage, Carlisle, PA

Clay, Lucius D. Papers. Library of Congress, Washington, DC.

Haganah Historical Archives, Tel Aviv. https://archives.mod.gov.il/sites/HaHagana/Eng/Pages/AbouttheHaganahHistoricalArchives.aspx.

Hilldring, John H. Papers. Gilder Lehman Library, New York

Israel Defense Forces Archive and Armored Corps Museum, Latrun

IDF Archives, Kiryat Ono, Tel Aviv. https://archives.mod.gov.il/sites/English/Pages/default.aspx.

Machal Archives. Center for Jewish History, New York

Museum of the Jewish Soldier in World War II, Latrun. https://www.jwmww2.org/en.

National Library of Israel, Jerusalem. https://www.nli.org.il/en.

Palmach Archives, Ramat Aviv, Tel Aviv. https://archives.mod.gov.il/sites/English/About/Pages/Palmah.aspx.

Shlomo Shamir Archive, Tel Aviv.

Truman, Harry S. Papers. Harry S. Truman Library, Independence, MO. https://www.trumanlibrary.gov/library/truman-papers.

US Army Center for Military History, Washington, DC

Works Cited

Allon, *Shield of David: The Story of Israel's Armed Forces.* New York: Random House, 1970.

———. *The Making of Israel's Army.* London: Valentine, Mitchell, 1970.

Arbel, Naftali. *The Sword and Plowshare: Israel, 1948–1968.* Tel Aviv: Amir, 1968.

———. *Jerusalem: Past and Present.* Tel Aviv: S. Friedman, 1969.

Beckman, Morris. *The Jewish Brigade: An Army with Two Masters, 1944–45.* Rockville Center, NY: Sarpedon, 1998.

Ben-Gurion, David. Diary. In Ben-Gurion, *Israel.*

Israel: A Personal History. New York: Funk & Wagnalls, 1971. Contains portions of Ben-Gurion's diary during the period of Marcus's recruitment and employment, which are cited by date or page in this edition.

Bercuson, David J. *The Secret Army*. New York: Stein & Day, 1983.

Berkman, Ted. *Around the World in 80 Years*. Carpinteria, CA: Manifest, 1998.

———. *Cast a Giant Shadow; The Story of Mickey Marcus, Who Died to Save Jerusalem*. Garden City, NY: Doubleday, 1962.

———. "In the Footsteps of Mickey Marcus." *Hadassah Magazine*, April 1962. Entered into *Congressional Record*, May 2, 1962, by Rep Emanuel Celler (D/Brooklyn).

Blum, Howard. *The Brigade: An Epic Story of Vengeance, Salvation, and World War II*. New York: Harper, 2001.

Borch, Fred L. "The Amazing Career of 'Mickey' Marcus." *Jewish Veteran*, Fall 2009, 14–15.

———. "David 'Mickey' Marcus." *On Point* 15, no. 3 (Winter 2010): 17–20.

———. "The Nuremberg Trials at 75: The International Military Tribunal and the Military Trials under Council Law No. 10 (1945–1949)." *Army Lawyer*, no. 6 (2020): 16–24. https://www.proquest.com/pqrl/docview/2549050151/52D5FC7D6C774EF7PQ/45.

Bourque, Steven A. *Tubby: Raymond O. Barton and the US Army*. Denton: University of North Texas Press, 2024.

Calhoun, Ricky-Dale. "Arming David: The Haganah's Illegal Arms Procurement Network in the United States, 1945–49." *Journal of Palestine Studies* 36, no. 4 (Summer 2007): 22–32.

Clay, Lucius D. *Decision in Germany*. New York: Doubleday, 1950.

Clifford, Clark. *Counsel to the President: A Memoir*. New York: Random House, 1991.

Cohen, Rich. *The Avengers: A Jewish War Story*. New York: Vintage, 2000.

Coles, Harry L., and Albert K. Weinberg. *Civil Affairs: Soldiers Become Governors*. Washington, DC: US Army Center for Military History, 1992. https://history.army.mil/html/books/011/11-3/CMH_Pub_11-3.pdf.

Collins, J. Lawton. *Lightning Joe: An Autobiography*. Baton Rouge, LA: LSU Press, 1979.

Collins, Larry, and Dominique Lapierre. *O Jerusalem!* New York: Simon & Schuster, 1972.

Dekel, Efraim. *Shai: The Exploits of Haganah Intelligence*. New York: Sagamore Press, 1959

Dunkelman, Ben. *Dual Allegiance: An Autobiography*. New York: Crown, 1976.

Dori, Yaakov. "His Name Was a Legend: A Tribute to Colonel Marcus (Stone)." *Palestine Post*, June 10, 1949.

Eastwood, Kathy. "Marcus—A Soldier for All Humanity." *Pointer View* 65, no. 21 (June 6, 2008): 7.

Eitan, Raful. *A Soldier's Soldier*. New York: SPI Books, 1992.

Erickson, Edgar L. "An Introduction to Military Government and Civil Affairs in World War II." Ms., ca. 1946. US Army Center for Military History, Washington, DC.

Ferencz, Ben. "Starting a New Life." https://benferencz.org/stories/1943-1946/starting-a-new-life.

———. "Detained for Impersonating an Officer." https://benferencz.org/stories/1946-1949/detained-for-impersonating-an-officer.

Finkelstein, Norman H. *American Jewish History*. Philadelphia: Jewish Publication Society, 2007.

Fredman, J. George, and Louis A. Falk. *Jews in American Wars*. New York: Jewish War Veterans, 1942.

Freeman, Michael. "The Forgotten Airman: Major General Oliver P. Echols and How He Won WWII." Master's thesis, School of Advanced Air and Space Studies, Air University, 2012. https://apps.dtic.mil/sti/tr/pdf/AD1019696.pdf.

Frommer, Myrna, and Harvey Frommer. *It Happened in Brooklyn: An Oral History of Growing Up in the Borough in the 1940s, 1950s, and 1960s*. New York: Harcourt, Brace, 1993.

———. "Zionism Yesterday," *Jewish Magazine*, June 1998. http://www.jewishmag.com/10mag/zionist/zionist.htm/

Gabel, Christopher R. *The U.S. Army GHQ Maneuvers of 1941*. Washington, DC: US Army Center for Military History, 1992. https://history.army.mil/html/books/070/70-41-1/CMH_Pub_70-41-1.pdf.

Grombach, John V. *The Saga of Sock: A Complete Story of Boxing*. New York: AS Barnes, 1949.

Grose, Peter. *Israel in the Mind of America*. New York: Knopf, 1983.

Halperin, Judith, and Phyllis Kreinik. *Mickey Marcus: The Story of Colonel David Marcus*. New York: Bloch, 1949.

Harper Encyclopedia of Military History. Edited by R. Ernest Depuy and Trevor N. Depuy. New York: HarperCollins, 1993.

Harrison, Gordon A. *Cross-Channel Attack: United States Army in World War II; The European Theater of Operations*. 1950. Reprint, Washington, DC: Office of the Chief of Military History, 1973.

Heiman, Leo. "David Marcus: Israel's Lafayette." *Congress Weekly*, July 21, 1958, quoted in "Extension of Remarks, Hon. Abraham J. Multer (Dem, Brooklyn)," 104 Cong. Rec. A8330 (daily ed. September 12, 1958).

Herzog, Chaim. *The Arab-Israeli Wars: War and Peace in the Middle East*. New York: Vintage Books, 1982.

———. *Living History: A Memoir*. New York: Pantheon, 1996.

Hoffman, Tom. *Benjamin Ferencz, Nuremberg Prosecutor and Peace Advocate*. Jefferson, NC: McFarland, 2014.

Hogan, David W., Jr. *A Command Post at War: First Army Headquarters in Europe, 1943–1945*. Washington, DC: US Army Center for Military History, 2000

"Honor Roll: Distinguished Service Medal to David Marcus, Colonel, J.A.G.," *Judge Advocate Journal* 2, no. 3 (Fall/Winter 1945): 30.

Hughes, Cici. "Spotlight on a Shadow: Col. David 'Mickey' Marcus, 1901–1948: A 75th Anniversary Tribute to the Class of '24." *Assembly* 57 (May/June 1999): 36–37.

Jacobson, Edward. "Two Presidents and a Haberdasher, 1948." *American Jewish Archives* 20, no. 1 (April 1968): 3–15. https://sites.americanjewisharchives.org/publications/journal/PDF/1968_20_01_00_doc_truman.pdf.

Karsh, Efraim. *The Arab-Israeli Conflict: The Palestine War 1948*. London: Osprey, 2002.

Katz, Samuel M. *Fire and Steel.* New York: Pocket Books, 1992

Kaune, Charles S. *The National Guard in War: An Historical Analysis of the 27th Infantry Division, (New York National Guard) in World War II.* Thesis, VMI, 1990.

Kimche, Jon, and David Kimche. *A Clash of Destinies: The Arab-Jewish War and the Founding of the State of Israel.* New York: Praeger, 1960.

Kitchen, K. A. *Pharaoh Triumphant: The Life and Times of Ramesses II.* Warminster, UK: Aris and Phillips, 1982.

Kramer, Martin. "The Forgotten Truth about the Balfour Declaration," *Mosaic Magazine*, June 5, 2017. https://mosaicmagazine.com/essay/2017/06/the-forgotten-truth-about-the-balfour-declaration/.

Krulewitch, Melvin L. *Now That You Mention It.* New York: Quadrangle, 1973.

Kurzman, Dan, *Ben-Gurion, Prophet of Peace.* New York: Simon & Schuster, 1983.

———. *Genesis 1948: The First Arab Israeli War.* New York: New American Library, 1970.

———. *Soldier of Peace: The Life of Yitzhak Rabin, 1922–1995.* New York: Harper, 1998.

Laffin, John. *The Israeli Army in the Middle East Wars, 1948–1973.* London: Osprey, 1982.

Limpus, Lowell M. "This Was Mickey Marcus." *Saturday Evening Post*, December 1, 1948, 29, 179–81.

———. "Lowell Limpus Obituary." *Assembly*, Spring 1958, 92–93.

Lorch, Netanel. *The War of Independence 1947-1949.* Hartford: Hartmore House, 1968 (1961).

Love, Edmund G. *The 27th Infantry Division in World War II.* 1949. Reprint, Nashville, TN: Battery Press, 1982.

Lustig, Doreen. "The Nature of the Nazi State and the Question of International Criminal Responsibility of Corporate Officials at Nuremberg: Revisiting Franz Neumann's Concept of Behemoth at the Industrialist Trials." *New York University Journal of International Law and Politics* 43, no. 4 (2011): 965–1044. https://nyujilp.org/wp-content/uploads/2013/02/43.4-Lustig.pdf.

Maginnis, John. *Military Government Journal: Normandy to Berlin.* Amherst: University of Massachusetts Press, 1971.

———. "My Service with Colonel Marcus." *American Jewish History* 69, no. 3 (March 1980): 301–24.

———. *Portrait of a Citizen-Soldier.* Great Neck, NY: Todd & Honeywell, 1981.

Mallin, Jay, and Robert K. Brown. *Merc: American Soldiers of Fortune.* 1979. Philadelphia: Casemate, 2018.

Marcus, Emma, and Ralph Schoenstein. "The West Pointer Who Built Israel's Army." *American Weekly*, February 10, 1957.

Marrus, Michael R. "Three Roads from Nuremberg, Seventy Years to the Day after the Start of the Epoch-Defining Trials, Three Jewish Advocates Stand above the Rest:

Jacob Robinson, Sir Hersch Lauterpacht, and Raphael Lemkin." *Tablet Magazine*, November 20, 2015. https://www.tabletmag.com/sections/arts-letters/articles/three-roads-from-nuremberg.

Melzer, Emanuel. "Revisionist Zionists." *The YIVO Encyclopedia of Jews in Eastern Europe*. https://yivoencyclopedia.org/article.aspx/Revisionist_Zionists.

Michelsohn, Benny. "Aluf David Marcus—the First General in the IDF and His Influence on the Two Armies." Museum of the Jewish Warrior in World War II. https://www.jwmww2.org/soldier.aspx?id=2741.

Michelsohn, Benny, and Fred L. Borch. "An American in the Israeli Army." *Military History*, Winter 2024. https://www.historynet.com/an-american-in-the-israeli-army/.

Millen, Raymond. *Bury the Dead, Feed the Living: The History of Civil Affairs/Military Government in the Mediterranean and European Theaters of Operation during World War II*. Carlisle, PA: Peacekeeping and Stability Operations Institute, 2019.

Millett, John D. *Organization and Role of the Army Service Forces*. Washington, DC: Office Chief of Military History, 1954.

Milstein, Uri. *A Nation Girds for War*. Vol. 1 of *History of the War of Independence*. New York: University Press of America, 1996.

Morris, Benny. *1948: The First Arab Israeli War*. New Haven : Yale, 2008.

———. *The Road to Jerusalem: Glubb Pasha, Palestine and the Jews*. London: I. B. Tauris, 2002.

Museum of the Jewish Warrior in World War II. "Liberation of the Concentration Camps." https://www.jwmww2.org/The_liberation_of_the_concentration_camps.

Nevins, Jack. "The Magnificent Mickey Marcus: Defender of Liberty." *Pointer* 37, no. 4 (Nov. 6, 1959): 6–7, 24–25.

"Declaring the State of Israel on May 14, 1948." *Newsweek*, May 24, 1948. https://www.newsweek.com/declaring-state-israel-may-14-1948-332152.

Olin, Chuck, dir. *Is Jerusalem Burning? Myth, Memory and the Battle of Latrun*. Tel Aviv: Chuck Olin Associates, PBS, 1998. https://digital.library.illinois.edu/items/163b0980-5cc8-0132-3334-0050569601ca-8.

———. *In Our Own Hands: The Hidden Story of the Jewish Brigade in World War II*. 1998; Chicago: Chuck Olin Associates, PBS, 1998. https://www.youtube.com/watch?v=_4Z4clCCkIg

Ossad, Steven L. "The Battle of Kadesh, 1300 BC: Public Relations Trumps Performance." https://www.stevenlossad.com/the_battle_of_kadesh__public_relations_trumps_performance_77536.htm.

———. "Last Battle of William Orlando Darby." *Army Magazine*, January 2003.

———. "Liberation of Nordhausen Concentration Camp." Warfare History Network, February 2019. https://warfarehistorynetwork.com/article/the-liberation-of-nordhausen-concentration-camp/.

———. *Omar Nelson Bradley, America's GI General, 1893–1981*. Columbia: University of Missouri Press, 2017.

———. "Out of the Shadow and Into the Light: Col. David 'Mickey' Marcus and US Civil Affairs in World War II." *Professional Bulletin of Army History* 98 (Winter 2016): 6–27.

Ossad, Steven L., and Don R. Marsh. *Major General Maurice Rose*. Lanham, MD: Rowman & Littlefield, 2003.

Oxford Companion to World War II. Edited by M. R. D. Foot and I. C. B. Dear. Oxford: Oxford University Press, 1995.

"The Palestine Situation." Summary of conclusions reached by representatives of CIA, State, War, and Navy in conference, May 5, 1948. CIA Reading Room. https://www.cia.gov/readingroom/docs/CIA-RDP67-00059A000200200011-5.pdf.

Parsons, Laila. *The Commander: Fawzi Al-Qawuqji and the Fight for Arab Independence, 1914-1948*. New York: Hill and Wang, 2017.

Penslar, Derek J. *Jews and the Military: A History*. Princeton, NJ: Princeton University Press, 2013.

Petersen, Arthur. Interview by Rabbi Charles Rosenzveig, August 5, 1986. Video recording, 1:14. Oral History Department, Zekelman Holocaust Center, Farmington Hills, MI. https://www.holocaustcenter.org/visit/library-archive/oral-history-department/petersen-arthur-l/.

Pick, Walter Pinhas. "Latrun." *Encyclopedia Judaica*. Farmington Hills, MI: Thomson Gale, 2007. https://www.encyclopedia.com/religion/encyclopedias-almanacs-transcripts-and-maps/latrun.

Pogue, Forrest C. *United States Army in World War II: European Theater of Operations, The Supreme Command*. Washington, DC: US Army Center for Military History, 1989. https://history.army.mil/html/books/007/7-1/CMH_Pub_7-1.pdf.

Popowycz, Jennifer. "Lunchbox Lecture: Holocaust by Bullets," July 6, 2022. National WWII Museum, New Orleans. https://www.nationalww2museum.org/about-us/notes-museum/lunchbox-lecture-holocaust-bullets.

———. "The Potsdam Conference," July 18, 2022. National WWII Museum, New Orleans. https://www.nationalww2museum.org/war/articles/potsdam-conference.

Porath, Zipporah. *Col. David (Mickey) Marcus: A Soldier for All Humanity*. New York: American Jewish Historical Society, 2010.

Pyle, Ernie. *Brass Hats*. 1943–44. Reprint, New York: Aeonian Press, 1978.

Rabin, Yitzhak. *The Rabin Memoirs*. Boston: Little, Brown, 1979.

Rashba, Gary L. *Holy Wars: 3,000 Years of Battles in the Holy Land*. Philadelphia: Casemate, 2011.

"Recognition of the State of Israel." Truman Papers. https://www.trumanlibrary.gov/library/online-collections/recognition-of-state-of-israel?section=2.

Reeder, Red. *Heroes and Leaders of West Point*. New York: Thomas Nelson, 1970.

Rogan, Eugene L., and Shlaim, Avi. *The War for Palestine: Rewriting the History of 1948*. 2001. Reprint, Cambridge: CUP, 2017.

Ruppenthal, Roland et. al., *Utah Beach to Cherbourg, 6–27 June 1944*. American Forces in Action 13. 1948. Reprint, Washington, DC: US Army Center for Military History, 1990. https://www.history.army.mil/html/books/100/100-12/CMH_Pub_100-12.pdf.

Royals, W. C. "Cast a Giant Shadow—by Ted Berkman." *Assembly* 21 (Summer 1962): 28–29.

Rubner, Michael. "Revisionist Zionism: The Founder, His Disciple and Their Chief Adversary." *Middle East Policy* 22, no. 2 (2015). https://mepc.org/journal/review-essay-revisionist-zionism-founder-his-disciple-and-their-chief-adversary.

Sacquety, Troy. "Major General John H. Hilldring." *Veritas* 12, no. 1 (2016). https://arsof-history.org/articles/v12n1_hilldring_page_1.html.

Schiff, Zeev. *A History of the Israeli Army, 1870–1974*. San Francisco: Straight Arrow, 1974.

Shamir, Shlomo. "Shamir Memoir, Background and Dates," n.d. Translated and edited by Yael Shamir Driver, September 13, 2022. Shamir Archive.

———. *The Battle for Jerusalem: How the Siege Was Lifted*. Jerusalem: Posner & Sons, 2001.

Shamir Driver, Yael. "Supplements to Col. (res.) Benny Michelsohn's Article on Colonel David Marcus," January 7, 2024. Museum of the Jewish Soldier in World War II. https://www.jwmww2.org/userfiles/file/2024/Supplementmarcus.pdf.

Shapira, Anita. "Historiography and Memory: Latrun, 1948." *Jewish Social Studies* 3, no. 1 (Autumn 1996): 20–61.

———. *Yigal Allon, Native Son: A Biography*. Philadelphia: University of Pennsylvania, 2004.

Shapiro, Stewart, "Architect of Victory: David 'Mickey' Marcus's Effect on *Zahal*." Student paper, West Point, 1995.

Slater, Leonard. *The Pledge*. New York: Pocket Books, 1971.

Stanton, Shelby L. *Order of Battle, U.S. Army, World War II*. Novato, CA: Presidio, 1984.

Stevenson, Charles G. "David Daniel Marcus Obituary." *Assembly* 7, no. 4 (January 1949): 15–18.

Stoil, Jacob. "The Haganah and SOE: Allies and Enemies—Irregular Warfare & Politics in Mandatory Palestine." Paper presented at Society for Military History annual meeting, May 11, 2012. https://www.academia.edu/1504354/.

Stone, I.F. *Underground to Palestine and Reflections Thirty Years Later*. New York: Pantheon, 1978.

Taylor, Telford. *The Anatomy of the Nuremberg Trials*. New York: Alfred A. Knopf, 1992.

———. *Final Report to the Secretary of the Army on the Nuernberg War Crimes Trials under Control Council Law No. 10*. Washington, DC: Government Printing Office, 1949. https://avalon.law.yale.edu/subject_menus/imt.asp#proc.

Tucker, Spencer C. "Moshe Sharett." In Tucker and Roberts, *Encyclopedia of the Arab-Israeli Conflict*, 3:906.

Tucker, Spencer C., and Priscilla Roberts, eds. *Encyclopedia of the Arab-Israeli Conflict*. 4 vols. New York: Bloomsbury, 2008.

Wandres, J. *The Ablest Navigator: Lieutenant Paul N. Shulman, USN, Israel's Volunteer Admiral*. Annapolis, MD: NIP, 2010.

Whelan, Richard. *Robert Capa: A Biography*. New York: Ballantine, 1985.

US Army. *Order of Battle of the United States Army, World War II: Pacific Theater of Operations, Divisions*. Paris: Office of the Theater Historian, 1945.

US Army. *27th Infantry Division: Pictorial History, 1940–1941*. Atlanta: Army-Navy, 1941.

US Department of State, Office of the Historian. "Creation of Israel, 1948." Milestones, 1945–1952. https://history.state.gov/milestones/1945-1952/creation-israel.

US Department of State. "The Arab-Israeli War of 1948." Milestones, 1945–1952. https://history.state.gov/milestones/1945-1952/arab-israeli-war.

US Holocaust Memorial Museum. "Recognition of US Liberating Army Units." *Holocaust Encyclopedia.* https://encyclopedia.ushmm.org/content/en/article/us-army-units.

———. "Benjamin (Beryl) Ferencz Describes How He Became Involved in Preparations for the Subsequent Nuremberg Proceedings." *Holocaust Encyclopedia.* https://encyclopedia.ushmm.org/content/en/oral-history/benjamin-beryl-ferencz-describes-how-he-became-involved-in-preparations-for-the-subsequent-nuremberg-proceedings

US Military Academy. *Official Register of the Officers and Cadets, US Military Academy for 1924.* West Point, NY: Association of Graduates, 1924.

Weiss, Amy. "1948's Forgotten Soldiers? The Shifting Reception of American Volunteers in Israel's War of independence," *Israel Studies* 25, no. 1 (Spring 2020): 149–73.

———. "The Spirit of 1776 in 1948: American *Machalnikim* and Israel's War of Independence." In *Armed Jews in the Americas*, ed. Raanan Rein and David M. K. Sheinin (Brill: Leiden, the Netherlands, 2021), 96–115.

Wouk, Herman. *The Hope and the Glory.* New York: Little Brown, 1993

Zabecki, David T. "David 'Mickey' Marcus." *Military History* 15, no. 1 (April 1998), https://www.historynet.com/david-mickey-marcus.

———. "David Marcus." In Tucker and Roberts, *Encyclopedia of the Arab-Israeli Conflict*, 2:664–65.

———. "Orde Charles Wingate." In Tucker and Roberts, *Encyclopedia of the Arab-Israeli Conflict*, 3:1085–86.

Ziemke, Earl F. *The U.S. Army in the Occupation of Germany, 1944–1946.* Washington, DC: US Army Center for Military History, 1990. https://history.army.mil/books/wwii/Occ-GY/.

NOTES

Introduction

1. Stevenson, "Marcus Obituary," 15.

2. Thucydides, *Peloponnesian War*, 5.89.

3. Marcus and Schoenstein, "West Pointer"; Heiman, "David Marcus."

4. Correspondence between Yael Shamir Driver and Ofer Bord, director, Heritage and Museums Unit, IDF, January 2021, Shamir Archive. There is no direct evidence of an extension of the contract during Marcus's second and final visit to Israel.

5. Dori, "His Name Was a Legend."

6. Journalist and Hollywood screenwriter Edward Oscar "Ted" Berkman (1914–2006) was born in Brooklyn and graduated with a BA from Cornell in 1933. He served in the OSS during World War II, including as chief of the Balkan–Middle East Foreign Broadcast Intelligence Service. Later he worked as a correspondent and was first to report on the destruction of the British Army headquarters in the King David Hotel, Jerusalem, by Jewish underground militias on July 22, 1946.

Even as a general guide to Mickey's life, Berkman's book is limited by poor organization, unidentified quotations, fictional narrative, and random jumps in chronology. When it comes to his time in Normandy, it's pure pulp fiction, completely unreliable and problematic, at best, about his experience, motivations, and actual contributions to the founding of the IDF. Since there has never been a critical biography of Marcus, however, generations of historians and biographers have treated many of Berkman's assertions as facts.

7. Moshe Sharret to Emma Marcus, ca. October 1962, Shamir Archive.

8. "Cast a Giant Shadow (1966)," *AFI Catalog of Feature Films*, https://catalog.afi.com/Film/22317-CAST-AGIANTSHADOW.

9. "Cast a Giant Shadow." Shavelson told *Daily Variety* that the IDF charged $300 per tank and $1,500—$2 a head—for a battalion of soldiers. The film's budget was $4 million, and it took seventy-four days to shoot. George Segal was initially considered for the role of Marcus, but it ultimately went to Kirk Douglas. Shooting in Israel started in mid-May 1965, but on the first day, due to rising tensions with Jordan, the rented Israeli forces—and their tanks—had to leave to do their real job. Other challenges included Arab snipers killing five civilians just a few blocks away, and mob scenes made even more chaotic by scores of multilingual extras.

10. "Cast a Giant Shadow (1966)," *AFI Catalogue of Feature Films*, https://catalog.afi.com/Film/22317-CAST-AGIANTSHADOW.

11. "Anonymous paper re General Marshall and negotiation with Jews," March 26, 1948, p. 2, Truman Papers, https://www.trumanlibrary.gov/library/research-files/anonymous-paper-re-general-marshall-and-negotiation-jews.

12. David Marcus, draft of letter to Ralph C. Smith, n.d., Shamir Archive.

13. Marcus to Hilldring, May 16, 1948, Hilldring Papers.

Prologue: The Return Bout

1. In letters to his wife, Marcus often signed himself "Mici," and she referred to him by that spelling, but his close friends called him Mick. Everyone from the neighborhood called him Little Mike to distinguish him from his older brother and hero Mike, and that eventually became Mickey, and sometimes Micky. His Boys High and West Point classmates embraced it from his arrival. So did everyone afterward.

2. "Indoor-Meet," *Howitzer* yearbook (West Point, NY: US Military Academy, 1922), 419. Mickey was the 1923 intercollegiate welterweight champion; Jazz Harmony was captain of the team that year, and a four-time West Point lightweight champion. He remained undefeated for the rest of his college career. Grombach was also collegiate heavyweight champion.

3. John V. Grombach correspondence, box 5, folder 10, Berkman Papers.

4. "Army Has Good Boxers," *New York Times*, February 8, 1923; and Berkman, *Cast a Giant Shadow*, 123.

5. Stevenson, "Marcus Obituary," 15; and "David Marcus, 'Micky,' " *Howitzer* yearbook (West Point, NY: US Military Academy, 1924), 204.

6. Robert Degen, "They Introduced the Manly Arts to West Point," *Assembly*, Spring 1967, 20, 36–38; and Greg Bishop, "Cadets Develop a Fighting Spirit," *New York Times*, April 8, 2010, https://www.nytimes.com/2010/04/09/sports/09boxing.html.

7. Limpus, "This Was Mickey Marcus," 27. The 1922 *Howitzer* misreported that Marcus suffered the injury during the fight. *Howitzer* yearbook (West Point, NY: 1922), 429.

8. "Class of 1924 Notes," *Assembly*, April 1945, 18.

Chapter 1. The Early Years

1. Stevenson, "Marcus Obituary," 16.

2. Marcus family genealogy at Geni.com on New York Public Library Website, 2022.

3. Julius Freeman to Ted Berkman, February 13, 1961, box 5, folder 11, Berkman Papers.

4. During the war, many congregants served in the armed forces; eight made the supreme sacrifice. In the postwar years the temple forged a connection with the Brooklyn Dodgers, whose Ebbets Field was close by. On Thanksgiving the team served dinner to hundreds of Jewish orphans brought by the Men's Club to the temple for the day.

5. Limpus, "This Was Mickey Marcus," 27.

6. Noah Chase to Emma, February 10, 1957, box 8, file 5, Berkman Papers.

7. Stevenson, "Marcus Obituary," 16.

8. Stevenson, 16; Stevenson to Berkman, February 8, 1961, box 5, file 1, Berkman Papers.

9. Stevenson to Berkman, February 8, 1961.

10. Reeder, *Heroes*, 32.

11. Shlomo Shamir, draft memoir, Shamir Archive.

12. Limpus, "This Was Mickey Marcus," 179; Stevenson, "Marcus Obituary," 16; and Berkman, *Cast a Giant Shadow*, 134.

13. "A Brief History of West Point," US Military Academy West Point, accessed November 8, 2023, https://www.westpoint.edu/about/history-of-west-point.

14. US Military Academy, *Official Register, 1924*, 4.

15. "Brief History of West Point"; Ossad, *Bradley*, 33–34.

16. Ossad, *Bradley*, 55–58; *Register of Graduates, United States Military Academy* (West Point: Association of Graduates, 1980), 344–50; and "Class of 1924 Notes," *Assembly*, April 1945.

17. Bradley, *A General's Life*, 49.

18. Omar Bradley, interview by Colonel Hanson, December 2, 1974, p. 34, Bradley Papers.

19. Reeder, *Heroes*, 32–33.

20. Ossad, *Bradley*, 57.

21. Bradley, interview, 35.

22. Stevenson, "Marcus Obituary," 16.

23. Berkman, *Cast a Giant Shadow*, 135.

24. Czar Dyer to Emma Marcus, January 25, 1949, box 5, file 11, Berkman Papers.

25. Stevenson, "Marcus Obituary," 16.

26. Emma Marcus, note to Ted Berkman, n.d., box 6, file 10, Berkman Papers.

27. Berkman, *Cast a Giant Shadow*, 135.

28. Henry Albert to Lowell Limpus, September 24, 1948, box 5, folder 10, Berkman Papers.

29. Albert to Limpus.

30. Charles Stevenson to Ted Berkman, n.d., box 5, file 10, Berkman Papers; and US Military Academy, *Official Register, 1924*, 37.

31. "Army Boxers Take Meet from Culver," *New York Times*, February 23, 1923; Stevenson, "Marcus Obituary," 16; Cici Hughes, "Spotlight on a Shadow," p. 4, box 14, folder 9, Machal Archives.

32. "The Mickey Marcus Memorial at West Point," *Jewish Link*, May 16, 2024, https://jewishlink.news/the-mickey-marcus-memorial-at-west-point/.

33. West Point //*Howitzer* 1924, (West Point, NY: Corps of Cadets of the US Military Academy, 1924), 204.

34. Porath, *Marcus*, 5.

35. Czar Dyer to Emma Marcus, January 25, 1949, box 5, file 11, Berkman Papers.

36. "History of the 16th Infantry Regiment," Sixteenth Infantry Regiment Association, https://16thinfassn.org/#.

37. John Grombach to Ted Berkman re: Lowell Limpus, January 11, 1949, box 6, file 7, Berkman Papers.

38. Limpus, "This Was Mickey Marcus," 180.

39. See Mac Coffman, *The Regulars*; and Grombach to Stevenson, n.d., box 6, folder 7, Berkman Papers.

40. Dozens of members of the class of 1924 resigned within five years of graduation, almost all returning to service during World War II. Among them were active reserve and New York National Guard Twenty-Seventh Infantry Division officers during the interwar period. "Class of 1924," *Register of Graduates of the US Military Academy*, 1980, 344–50; and Limpus, "This Was Mickey Marcus," 29. Limpus was elected an "official" member of the Thundering Herd.

41. Czar Dyer to Emma Marcus, January 25, 1949, box 5, file 11, Berkman Papers. Colonel Nicholas W. Campanole (1881–1955) was a decorated officer of the Great War and linguist who rose from private to Patton's Third Army staff.

42. Frommer and Frommer, *It Happened in Brooklyn*, 49–50; and Frommer and Frommer, "Zionism Yesterday."

43. Mickey Marcus to George Medalie, box 6, file 7, Berkman Papers.

44. Thomas B. Dewey to Emma Marcus, February 21, 1949, box 8, file 6, Berkman Papers.

45. Berkman, *Cast a Giant Shadow*, 184–85; Limpus, "This Was Mickey Marcus," 180; Reeder, *Heroes*, 103.

46. Charlie Stevenson, comments at the Gibborim Society meeting, 1959, in *Congress Weekly*, July 21, 1958, cited in "Extension of Remarks, Thurs August 7 1958, by Rep. Abraham J. Multer," Congressional Record Appendix, A8330.

47. "Welfare Island Raid Bares Gangster Rule over Prison; Weapons, Narcotics Found," *New York Times*, January 25, 1934; and Stevenson, "Marcus Obituary," 16.

48. "M'Cormick Raids Welfare Island, Smashes Gangster Rule of Prison; Warden Relieved, Deputy Seized," *Herald Tribune*, January 25, 1934; Berkman, *Cast a Giant Shadow*, 184; and Limpus, "This Was Mickey Marcus," 180.

49. "Welfare Island Raid," *New York Times*, January 25, 1934; Berkman, *Cast a Giant Shadow*, 184; Limpus, "This Was Mickey Marcus," 180; "Dodge Subpoenas M'Cormick on Raid," *New York Times*, February 4, 1934.

50. Limpus, "This Was Mickey Marcus," 180.

51. Limpus.

52. "Blackwell's Island (1939)," *AFI Catalog of Feature Films*, accessed November 8, 2023, https://catalog.afi.com/Catalog/moviedetails/8125; "Warner Schedules 'Boy Meets Girl' for Cagney," *New York Times*, January 5, 1938; Berkman, *Cast a Giant Shadow*, 189; Emma Marcus, notes about January 5, 1938, departure for Hollywood, box 6, file 7, Berkman Papers. An early draft of the Blackwell's Island screenplay credited David Marcus as author, but his name was eliminated from later drafts, and the extent of his participation in the final film remains unclear. According to the *AFI Catalog*, the story was inspired by Austin MacCormick's 1934 raid on the Welfare Island prison. It also reported that Mickey had been the film's technical adviser, which

Emma corroborated earlier in her correspondence with Berkman. Warner Bros. held its first press showing at Welfare Island.

53. Franklin F. Russell to Emma Marcus, June 17, 1948, box 6, file 7, Berkman Papers.

54. Rose Sanker to Emma Marcus, November 1, 1960, box 5, file 8, Berkman Papers.

55. Statement of Special Prosecutor Thomas E. Dewey, June 8, 1936, box 6, file 7, Berkman Papers.

56. Limpus, "This Was Mickey Marcus," 180.

Chapter 2. World War II

1. Stevenson, "Marcus Obituary," 16. On the role of the JAG Corps, see US Army, "Protect Our Nation in Army Law," https://www.goarmy.com/careers-and-jobs/specialty-careers/law.html.

2. Borch, "David 'Mickey' Marcus;" Stevenson, "Marcus Obituary," 16; Berkman, *Cast a Giant Shadow*, 181–83; "Women Hysterical as Troops Depart," *New York Times*, October 24, 1940; and "Kissing the Girl Goodbye," *Brooklyn Eagle*, October 24, 1940, 2.

3. Reeder, *Heroes*, 104; Fiorello La Guardia, note to Mickey, May 2, 1940, box 6, folder 7, Berkman Papers.

4. Obituary for John Haskell, *New York Times*, November 14, 1987, http://www.nytimes.com/1987/11/14/obituaries/john-hf-haskell-83-ex-finance-executive.html

5. See especially Love, *27th Infantry Division*. For an example of these duties at division level, see also Bourque, *Tubby*.

6. Love, *27th Infantry Division*. See also Gabel, *U.S. Army GHQ Maneuvers*.

7. William H. Haskell, "Promotion of outstanding officers," HQ 27th Infantry Division, October 13, 1941, in Michelsohn, "Aluf David Marcus."

8. Love, *27th Infantry Division*.

9. Borch, "David 'Mickey' Marcus," 17–20.

10. Office of the Provost Marshal General, US Army Website, accessed November 8, 2023, https://api.army.mil/e2/c/downloads/287193.pdf.

11. Office of the Provost Marshal General.

12. Eric Pace, "Gen. Ralph C. Smith, Honored for War Bravery, Dies at 104," *New York Times*, January 26, 1998.

13. Pace, "Gen. Ralph C. Smith"; and Sharon Tosi Lacey, " 'Howlin Mad' WWII Marine General Goes to War with the Army," HistoryNet, March 30, 2011, https://www.historynet.com/howlin-mad-wwii-marine-general-goes-to-war-with-army/. Smith was relieved, according to the Marine commander, for his failure to advance, which exposed the flanks of the Marine Corps divisions. The army board, without outside members, fully exonerated Ralph Smith. By then Mickey had departed the division, but he maintained his respect for Ralph Smith for the remainder of his life.

14. Borch, "David 'Mickey' Marcus"; and Borch, "Amazing Career."

15. Ossad, "Out of the Shadow"; and Ossad, "Last Battle of William Orlando Darby."

16. Stevenson, "Marcus Obituary," 17.

17. Coles and Weinberg, *Civil Affairs*, 673–77.

18. 12th Army Group, Report of Operations, Final After-Action Report, vol. 7, pp. 21–27, G-5 Section, 1945.

19. Coles and Weinberg, *Civil Affairs*, 1–30; Millett, *Army Service Forces*, 148–54.

20. Edgar L. Erickson to Ted Berkman, March 28, 1961, box 6, folder 7, Berkman Papers.

21. There are a half dozen references to Hilldring in Ben-Gurion's diary and in documents in the Shamir Archive, including a draft contract for consultant employment with the Jewish Agency referring to General Hilldring's involvement.

22. Stevenson, "Marcus Obituary," 17; Borch, "David 'Mickey' Marcus"; and Borch, "Amazing Career."

23. Limpus, "This Was Mickey Marcus," 29, 179; "Honor Roll," *Judge Advocate Journal*; and "Col. Marcus Wins DSM; Aided in Surrenders," *New York Times*, May 18, 1945.

24. "The Cairo Conference, 1943," US Department of State Archive, 2001–2009, https://2001-2009.state.gov/r/pa/ho/time/wwii/107184.htm.

25. "Cairo Conference."

26. For general background on civil affairs and military government, see Ziemke, *Occupation of Germany*; and Coles and Weinberg, *Civil Affairs*.

27. First Army, Report of Operations, 23 February—8 May 1945, G-5 Section, annex 3 (Washington DC: Government Printing Office, 1946), p. 77.

28. 12th Army Group, Report of Operations, Final After-Action Report, vol. 7, G-5 Section (Washington, DC: Government Printing Office, 1946), p. 11.

29. First Army, Report of Operations, 23 February—8 May 1945, G-5 Section, Annex 3, pp 77-85, 1945; 12th Army Group, Report of Operations, Final After-Action Report, Volume VII, G-5 Section, pp. 11-27, pp 129-130, Appendices 2, 3, 5

30. Citation, Award of Military Commander, Order of the British Empire, quoted in Berkman, *Cast a Giant Shadow*, 161.

31. "Class of 1924 Notes," *Assembly* 4, no. 1 (April 1945): 18; and Berkman, *Cast a Giant Shadow*, 22.

32. "The British do not seem to be preparing themselves for the new plan but Americans prefer a directive which avoids seeming agreement with FCNL (French Committee of National Liberation)." Internal memo, September 17, 1943, in Coles and Weinberg, *Civil Affairs*, 661.

33. Coles and Weinberg, 661.

34. Coles and Weinberg, 136–37.

35. Ossad, "Shadow," 10-11.

36. Stevenson, "Marcus Obituary," 17.

37. Berkman, *Cast a Giant Shadow*, 27.

38. Maginnis, "My Service with Marcus," 303, 305.

39. 12th Army Group, Report of Operations, G-5, p. 21.

40. Coles and Weinberg, *Civil Affairs*, 722–25.

41. Ossad, "Shadow," 12.

42. 12th Army Group, Report of Operations, G-5, p. 6.

43. Ziemke, *Occupation of Germany*, 62.

44. Maginnis, *Journal*, xiv.

45. Pogue, *United States Army*, 83.

46. The four categories of detachment were prefixed from A to D in decreasing order of size (and importance). The C and D detachments, operating in smaller places, formed the bulk of the units, occasionally offering unique field and administrative challenges; the A and B detachments were the most desirable in terms of locations and advancement potential. "A" detachments were assigned to major cities, including national capitals, and regarded as the elite. For example, First US Army Detachment A1B1 was assigned to Cherbourg, the main Normandy port, and a major objective of Overlord.

47. Maginnis, *Journal*, 3–4; Maginnis, "My Service with Marcus," 302; and Maginnis, *Portrait of a Citizen-Soldier*, 43–44.

48. Maginnis, *Journal*, 3–4; Maginnis, "My Service with Marcus," 302–3.

49. Maginnis, "My Service with Marcus," 303.

50. Maginnis, *Journal*, 4–5; Maginnis, "My Service with Marcus," 303; and Maginnis, *Portrait of a Citizen-Soldier*, 45.

51. Maginnis, "My Service with Marcus," 315.

52. Reeder, *Heroes*, 101.

53. Maginnis, "My Service with Marcus," 306.

54. Maginnis, *Journal*, 4–5; and Maginnis, "My Service with Marcus," 305.

55. Maginnis, "My Service with Marcus," 307–8, 310.

56. Mickey's suspicion was correct, as Omar Bradley makes clear in his several accounts of Overlord strategy.

57. Maginnis, "My Service with Marcus," 308.

58. Maginnis, 309.

59. Maginnis, *Portrait of a Citizen-Soldier*, 46; and Maginnis, *Journal*, pp. 6.

60. Maginnis, "My Service with Marcus," 310.

61. James S. Thurmond, "Report of Service on TD With 82d Airborne Div, 23 May 44 to 14 Jun 44," in Coles and Weinberg, *Civil Affairs*, 722–24. The G-5 section at First Army was the oldest such section in continuous existence during the war activated on November 5, 1943, by Colonel Damon M. Gunn and his Exec, Major Thurmond.

62. Maginnis, *Portrait of a Citizen-Soldier*, 47; and Maginnis, "My Service with Marcus," 311.

63. Coles and Weinberg, *Civil Affairs*, 722–25.

64. Harrison, *Cross-Channel Attack*, 187, 280.

65. Maginnis, *Journal*, 8; and Maginnis, "My Service with Marcus," 311. Taylor presided at Mickey's West Point funeral. He is the only graduate buried in the academy cemetery who died fighting under a foreign flag.

66. Maginnis, *Journal*, 9; and Maginnis, "My Service with Marcus," 311–12.

67. Collins, *Lightning Joe*, 205.

68. Maginnis, "My Service with Marcus," 311–13.

69. Maginnis, *Journal*, 9; Maginnis, "My Service with Marcus," 312; and Maginnis, *Portrait of a Citizen-Soldier*, 48-50.

70. Ruppenthal, *Utah Beach to Cherbourg*, 92.
71. Ruppenthal.
72. Maginnis, "My Service with Marcus," 313; and Maginnis, *Portrait of a Citizen-Soldier*, 51.
73. Ossad and Marsh, *Maurice Rose*, 300–330.
74. Maginnis, "My Service with Marcus," 316.
75. 12th Army Group, Report of Operations, Final After-Action Report, Annex 1.
76. First US Army, Civil Affairs Section, "The Beachhead Phase Presents No Severe Civil Affairs Problems," memo, in Coles and Weinberg, *Civil Affairs*, 725.
77. Maginnis, *Portrait of a Citizen-Soldier*, 55.
78. Maginnis, *Journal*, 28.
79. Berkman, *Cast a Giant Shadow*, 27–28.
80. Maginnis, "My Service with Marcus," 318.
81. First US Army, "Beachhead Phase," 725.
82. Maginnis, "My Service with Marcus," 319.
83. Berkman, *Cast a Giant Shadow*, 34.
84. Royals, "Cast a Giant Shadow," 28; and Berkman, *Cast a Giant Shadow*, 35.
85. "Class of 1924 Notes," *Assembly* 4, no. 1 (April 1945): 18.
86. Berkman, *Cast a Giant Shadow*, 35.
87. Limpus, "This Was Mickey Marcus," 28–29, 179–81.
88. Berkman, *Cast a Giant Shadow*, 36
89. Royals, "Cast a Giant Shadow," 28; and Berkman, *Cast a Giant Shadow*, 37.
90. Berkman, *Cast a Giant Shadow*, 30–41.
91. "Honor Roll," *Judge Advocate Journal*; Borch, "David 'Mickey' Marcus."
92. Pyle, *Brass Hats*, 306.
93. Ossad and Marsh, *Maurice Rose*.
94. Stevenson, "Marcus Obituary," 17.
95. *Oxford Companion to World War II*, s.v. "Dumbarton Oaks conference," 312.
96. "History," Dumbarton Oaks Library and Collection, Washington DC, https://www.doaks.org/about/history.
97. *Oxford Companion*, s.v. "Octagon," 829.
98. *Oxford Companion*, s.v. "Argonaut," 54.
99. "The Yalta Conference, 1943," US Department of State Archive, 2001–2009, https://2001-2009.state.gov/r/pa/ho/time/wwii/93273.htm.

Chapter 3. The Occupation of Germany

1. Clay, *Decision in Germany*, 5–6.
2. Clay, 5.
3. Reeder, *Heroes*, 57–60.
4. Clay, 5.
5. Clay, 5.
6. Fred Borch, Colonel David D. "Mickey" Marcus, Distinguished Member of the Civil Affairs Regiment, Induction Ceremony, Fort Liberty, NC, October 26, 2017. Program biography available at https://www.swcs.mil/Portals/111/ca_marcus.pdfBorch.

7. *Assembly*, April 1946, 30; "Brooklyn Man Assisted in V-E Day Negotiations," *Brooklyn Eagle*, May 16, 1945.
8. Borch, "David 'Mickey' Marcus" and "Amazing Career."
9. Freeman, "Forgotten Airman," 170–74.
10. Freeman, 183–84.
11. Freeman, 158.
12. Freeman, 158.
13. Maginnis, "My Service with Marcus," 319.
14. Maginnis, *Journal*, 245.
15. Buchenwald was liberated on April 11, 1945, by soldiers of the Sixth Armored Division, https://encyclopedia.ushmm.org/content/en/article/the-6th-armored-division; Dachau was liberated on April 29 by elements of the Forty-Second, Forty-Fifth, and Twentieth Armored Divisions, https://encyclopedia.ushmm.org/content/en/timeline-event/holocaust/1942-1945/liberation-of-dachau. US Holocaust Memorial Museum.
16. Maginnis, "My Service with Marcus," 319–33.
17. See especially US Holocaust Memorial Museum, "Liberating Units" https://encyclopedia.ushmm.org/tags/en/tag/liberating-units; and Museum of the Jewish Warrior in World War II, "Liberation of the Concentration Camps." https://www.jwmww2.org/The_liberation_of_the_concentration_camps.
18. Ossad, "Liberation of Nordhausen."
19. US Holocaust Memorial Museum, "Liberating Army Units"; and Ossad, "Liberation."
20. "Potsdam," *Oxford Companion*; Popowycz, "Potsdam Conference." National World War II Museum, https://www.nationalww2museum.org/war/articles/potsdam-conference.
21. "The Cairo Conference, 1943," US Department of State Archive, 2001–2009, https://2001-2009.state.gov/r/pa/ho/time/wwii/93275.htm; and Popowycz, "Potsdam Conference.
22. Maginnis, "My Service with Marcus," 320–21.
23. Maginnis, 320-321.
24. Maginnis, "Service," 320; Maginnis, *Journal*, 324-325.
25. "Earl G. Harrison," US Holocaust Memorial Museum Encyclopedia https://encyclopedia.ushmm.org/content/en/article/earl-g-harrison-biography?parent=en%2F11820; "Displaced Persons – Jewish," Yad Vashem Museum https://www.yadvashem.org/odot_pdf/Microsoft%20Word%20-%206273.pdf; "Jews in US Camps Held Ill-Treated; Military Government Men in Germany Are 'Incompetent,' Chaplain Declares," *New York Times*, November 2, 1945.
26. "The Harrison Report," https://encyclopedia.ushmm.org/content/en/article/the-harrison-report; "Jews in US Camps."
27. "Jews in US Camps."
28. Maginnis, *Journal*, 328.
29. Maginnis, "My Service with Marcus," 321–22.
30. Maginnis, 320.

31. This was just over two years before the formal presentation of the decoration at the British Embassy in Washington in mid-April 1948.

32. Maginnis, "My Service with Marcus," 301–24.

33. Taylor, *Final Report.*

34. "Nuremberg Trials Final Report Appendix D: Control Council Law No. 10," Yale Law School Avalon Project, https://avalon.law.yale.edu/imt/imt10.asp#art2; and John Hilldring to Lucius Clay, January 22, 1946, box 6, file 10, Berkman Papers.

35. Taylor, *Final Report*; and Hilldring to Clay.

36. Borch, "Nuremberg Trials at 75."

37. Marrus, "Three Roads from Nuremberg."

38. Marrus.

39. Lustig, "Nature of the Nazi State."

40. Taylor, *Anatomy*, ch. 11, sec. 9.

41. Taylor.

42. Petersen, video interview.

43. "Subsequent Nurenberg Proceedings, Case #9, The Einsatzgruppen Case," USHMM, https://encyclopedia.ushmm.org/content/en/article/subsequent-nuremberg-proceedings-case-9-the-einsatzgruppen-case; and "Ben Ferencz and the Einsatzgruppen Trial," USHMM, https://encyclopedia.ushmm.org/content/en/gallery/ben-ferencz-and-the-einsatzgruppen-case

44. Popowycz, "Holocaust by Bullets."

45. Ferencz, "Starting a New Life"; Ferencz, "Detained for Impersonating an Officer"; and Hoffman, *Benjamin Ferencz*, 106–7.

46. Thomas Greene to Lord Wright, July 22, 1946, in *Foreign Relations* 8 (1946): 438–40.

47. "Benjamin (Beryl) Ferencz," US Holocaust Memorial Museum.

48. Thomas Greene, memo to Lord Wright, July 22, 1946, in *Foreign Relations* 8 (1946): 438–40.

49. Hilldring made several recommendations, as did Clay, countersigned by other officers.

50. Stevenson, "Marcus Obituary," 16–17; Berkman, *Cast a Giant Shadow*, 45.

Chapter 4. "Code Name: Michael Stone"

1. According to Shamir, Ben-Gurion offered him the position of chief of staff after the war. Information on Shlomo Shamir in this section is based on Shamir's memoir, edited and translated by his daughter, Yael Shamir Driver. Other sources include Driver, "Supplements," personal correspondence, multiple phone contacts, and in-person interviews with Driver and the author, 2021–24.

2. Shamir, "Memoir."

3. History of the Yishuv's participation in the British forces in World War II is based on correspondence and conversations between the author with Yael Shamir Driver and documents in the Shamir Archive, verified by general references on the period. Note: Ari Ben Canaan, the Palestinian Jew with service in a British Royal Transport company in the film *Exodus*, is an accurate representation of these troops.

4. Shamir, "Memoir"; "Shlomo Shamir," Museum of the Jewish Soldier in World War II, https://www.jwmww2.org/soldier.aspx?id=2776.

5. The Forty-First Cavalry Reconnaissance Squadron of the US Eleventh Armored Division, US Third Army, liberated Mauthausen subcamps Gusen and Melk on May 5, 1945, the Eightieth Infantry Division took Ebensee on May 6, and the Eleventh Armored Division entered the main Mauthausen concentration camp on May 7 (https://encyclopedia.ushmm.org/content/en/article/the-11th-armored-division). Bergen-Belsen was liberated by the British Eleventh Armoured (Red Bull) Division on April 15, 1945 (https://encyclopedia.ushmm.org/content/en/article/the-11th-armoured-division-great-britain). The first Belsen trial was held in September at British HQ, Luneburg. Imperial War Museum, "Belsen on Trial, 1945," https://www.iwm.org.uk/history/belsen-on-trial-1945.

6. Shamir, "Memoir."

7. "Jewish Brigade Group," United States Holocaust Memorial Museum Website, Washington, DC https://encyclopedia.ushmm.org/content/en/article/jewish-brigade-group.

8. Shamir, "Memoir"; and Shamir, "Supplements."

9. After further command assignments in the 1948 war, Shamir led Israel's navy and then Israel's air force. Retiring from the military in 1952, he eschewed politics and began a career as a successful public servant, establishing and developing Israel's phosphate mining business and then administering the Israel Land Authority. Later in life he completed his university education in Israel and at Harvard Business School and published his account of the battles of Latrun, which includes his memories of events related to Mickey Marcus. Shamir remained in touch with Emma Marcus until she died. At her request, he cooperated with Ted Berkman for his biography of Marcus. In 1949 Ben-Gurion asked Gershon Rivlin, the head of IDF magazine *Marachot*, to assign a writer for an article about Mickey on the anniversary of his death. The assignment went to Zipporah Porath (née Borovsky), a young American journalist who had been in Jerusalem with the Haganah during the siege. The project was never completed, but six decades later Porath revisited her notes and wrote a brief pamphlet about Mickey, quoting her interviews with people who knew him, starting with Shamir. Though filled with errors both large and small that are consistent with the general image of Marcus, her short work offers a contemporary picture of peoples' reactions to the man. The booklet is used by Israel's Consulate in response to inquiries about Marcus. Porath, *Marcus*.

10. Shamir, "Memoir"; Oxford Reference, s.v. "Jewish Agency," https://www.oxfordreference.com/display/10.1093/oi/authority.20110803100020443.

11. J. Wandres, *Ablest Navigator*, 34–34. Sinatra was a well-known Zionist sympathizer and had a supporting role in the movie *Cast a Giant Shadow*.

12. Slater, *The Pledge*, 71–75; Calhoun, "Arming David."

13. Under FOIA requests, numerous FBI and CIG memos during 1947–48, describe comprehensive surveillance of Zionist leaders and Jewish Agency arms procurement activities by various national security and local police. The British also conducted surveillance in the United States with the knowledge and acquiescence of the American IC.

14. Al Schwimmer, founder of Israel Aircraft Industries, who played a major role in smuggling aircraft to the IDF, was prosecuted and lost citizenship. He was later pardoned by President Clinton. "Al Schwimmer, NY Born Father of Israel's Aerospace Industry, Dies at 94," *Haaretz*, June 12, 2011, https://www.haaretz.com/2011-06-12/ty-article/al-schwimmer-ny-born-father-of-israels-aerospace-industry-dies-at-94/0000017f-dbe8-d856-a37f-ffe8d6990000.

15. Shamir, "Memoir."

16. Slater, *The Pledge*, 88–94.

17. "Contemplated Transformation of Haganah into Army," Central Intelligence Group report, October 10, 1947, declassified 08/09/1998, https://www.cia.gov/readingroom/docs/CIA-RDP82-00457R001000140001-8.pdf.

18. US Department of State, "Creation of Israel."

19. Efforts to illegally procure and ship arms by Irgun and other Revisionist groups were a subject of IC surveillance documented by FOI-requested CIA documents during the 1980s.

20. Yael Shamir Driver, personal correspondence with the author; Shamir, "Memoir"; and Driver, "Supplements."

21. Shamir, "Memoir"; and Driver, "Supplements."

22. "David Ben Gurion," Jewish Agency for Israel, https://archive.jewishagency.org/leaders/content/25952/

23. Kramer, "Forgotten Trust." For the NILI spy ring, see *Encyclopedia of Jewish Women*, s.v. "Sarah Aaronsohn," https://jwa.org/encyclopedia/article/aaronsohn-sarah.

24. United Nations, "Origins and Evolution of the Palestine Problem: 1917–1947 (Part I)," https://www.un.org/unispal/history2/origins-and-evolution-of-the-palestine-problem/part-i-1917-1947/; "Alfred Dreyfus and the Dreyfus Affair," US Holocaust Memorial Museum, https://encyclopedia.ushmm.org/content/en/article/alfred-dreyfus-and-the-dreyfus-affair.

25. "David Ben Gurion," Jewish Agency for Israel, https://archive.jewishagency.org/leaders/content/25952/

26. Ben-Gurion, *Israel.*

27. Karsh, *Arab-Israeli Conflict*, 22–25.

28. "Haganah History," Haganah Heritage Organization Website, https://haganah.org.il/story/thecantryarmy/; "Synopsis of Palmach History," Palmach Museum, https://palmach.org.il/en/history/about/; "Palmach," Encyclopedia of the Arab Israeli Conflict, 2008, 800–801.

29. See especially Stoil, "The Haganah and SOE."

30. Melzer, "Revisionist Zionists," https://yivoencyclopedia.org/article.aspx/Revisionist_Zionists; and Rubner, "Revisionist Zionism," https://onlinelibrary.wiley.com/doi/abs/10.1111/MEPO.12136. *The Revolt* was also the title of Begin's history of the uprising against the British.

31. Both events were dramatically fictionalized in Leon Uris's book *Exodus*, about the months before the partition vote in November 1947, as well as the book's movie version.

32. Teddy Kolleck, letter to the editor, *New York Times*, September 28, 1981.

33. "Chaim Laskov," Jewish Soldiers of World War II Museum, https://www.jwmww2.org/soldier.aspx?id=2728; Chaim Herzog, https://www.jwmww2.org/soldier.aspx?id=2890; Chaim Herzog, Member of Knesset Bio, https://main.knesset.gov.il/en/MK/APPS/mk/mk-personal-details/391.

34. Shamir, "Memoir."

35. Shlomo Shamir, correspondence about a visit to Haganah training center in the Yishuv, 1942, Shamir Archive.

36. Rabin, *Memoirs*, 19–20.

37. Allon was receptive to Marcus, and his genuine affection was a bridge to the Palmach. Emma visited with the Allons when she visited Israel. See especially Shapira, *Allon, Native Son.*

38. Ben-Gurion diary, April 26–27, 1948.

39. Allon, *Shield of David*, 102–6; Shamir's wife Mina, later a judge in Israel, translated a book about Wingate's adventures in Africa.

40. Zabecki, "Orde Charles Wingate," *Encyclopedia,* 1085–86.

41. Shamir, "Memoir."

42. Shamir.

43. Shamir; and Milstein, *A Nation Girds for War*, 322.

44. Shamir, "Memoir"; and Driver, "Supplements."

45. Emma's notes to Berkman, box 6, folder 7, Berkman Papers; and Berkman, *CAGS*, 45.

46. Fiorello La Guardia to David Marcus, April 1946, box 6, folder 12, Berkman Papers.

47. Emma Marcus, notes, box 6, folder 12, Berkman Papers, 948; obituary for Rabbi Sidney Tedesche, *New York Times*, May 19, 1962.

48. Berkman, *Cast a Giant Shadow*, 46.

49. Tucker, "Moshe Sharett."

50. Shamir, "Memoir"; Driver, "Supplements"; obituary for Murray Gurfein, *New York Times*, December 18, 1979.

51. Hilldring played a secret part in the Haganah search for military consultants. Ben-Gurion diary, December 30, 1947; and David Marcus, handwritten and typed proposed contract for Ralph C. Smith, Shamir Archive.

52. Bercuson, *Secret Army*, 52.

53. Bercuson, 52; Yael Shamir Driver, correspondence with Israel Museum, no. 13, January and September 2021, Shamir Archive.

54. Sacquety, "John H. Hilldring."

55. News coverage of Hilldring's appointment in 1948, and his subsequent decision not to serve, uniformly describe him as sympathetic to the Jewish position. Marshall's opposition to partition is well documented in numerous biographies of Truman, the "Recognition of the State of Israel" collection at the Truman Library (https://www.trumanlibrary.gov/library/online-collections/recognition-of-state-of-israel?section=2), and in the memoirs of those involved, especially Truman presidential adviser Clark Clifford's *Counsel to the President.*

56. Danton Walker, "The Barberry Room, on Broadway," *New York Daily News*, March 11, 1956; "Job 362, Barberry Room (Elbow Room), 1937–1957," Norman Bel Geddes Database, University of Texas, https://norman.hrc.utexas.edu/NBGPublic/details.cfm?ID=294; Terry Turcco, "Good-bye, Omni Berkshire Place NYC, the Hotel Where Rodgers & Hammerstein Hatched "Oklahoma!" *Hotel History, Hotel Openings and Closings*, July 13, 2020, https://overnightnewyork.com/hotel-openings-and-closings/good-bye-omni-berkshire-place-nyc-the-hotel-where-rodgers-hammerstein-hatched-oklahoma/.

57. Berkman, *Cast a Giant Shadow* (46), puts the initial recruitment meeting place in Yablok's suite of offices, and the movie places the recruitment in Macy's, near Christmas time. Both are refuted by official Israel sources (Israel Defense Forces History Museum newsletter, December 2020) and Shamir's various written versions, as well as a letter from Moshe Sharett to Emma Marcus in October 1962 as a response to Berkman's version (letter in the Shamir Archive). Ex Lieutenant Colonel Morton Strauss, an army friend of Mickey, was a witness to at least one meeting between Shamir and Mickey at Mickey's office and accompanied the two men to see General Ralph C. Smith in San Francisco in November 1947. That was corroborated by Shamir in his memoir. Strauss may have been the source of Berkman's version, and he appeared on a list of possible staff officers along with Shamir's comment, "Subject to General Smith's approval." Shamir Archive.

58. Shamir, "Memoir."

59. According to a draft letter to General Smith in early December bearing Mickey's signature, the contract was $1,000 per month for general officers, and $750 for adjutants and staff. David Marcus to Ralph C. Smith, December 1947, Shamir Archive.

60. Shamir, "Memoir."

61. Every serious account of Shamir's assignment, regardless of overall accuracy, correctly mentions that all the candidates on Shamir's ultimate target list were concerned about potential problems with their pensions.

62. Shamir's annotated list of 24 candidates is in the Shamir Archive.

63. Shamir, "Memoir."

64. Handwritten note on Shamir's list of 24 prospects, Shamir Archive; Ted Berkman, whose account of events differs dramatically from Shamir's version, used Strauss as a source, and Shamir confirms Strauss's involvement in his memoir.

65. All the various accounts of the recruitment stress this point. The original list included Harry Collins, the Liberator of Dachau, who defied convention by appointing a rabbi as chaplain of the Forty-Second Infantry Division and showed open sympathy to the survivors of the Holocaust.

66. Shamir, "Memoir."

67. "1947: The International Community Says YES to the Establishment of the State of Israel," Israel Ministry of Foreign Affairs, https://mfa.gov.il/Jubilee-years/Pages/1947-UN-General-Assembly-Resolution-181-The-international-community-says-Yes-to-the-establishment-of-the-State-of-Israel.aspx.

68. US Department of State, "Creation of Israel"; and Shamir, "Memoir."

69. Shamir, "Memoir."

70. US Department of State, "Creation of Israel."

71. Units of the Arab Legion eventually captured East Jerusalem, including the Jewish Quarter in the Old City and the west bank of the Jordan River. The same area was liberated by IDF forces in June 1967.

72. Documents about this program were later declassified in the 1980s, painting an incredibly dark chapter of American intelligence history.

73. Shamir, "Memoir."

74. Porath, *Marcus*, 5.

75. Porath, 5; Berkman, *Cast a Giant Shadow*, 58.

76. Shamir, "Memoir."

77. Shamir.

78. Prominent examples include the Muslim spiritual leader (Mufti) of Jerusalem, a member of the prominent Palestinian Husseini family, and Anwar Sadat, who later led Egypt into war in 1973 and then signed the first formal Peace Agreement with Israel in 1977.

79. Porath, *Marcus*, 5–6.

80. Porath.

81. Shlomo Shamir, desk calendar notation for December 30, 1947, Shamir Archive.

82. Milstein, *A Nation Girds for War*, 322–24.

83. David Ben-Gurion, telegram to Shlomo Shamir, January 13, 1948, Shamir Archive. Bernard Baruch was a wealthy Jewish financier and longtime Democratic adviser to Roosevelt and Truman.

84. Bercuson, *Secret Army*, 52–54, 240.

85. Karsh, *Arab-Israeli Conflict*, 10; and Laffin, *Israeli Army*, 10–12.

86. Shamir, "Memoir"; and Shamir to Berkman, December 28, 1961, Shamir Archive.

Chapter 5. Mickey Marcus and the Jewish Army

1. Yossi Melman, "What Did America's First Envoy Think of Israel?" *Jerusalem Post*, April 21, 2017, https://www.jpost.com/israel-news/diary-of-first-us-envoy-to-israel-revealed-488465.

2. Micky Marcus to Emma Marcus, February 2, 1948, David Marcus files, Personal Letters, Machal Archives.

3. A translation of the Hebrew entry in Ben-Gurion's diary for February 3, 1948, is quoted in Shamir, "Memoir."

4. Shamir, "Memoir."

5. Porath, *Marcus*, 7-8.

6. Porath, 7.

7. Porath, 8.

8. Lorch, *War of Independence*, 59.

9. Porath, *Marcus*, 9.

10. Porath, 10.

11. Porath, 7.

12. Secretary of Defense to Secretary of State, Office of the Historian, US Department of State, April 19, 1948, https://history.state.gov/historicaldocuments/frus1948v05p2/d160.

13. US Department of State, "Creation of Israel."

14. Jacobson, "Two Presidents and a Haberdasher"; and "Recognition of the State of Israel," Truman Papers.

15. Porath, *Marcus*, 13.

16. Porath, 16; "List of 10 Officers Referenced by American Rabbis," Shamir Archive.

17. Porath, *Marcus*, 17.

18. US Department of State, "Creation of Israel."

19. Jacobson, "Two Presidents and a Haberdasher."

20. David Ben-Gurion, diary entry (in Hebrew), March 12, 1948, Ben-Gurion Archive, https://bengurionarchive.bgu.ac.il/en/search-api/bg_arc/223975; David Marcus, report to Haganah, March 16, 1948, Shamir Archive.

21. Schiff, *History of the Israeli Army*; and Jacobson, "Two Presidents and a Haberdasher."

22. Marcus, report to Haganah.

23. Marcus.

24. Marcus.

25. Boatner, *Encyclopedia of the American Revolution*, 1055–58.

26. Porath, *Marcus*, 2.

27. Berkman, *Cast a Giant Shadow*, 98–100; and Marcus, report to Haganah.

28. Marcus, report to Haganah; and Michelsohn, "Aluf David Marcus."

29. Most sources, including Berkman, Limpus, Zabecki, and USASOC, use some variation of the "from memory" narrative of writing the training manuals, beginning with Zipporah Porath's original interview subjects. Porath, *Marcus*, 19. Notable exceptions are Stevenson's obituary and Fred Borch's signed articles.

30. Michelsohn, "Aluf David Marcus."

31. Marcus, report to Haganah.

32. "Lectures for Commanders by (Mickey Stone) [David Marcus]," National Library of Israel; and Marcus, report to Haganah.

33. Jacobson, "Two Presidents and a Haberdasher"; and US Department of State, "Arab-Israeli War of 1948."

34. Ben-Gurion diary, May 10–15, 1948, 91–93.

35. Jacobson, "Two Presidents and a Haberdasher."

36. US Department of State, "Creation of Israel."

37. US Department of State; and Jacobson, "Two Presidents and a Haberdasher."

38. US Department of State, "Creation of Israel."

39. US Department of State; and Schiff, *History of the Israeli Army*, 32–35.

40. Porath, *Marcus*, 20.

41. Regina Gabel to Emma Marcus, n.d., box 6, file 6, Berkman Papers.

42. "Palestine Situation"; and Porath, *Marcus*, 20.

43. Emma Marcus, desk calendar, April–May 1948, box 6, files 3, 6, 11, 12, Berkman Papers.

44. Porath, *Marcus*, 21.

45. Porath.

46. Porath, 10; and Marcus, report to Haganah.

47. Porath, *Marcus*, 10; and Marcus, report to Haganah.

48. "Recognition of the State of Israel," Truman Papers; and Jacobson, "Two Presidents and a Haberdasher."

49. Emma Marcus, notes and desk calendars, box 6, files 3, 7, 11, 12, Berkman Papers.

50. Emma Marcus to Ted Berkman, October 10, 1961, box 6, file 6, Berkman Papers.

51. Emma Marcus, notes to Berkman regarding the OBE, n.d., box 6, file 11, Berkman Papers. Both the book and movie *Cast a Giant Shadow* dramatize the event and intimate that the British knew Marcus's identity during his first visit to Palestine.

52. Porath, *Marcus*, 10.

53. Marcus, notes and desk calendars, box 6, files 11, 12.

54. Krulewitch, *Now That You Mention It*, 147–50.

55. Marcus to Berkman, October 10, 1961.

56. Marcus to Berkman, n.d., box 6, file 11.

Chapter 6. "Aluf Michael Stone" and the Siege of Jerusalem

1. Heiman, "David Marcus."

2. Porath, *Marcus*, 24.

3. Ben-Gurion diary, May 10, 1948, 91.

4. Jacobson, "Two Presidents and a Haberdasher."

5. "The Palestine Situation," summary of conclusions reached by representatives of CIA, State, War, and Navy in conference May 5, 1948, "Approved for Release, CIA, August 8, 2001; Porath, *Marcus*, 20.

6. Jacobson, "Two Presidents and a Haberdasher."

7. "Declaring the State of Israel."

8. "Declaration of Israel's Independence."

9. Porath, *Marcus*, 23.

10. Berkman, *Cast a Giant Shadow*, 224.

11. US Department of State, "Creation of Israel."

12. Herzog, *Arab-Israeli Wars*, 47–48; Allon, *Shield of David*, 206–8; Laffin, *Israeli Army*, 7–8; and Michelsohn, "Aluf David Marcus."

13. Michelsohn.

14. Shamir, "Memoir"; Shlomo Shamir to Ted Berkman, February 28, 1961, Shamir Archive.

15. Porath, *Marcus*, 25.

16. Michelsohn, "Aluf David Marcus."

17. Michelsohn; and Lorch, *War of Independence*, 240.

18. Michelsohn, "Aluf David Marcus"; and Ben-Gurion, *Israel*, 108.

19. Michelson, "Aluf David Marcus"; Porath, *Marcus*, 25–26.
20. Porath, *Marcus*, 25; Whelan, *Robert Capa*, 334–36.
21. Shamir, "Memoir," 4; and Porath, *Marcus*, 25–26.
22. Ben-Gurion diary, May 23, 1948, 115–16.
23. Michelsohn, "Aluf David Marcus."
24. Michelsohn; and Ben-Gurion diary, 110.
25. Michelsohn, "Aluf David Marcus."
26. Porath, *Marcus*, 26.
27. Ben-Gurion diary, May 28, 1948, 119.
28. Ben-Gurion diary, May 16, 1948; and Michelsohn, "Aluf David Marcus."
29. Lorch, *Israel's War of Independence*, 218–20; Herzog, *Arab-Israeli Wars*, 63; Michelsohn, "Aluf David Marcus."
30. Collins and Lapierre, *O Jerusalem!* 332–34.
31. Pick, "Latrun."
32. Lorch, *Israel's War of Independence*, 219–20; Depuy, *Elusive Victory*, 64.
33. Lorch, *Israel's War of Independence*, 220; Depuy, *Elusive Victory*, 63; Herzog, *Arab-Israeli Wars*, 63–65.
34. Lorch, 221–26.
35. Ben-Gurion diary, 109.
36. The claims about massive casualties during Bin Nun Alef and Bin Nun Bet and the sacrifice of Holocaust survivors, haunted Israeli politics and divided people for many decades. See esp. Shamir, *Battle for Jerusalem*, for the commander's view; 139 soldiers were killed in action in the two engagements.
37. Ben-Gurion diary, May 28, 1948, 119.
38. Lorch, *War of Independence*, 221–26; and Ben-Gurion diary, June 13, 1948, 125.
39. Shamir, "Memoir;" Driver, "Supplements."
40. One *aluf* kept his family name to honor a living parent.
41. Shamir, *Battle for Jerusalem*, 200–203.
42. Lorch, *War of Independence*, 223–26; *Herzog*, Arab-Israeli Wars, 62–63; Shamir, *Road to Jerusalem*, 201.
43. Michelsohn, "Aluf David Marcus."
44. Michelsohn, "Aluf David Marcus"; Michelsohn and Borch, "An American in the Israeli Army," 45; Lorch, *War of Independence*, 225–27.
45. Numerous sources, including Shamir, "Memoir"; Zabecki, *Military History*; Kimche and Kimche, *Clash*, 193–95.
46. Michelsohn, "Aluf David Marcus."
47. "The Arab-Israeli Wars," *Harper Encyclopedia of Military History*, 1335–38; Karsh, *Arab-Israeli Conflict*, 11; Schiff, *History of the Israeli Army*, 39–44; Michelsohn, "Aluf David Marcus."
48. Whelan, *Robert Capa*, 334–36.
49. Porath, *Marcus*, 29; Shamir, "Memoir."
50. Porath, 28.
51. Michelsohn, "Aluf David Marcus"; and Whelan, *Robert Capa*, 337.

52. "Shapira's Official Investigation into Marcus' Death," Shamir Archive.

53. "Dr. Meron Issachari," Haganah Archive.

54. Dr. Meron Issachari, "Death of Stone Autopsy Report," June 11, 1948, Shamir Archive. After the war, Dr. Issachari established Israel's School of Military Medicine.

55. Porath, *Marcus*, 30–31.

56. " 'I Shot Aluf Marcus' Sentry Speaks Up," *Jerusalem Post*, March 22, 1983.

57. Stevenson, "Marcus Obituary," 16; and Emma Marcus, "The West Pointer Who Built Israel's Army," *Knoxville (TN) Journal*, February 10, 1957.

58. Wolf Blitzer, "I Owe a Lot to Mickey Marcus, Rabin Says at Graveside Ceremony," *Jerusalem Post*, December 18, 1987; "Shapira's Investigation;"

59. "Marcus Funeral at West Point," *New York Times*, July 2, 1948; Limpus, "This Was Mickey Marcus," 181.

60. Each graduate of the US Military Academy is assigned a Cullum number, named for Brevet Major General George W. Cullum, 1833, initiator of the register that describes the biographies of every graduate.

61. "Plans Told to Perpetuate Memory of Col. Marcus," *New York Herald Tribune*, February 24, 1949; "America and Israel Honor the Memory of Colonel David Marcus," *Assembly* 14, no. 2 (July 1955): 28.

62. "The Armistice Agreements," Israel, Ministry of Foreign Affairs, Foreign Policy Historical Documents, https://www.gov.il/en/pages/the-armistice-agreements.

63. Ministry of Defense, IDF and Defense Establishment Archives, https://archives.mod.gov.il/sites/English/Exhibitions/David_Ben_Gurion_and_the_IDF/Pages/The-end-of-The-War-of-Independence.aspx.

64. "Israel Defense Forces," *Encyclopedia Judaica*, 518.

Chapter 7. Assessment and Legacy of Mickey Marcus

1. These ceasefire agreements ended hostilities on each front but did not, and were not intended to, establish permanent borders.

2. "ADL's Annual Assessment of Anti-Israel Activism on U.S. College Campuses," Anti-Defamation League, https://www.adl.org/resources/report/anti-israel-activism-us-campuses-2022–2023.

3. Jerry Klinger, "From the Old Maccabees to the New Maccabees: 'A Wrong Made Right,' " *Times of Israel*, January 28, 2019, https://blogs.timesofisrael.com/from-the-old-maccabees-to-the-new-maccabees-a-wrong-made-right/.

4. Porath, *Marcus*, 5.

5. "Our Mission," Israeli Defense Forces, https://www.idf.il/en/mini-sites/our-mission-our-values/.

6. "Al Schwimmer, NY Born Father of Israel's Aerospace Industry, Dies at 94," *Haaretz*, June 12, 2011, https://www.haaretz.com/2011-06-12/ty-article/al-schwimmer-ny-born-father-of-israels-aerospace-industry-dies-at-94/0000017f-dbe8-d856-a37f-ffe8d6990000. A number of those who fought or performed noncombat services for Israel suffered consequences ranging from fines to imprisonment. Al Schwimmer was the most prominent case. He smuggled transport and fighter aircraft and recruited many of the personnel that established the Israel Air Force. He was tried, convicted,

and stripped of his American citizenship in absentia until pardoned by President Clinton in 2000.

7. USASOC website profiles of David Marcus, https://www.swcs.mil/Portals/111/ca_marcus.pdf, and his boss John H. Hilldring, https://arsof-history.org/articles/v12n1_hilldring_page_1.html.

8. Weiss, *Spirit of 1776*, 96–98, 100–110; and Penslar, *Jews and the Military*, 225–32.

9. Scholars date Ramses II the Great, the Exodus Pharaoh, to ca. 1300–1200 BC. See Kitchen, *Pharaoh Triumphant*; and Ossad, "Battle of Kadesh."

Chronology of the Life of "Mickey" Marcus

1. David Marcus's birth certificate, signed by the delivering physician in the state of New York on February 23, 1901, lists that day as Marcus's birth date. Ancestry.com. Other sources cite his birth date as Washington's birthday (celebrated on the fourth Friday in February), which was February 22 that year. West Point records (distinct from alumni or *West Point Post* publications), including US Military Academy, *Official Register, 1924*, 93, and the Collum Register #7368 (David Marcus), list February 22, 1901. Many other references, including Berkman (125) and Israel sources (IDF website) incorrectly list 1902 as his birth year.

Principal Awards and Decorations

1. *Brooklyn Daily Eagle*, December 2, 1945.
2. *Assembly*, October 1945, 3.

INDEX

Page numbers in *italics* indicate illustrations